Process-Based Management Systems for High Reliability Organizations

by

John Paciga and Germaine Watts

All rights reserved

First Edition

Copyright © 2016 by John Paciga and Germaine Watts

For information about permission to reproduce selections from this book, contact:

Intelligent Organizational Systems, Inc.

Germaine.Watts@IntelOrgSys.com

Library of Congress Cataloging-in-Publication Data

Paciga, John and Watts, Germaine

Integrated Management Systems for High Reliability Organizations/John Paciga, Germaine Watts

1st Edition

iv. 330 p., | c25 cm.

Includes bibliographical references.

ISBN-13: 978-1533174475

1. Management. 2. Management Systems. 3. Continual Improvement.

4. Human Systems 5. Meaning-Making. I. Title.

Published by: Intelligent Organizational Systems, Inc.

Bayswater, New Brunswick, Canada, E5S 1M4

IntelOrgSys.com

"The more we all know, the better we collectively become."

— Daniel J. Keys, Artist

Preface

All organizations require an effective management system. This is particularly important for high reliability organizations that require safety, defense-in-depth, and resilience, while utilizing the inherent intelligence and agility of people to undertake improvements and cope with unanticipated events. Such organizations have a greater obligation than most to ensure public safety and meet regulatory requirements.

Experience shows that creating such a system is difficult from the traditional point of view of quality assurance simply because the field has evolved significantly. This includes an expanded focus on risk management, risk informed decision-making and resilience-sustainability-agility.

Our decision to write this handbook arose from observations during our work on management systems and safety culture within the nuclear industry:

- Although many standards for management systems exist, none provide systematic instructions on how to develop an integrated, process-based management system
- Where practical information exists, it typically focuses on a specific topic, hence a complete picture is scattered across many sources
- The role of meaning-making is absent from discussions of organizational effectiveness and safety culture
- The role of the human system is also absent beyond general statements on leadership commitment and organizational culture.

The purpose of this handbook is to share our experience on taking a systemic and systematic approach to developing an integrated process-based management system which encompasses the essential elements listed above. In order to do this effectively, we provide a necessary basis in the theory of management systems followed by a step-by-step approach to establishing and improving such a system. The appendices provide tools and templates to support hands-on application of the approach outlined in this handbook.

Table of Contents

Preface..Error! Bookmark not defined.

Chapter 1 Introduction 1

Part A Foundations 10

Chapter 2 The Roots of High Performance 11

Chapter 3 Organizational Evolution and Design 42

Chapter 4 Leadership, Teams and Culture 60

Chapter 5 Team Selection, Performance and Propensities 74

Chapter 6 Process-based Management Systems 89

Part B Application 115

Chapter 7 Assess Organizational Readiness and Capacity 116

Chapter 8 Establish an Excellence Team and Project Team 129

Chapter 9 Establish a Top Level Model and Organizational Design ... 146

Chapter 10 Establish Architectural Controls 158

Chapter 11 Establish a Mapping Methodology 167

Chapter 12 Establish Document Standards and Controls 185

Chapter 13 Assign Process Owners and Develop a Roadmap 198

Chapter 14 Develop Processes, Confirm Alignment, and
    Establish Mobilizing Metrics 210

Chapter 15 Conduct Pilots, Train and Implement 221

Chapter 16 Monitor, Assess, and Improve/Innovate 226

Chapter 17 Summary 239

Glossary of Terms 242

References and Resources 247

Acknowledgements 251

Appendix A Motivation A-1

Appendix B Behavioural Factors, Career Themes, and Leadership Styles A-6

Appendix C Leadership Style by Stage of Evolution A-11

Appendix D Organizational Design Principles A-26

Appendix E Samples of Management System Models A-30

Appendix F Organizational Assessment Questionnaire **A-37**

Appendix G Process Description Worksheet **A-52**

Appendix H Table of Contents – Organizational Design Basis Document **A-54**

Appendix I Table of Contents – Management System Manual **A-55**

Appendix J Example of a Graded Approach **A-57**

Appendix K Tips for Writing Effective Process and Procedural Documents **A-59**

Appendix L Human Performance Enhancers and Error Reduction Tools **A-62**

Appendix M Selecting Mobilizing Metrics **A-66**

Chapter 1

Introduction

IN THIS CHAPTER

Embarking on a journey to develop an Integrated Management System (IMS) is a large scale organizational change initiative that results in new ways of doing business. It has many benefits for individuals, teams and the entire organization, but the journey can be long and challenging. Engagement and communication are key elements for helping people understand and embrace a different vision of organizational life. Depending on the starting point, the initiative may be one of the largest change management projects ever undertaken by the organization's leadership.

This handbook is intended as a practical guide rather than an academic textbook on developing an IMS. Nevertheless, some essential 'schooling' is necessary to attain proficiency at putting the underlying concepts into practice. To facilitate the learning and doing journey, the handbook is divided into two parts.

- Part A (supplemented by appendices) provides foundational material intended to deepen understanding of key elements of management and organizational systems. It serves as reference material for organizational learning as the implementation process unfolds. We recommend that readers inclined to begin with a 'boots on the ground' approach avoid the urge to skip Part A.

- Part B (also supplemented by appendices) provides specific development and implementation strategies and activities that may be used for organizations embarking on the integrated management system journey. It can also be used to remedy gaps in organizations experiencing difficulties.

Part B is written as a step-by-step process that addresses the what, why, and how of each step in the complex process of implementing a comprehensive integrated management system. Each section has pointers on change management, including communication and success factors to help developers guide the organization's learning process.

MANAGEMENT SYSTEMS

A typical response to the question – What is a management system? – is that it is a system of processes established to ensure workers achieve desired levels of safety and quality. Workers are trained to follow policies and procedures, and managers and supervisors provide direction and oversight to ensure the work is accomplished as intended.

A more comprehensive view takes an integrated systems perspective in which processes are not only designed by and resourced with trained staff, but are grouped for natural synergies to create a coherent organizational structure. In addition, it includes elements such as resourcing decisions that emphasize innate abilities as well as learned competencies to ensure the organization has the capacities needed to function as required. The focus is on helping people make sense of organizational requirements and practices as a fundamental way to promote coherence across systems. Training builds on individual strengths and intrinsic motivation to achieve superior levels of performance. Management roles are structured to mine the intelligence of the organization to bring out the best in people.

This is not a minor distinction. In the more traditional view, quality is achieved through constraints and controls. The approach is inherently invested in shaping behaviours to meet standards and expectations.

In the second view, the capacities of the workforce to make sense of their environment along with their natural motivation, problem-solving and relational skills are aligned along process lines to create a self-actualizing system. This approach is more complex to understand because it adds as design variables, the dimensions of human capability, context and how individuals and groups make sense of things. It will, however, achieve consistently higher levels of quality because individuals are personally invested through the gratification of doing what they enjoy and do well. High performance organizations don't treat people merely as a means of production, but as the source of intelligence, conscience, resourcefulness, and connectivity.

We encourage users of this handbook to think about their management system from this more encompassing perspective. In the coming chapters we will place as much emphasis on the human and organizational aspects of the management system, as on the processes that are intended to support and guide peoples' efforts since everything accomplished within organizations is ultimately achieved by people.

A SYSTEMIC VIEW

Organizations involve a continuous interplay of six complex, often messy, systems (Figure 1-1):

1. The hard or soft technology on which the organization is based
2. The human system which includes the innate propensities (talents), learned competencies, meaning systems and behaviours of individuals, teams, and leaders
3. The organizational structure established to coordinate relationships
4. The processes used to operate and manage the organization
5. The outcomes and impacts resulting from the organization's activities, and
6. An evolving external context driven by customers, competitors, regulators, the public, and other internal and external forces.

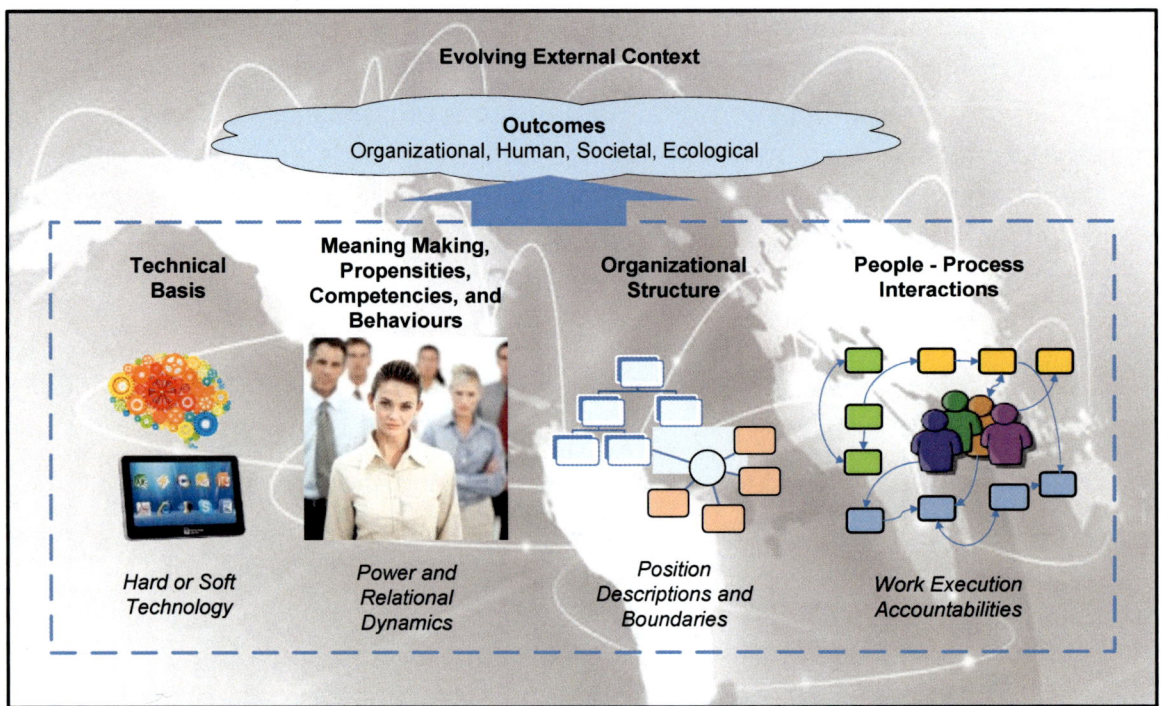

Figure 1-1: Organizational functionality depends on six simultaneously interacting, complex systems working together

The main purpose of an Integrated Management System (IMS) is to establish a degree of coherence among these six systems. Ideally it serves to integrate the organization at four distinct levels: meaning-purpose level, relational-relationship level, activity-task level, and outcome level. This approach helps to overcome the biggest challenge to successful implementation, namely that documentation of processes and procedures is seen as the end in itself, rather than simply a part of a total integrated management system. An IMS is only effective if members of the organization buy in and use what is documented to guide and integrate their day-to-day decisions and actions.

PROCESS OR PROGRAM BASED?

No matter whether you are an entrepreneur starting a new business, or an experienced manager, at some point you come face-to-face with the effectiveness of your management system. In the short term people can often function in 'project mode' moving from task to task or crisis to crisis with seeming success; however, this isn't sufficient for sustainability, particularly in high-reliability organizations. The management system serves as an essential framework for sustainability and performance improvement. In high reliability organizations, a robust management system is essential for safety, not just at the worker level, but also to support risk-informed decision making at senior levels.

Organizations that require consistent outcomes tend to favour process-based systems over program-based systems. The benefits of an integrated, process-based management system are far more profound than its use as a management tool to control the work of direct reports and front-line workers. It:

- Enhances communication through simplicity and uniformity
- Reduces duplication by establishing common processes
- Reduces documentation effort
- Improves quality, reliability, efficiency, and effectiveness of implementation
- Establishes clear accountabilities, authorities, and responsibilities
- Simplifies management and external oversight
- Serves as a basis for organizational design to align organizational functionalities, structure, interfaces, and talent distributions
- Increases the transparency of resource allocation
- Improves identification, mitigation, and resolution of risks
- Enhances employee participation and ownership, leading to reduced stress and greater creativity
- Enables accelerated, more focused training
- Enhances stakeholder understanding and satisfaction
- Improves return on improvement and change initiatives
- Increases financial viability through lower costs, improved productivity and creativity
- Serves as a key repository of information and knowledge management
- Serves as a requisite framework for continual improvement
- Serves as a requisite framework for training and development, including leadership development
- Shifts focus from compliance monitoring to performance-based monitoring
- Helps management understand the organization as coupled systems and how work fits together and flows.

The list applies equally and as importantly to the work of senior managers and executives.

DEFINING 'THE SYSTEM'

To ensure a systemic and systematic approach to the six systems introduced in Figure 1-1, we will tie some of our discussion to a more explicit model (Figure 1-2) that describes the essential elements of any organization.

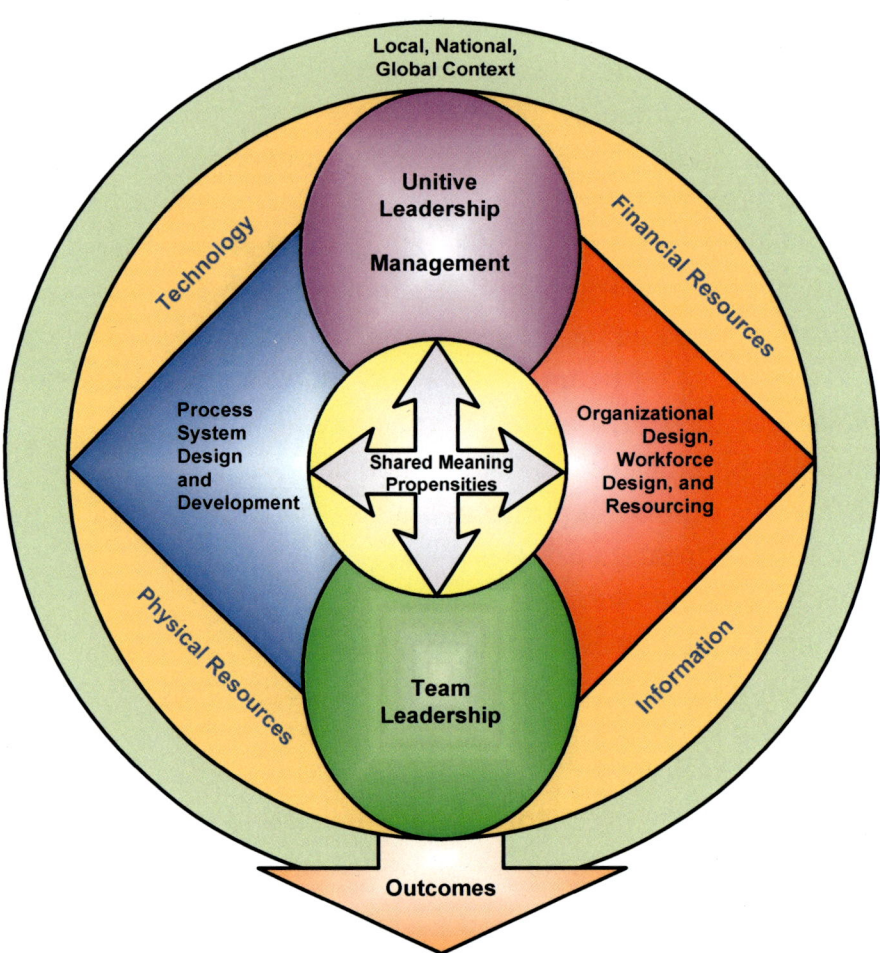

Figure 1-2: Key elements of an organization

The elements in the model relate to:

External Operating Context – Local, National and Global

- Influence of clients, regulators, the public, and society
- Environmental and ecological context.

Human System

The human system is comprised of several elements within the model.

- Unitive leadership that looks strategically at systemic and systematic integration
- Management that involves interface issues and staff engagement activities
- Shared meaning and culture within the organizational context
- Propensities or natural inclinations and talents across the organization at the individual and team levels
- Team leadership that involves the localized organization of work at all levels of the organization
- Organizational design, workforce design, and resourcing.

Process System

- Process system (governance, executive, core, and support) requirements and controls.

Technology, Infrastructure and Support

- Technology (both primary and support)
- Financial resources
- Information resources
- Physical resources.

Outcomes

- The nature and value of organizational impacts.

Outcomes extend beyond products and business (profit, market share, growth, risk, etc.) to include human (development, health, wellness, compensation, security, etc.), organizational (reputation, productivity, quality, diversity, locations, etc.), ecological, and societal (contribution, job creation, etc.) outcomes.

Together, these elements represent how organizational members understand their context and distribute their time, attention and effort. This is particularly true from a senior management perspective where final accountability for efficacy of the system resides.

THIS HANDBOOK

This handbook will help your organization develop an integrated, process-based management system specific to your needs, while making use of best practices for high reliability organizations. To that end, we will introduce and explore emerging concepts involving meaning systems, human systems, propensities, and unitive leadership. We will also revisit some ingrained patterns of thinking, many of which derive from quality management, and if implemented in a traditional manner may actually limit an organization's ability to achieve significant improvements. These include:

- The Plan-Do-Check-Act (PDCA) cycle
- Corrective action identification and management
- Operating experience and benchmarking
- Continual improvement.

We will explore other models, including an organizational evolution model that illustrates the transition from a technical-focused leadership approach to one that integrates the systems that influence and enable the organization.

We will discuss design paradoxes for management systems such as the need to balance codification with organizational resilience. Reliance on standardized processes and procedures is the means to minimizing risks during normal operations and predicted off-normal conditions. At the same time, procedural adherence must not substitute for deep understanding of technical systems, or interfere with the level of collaboration and mindful adaptation needed from people during complex emerging situations.

Finally, we will demonstrate a streamlined documentation approach that any organization can use to ensure that their integrated management system is user-friendly.

The next five chapters (Part A) cover foundational material related to management systems. These include:

Chapter 2. Meaning Systems

Chapter 3. Organization Evolution and Design

Chapter 4. Leadership, Teams and Culture

Chapter 5. Team Selection, Performance and Propensities

Chapter 6. Process-based Management Systems.

As mentioned earlier, the practical steps in Part B build on the discussions in Part A, therefore we recommend you read these chapters in sequence.

Part A
Foundations

Chapter 2
The Roots of High Performance

IN THIS CHAPTER

To understand how organizations of any type really work, we need to start with a few foundational concepts that shape human decision-making and action. In this chapter we explore key elements that drive high performance. In order for the management system to enable and support high performance, these elements have to be considered and embedded in the system at the design stage:

- Culture
- Human Systems
- Meaning-making
- Motivation
- Propensities
- Social Dynamics and Shared Space
- Flow
- Diversity
- Self in Action.

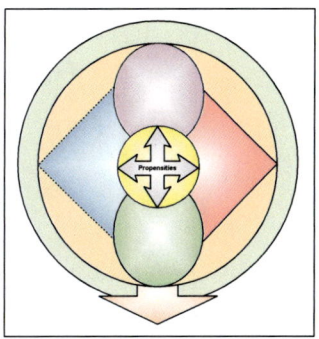

Culture

Figure 2-1 shows a modified version of the classic iceberg model of culture developed by Edgar Schein (2010). The top level consists of the observable manifestations or artifacts of the culture. For example, they include the organization's structure, management system, observable behaviours, and organizational outcomes.

The second level includes the espoused values intended to serve as guiding principles for the culture. This includes organizational plans, strategies, norms and intended ways of doing things as determined by the leadership team.

The third level consists of the underlying assumptions related to how the culture perceives reality. This layer represents the deepest drivers of culture on which people base their reasoning and actions. It includes meaning systems, propensities, beliefs, perceptions and reasoning patterns. These may or may not align with the top two levels.

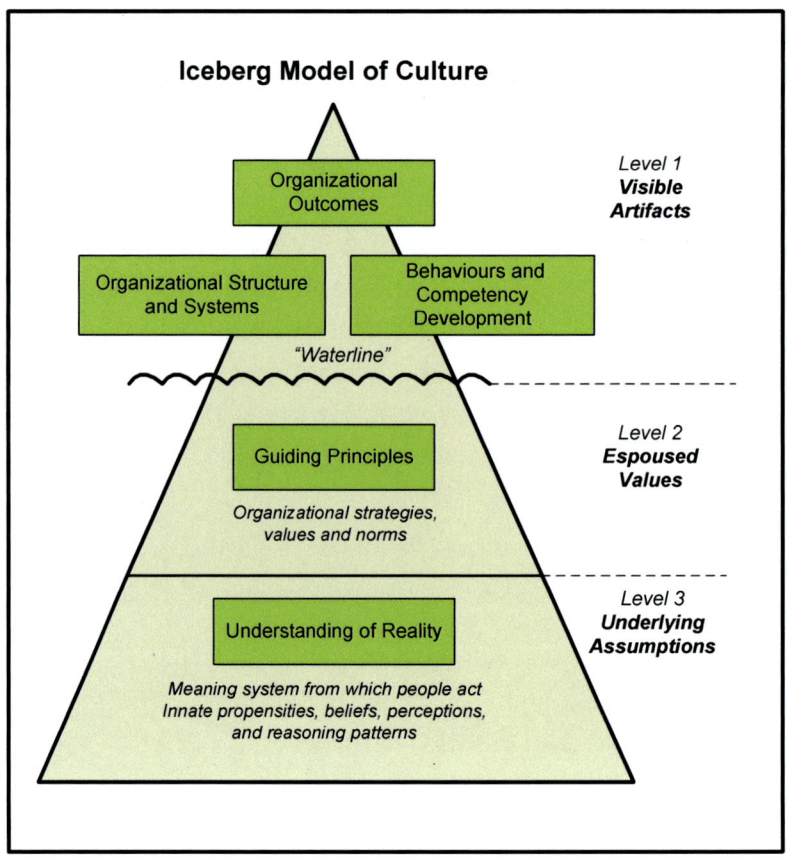

Figure 2-1: The Schein iceberg model of culture

Anthropologist Clifford Geertz said "culture is the creation of meaning through which human beings interpret their experiences and guide their actions". This holds true for any collection of people, be they family, community, organization or nation state. Each has a unique culture driven by individual and collective meaning systems. For example, religious beliefs, political philosophies, and free market versus controlled economies represent different meaning systems.

Significant attention has been paid to culture as a key variable in shaping organizational effectiveness since the 1980s. While initially touted as the means to ensuring business success, culture has since become understood as a complex phenomenon that can be influenced, but cannot be controlled to achieve desired outcomes. Part of this has to do with the realization that culture is deeply rooted in invisible meaning systems within and beyond the organization's boundaries and as such are not easily understood or managed.

In this handbook we prefer to use two terms: human system and meaning system, rather than culture because these terms invite a more penetrating view of how individuals, teams, and organizations relate and make meaning. A human system/meaning system approach lends itself to diagnostic tools and approaches that are more precise than generic culture assessments. In addition, by working with these two distinct concepts, management system developers are better able to shape a comprehensive system that closely aligns with the needs and desired outcomes of the organization.

HUMAN SYSTEMS AND MEANING MAKING

From an organizational perspective, the human system describes the way people interact with the social, physical, and formal organizational context in which they find themselves. The human system is the culture producing entity. We introduced the elements of the human system in Figure 1-2, and will explore each of them in later chapters. Our definition for human system is shown in the following box.

> ### *DEFINITION: Human System*
>
> A ***human system*** is a multi-dimensional, self-regulating interplay of meaning-making, intentions, relationships, and capabilities at the team, organizational, and societal levels.

Meaning systems are the underlying drivers of decision-making and action within a human system. Individuals operate on the basis of personal beliefs or theories they have about themselves, about others, about the world of situations they encounter, and their relationship to each. These beliefs or theories form distinct meaning systems that allow individuals to give meaning to the world around them and to their experiences, as well as to set goals, plan activities, and order their behavior.

Meaning systems usually contain descriptive beliefs as well as motivational or prescriptive beliefs. The major descriptive aspects of a meaning system are concerned with the nature of the person (e.g., I am competent); the nature of the world (e.g., the world is just), and propositions relating the two (e.g., I can change the world). Meaning systems develop in order to meet basic motives: 1) a stable and coherent sense of self, 2) a favourable balance of pleasure and pain in the forseeable future, 3) a favorable balance of self-esteem, 4) a favourable relationship with significant others. We define meaning system in the following box.

DEFINITION: Meaning System

A ***meaning system*** is an inner sense-making and response-formulating strategy evolved from assimilating perceived external cues over the course of one's life.

Most of us don't think about our meaning system even though it underlies almost every aspect of our individual, team, organizational and societal functioning. Individual meaning systems manifest as dominant tendencies and preferences as well as blind spots. Differences in meaning systems can give rise to misunderstanding or conflict, yet are also a rich source of ideas and opportunities. In organizations, poorly integrated meaning systems create dysfunction rather than leverage the capabilities inherent in diversity.

Each of us has developed a unique meaning system over time from a myriad of factors related to our innate capabilities, culture, heritage, education, environment, preferences, experiences, and relationships with family and others (Figure 2-2). Our meaning system continually evolves, with some elements deeply rooted, and others subject to re-evaluation based on new experiences and information (Figure 2-3).

Meaning systems are the birthplace of intention. Intention in turn drives attention, connectedness, and action. Meaning systems are related to social-emotional-physical security and survival. At a deep level they are a hook to an interior sense of self, innate propensities, feelings and emotions. They are a key to surfacing intrinsic motivation and with it, discretionary effort.

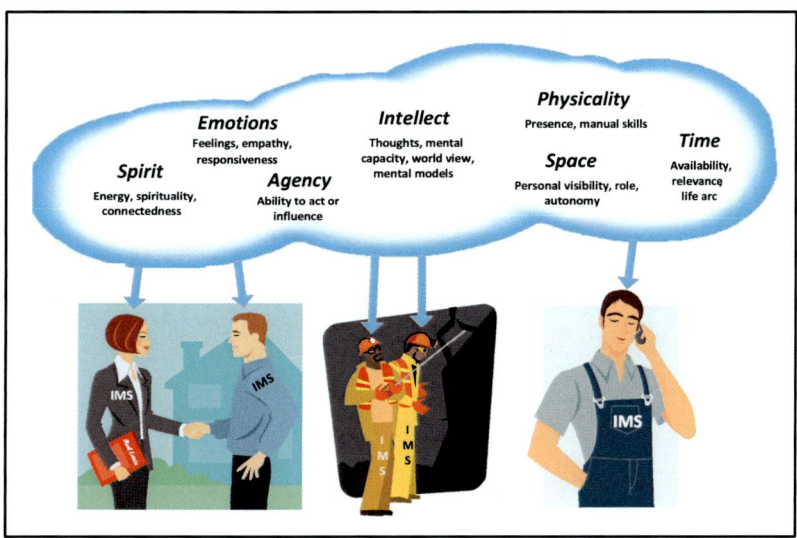

Figure 2-2: Our individual meaning systems are unique

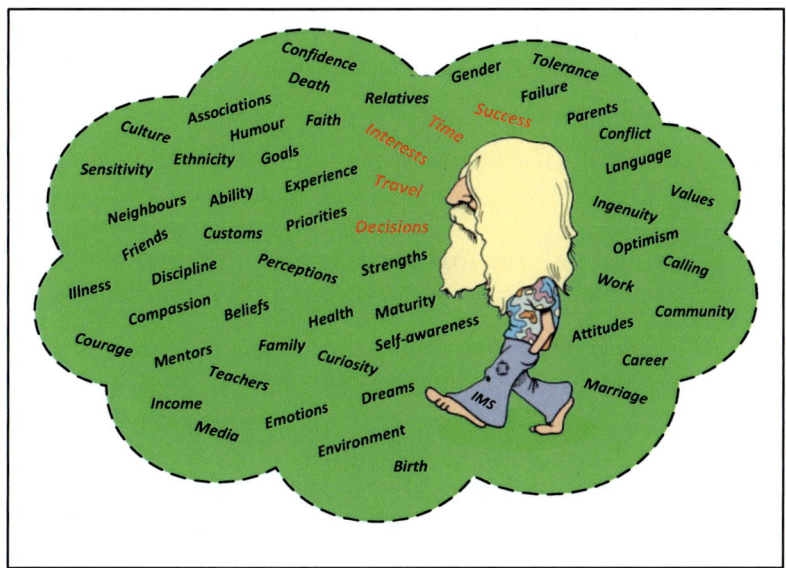

Figure 2-3: Our meaning systems continually evolve

Not only are individual meaning systems unique, they are often surprisingly different. For example, a clever HSBC Bank ad (Figure 2-4) illustrates that computers and babies may mean work to one person, and play to another. The accompanying caption states that "A different point of view is simply the view from a place where you're not". In other words, our meaning system drives our point of view.

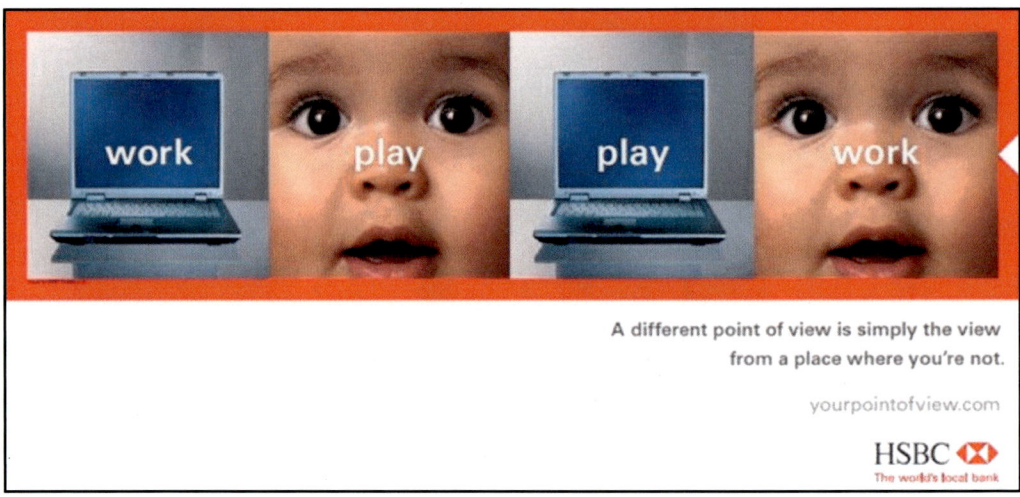

Figure 2-4: HSBC advertisement illustrating different meaning systems

An example of conflicted meaning systems can be found in the Camel "Discover More" cigarette ads showing a picture taken at dusk in which a torch handler deftly traces an illuminated outline of a camel (Figure 2-5A). In Germany, the words "Smoking can kill" appear in stark letters beneath the ad as required by law (Figure 2-5B).

The meaning created by the juxtaposition of "discover more" and "smoking can kill" probably wasn't foreseen by the ad designers. 'Enjoy each moment' or a similar phrase might have reduced the dissonance, although 'enjoy it while you can' might have appeared too cynical. The ad has since disappeared.

When one adds cultural influences, divergence can be significant. What is accepted as safe, for example, may differ greatly from country to country, since relative safety depends not only on individual perceptions of risk, but risk as perceived within the organizational and societal culture.

Figure 2-5A:

Camel cigarette ad as originally conceived

Figure 2-5B:

Camel cigarette ad as presented to the German public

Effective ad campaigns not only account for, but are designed to leverage or manipulate meaning systems. A study of extreme consumers indicated that 100% of them "personally identify with and say they gain meaning from a favorite brand" [Harvard Business Review 2010]. This was higher than any other attribute in the study. By extension, people who personally identify with and gain meaning from their organizations will be more inclined to support the activities of the organization.

Although we have highlighted individual meaning systems, organizations also have collective meaning systems that are created through the interactions of individual meaning systems with the overall intention of the organization. Misalignment between the collective meaning system and individual meaning systems can make or break an organization (see box).

> ### *Why meaning systems matter to organizations*
>
> A clearly articulated meaning system enables an organization to consciously design its processes and structures to support implementation of its intended culture and purpose. Employees and customers who relate to the organization's meaning system will actively support its goals. Practices that conflict with or undermine an organization's meaning system inevitably give rise to internal conflicts that reduce effectiveness.
>
> ***Principle in action:*** Reflect on and communicate the underlying meaning of your organization's purpose and actions. Ensure that the management system reflects and promotes the organization's desired meaning system.

MOTIVATION

A spirited management pitch to motivate employees may simply incite derision in some people. Why? The simple answer is that motivation is tightly tied to individual meaning systems – what motivates Robert may demotivate Sally. Understanding that people, in the end, can only motivate themselves, is essential to understanding individual performance and organizational dynamics.

Each of us is motivated by different things. It isn't as simple as saying that fortune, love, and the good life portrayed in TV commercials summarize human motivators. Yet even though it's more complicated, our underlying motivational pattern is still decipherable. Appendix A provides methods for you to explore your own motivational preferences. Try it before you read on.

Some of us pay close attention to what is happening inside us from moment to moment, noticing our thoughts and feelings. Some of us pay attention to what is happening within our immediate family and community of friends. Others are highly attuned to what is going on in the broader world; what is making news, who is being affected or infected by what, and who is trying to do something about it. Some of us merely watch life's script play out before our eyes, as if powerless to influence the unfolding drama.

We'll start deciphering these different approaches using Table 2-1, in which we consider motivation in three categories shown by the columns. Those of us who pay close attention to our inner well-being and self-determination tend to be motivated by feelings of personal competence, autonomy, and relatedness listed in column 1 (intrinsic motivation). We shape our behaviors based on this internal monitoring. For example, emergence from childhood is often a quest for demonstrating competence – from learning to ride a bike, to gaining the freedom to drive the family car, to building friendships beyond our family and neighbors.

Table 2-1: Perspectives on Human Motivation

Intrinsic Motivation (Interior space) *Focus on inner well-being and self-determination*	**Inter-subjective Motivation** (Shared space) *Focus on engagement and appreciation*	**Extrinsic Motivation** (Visible/public space) *Focus on impact and outcome*
Competence	Recognition	Achievement
Autonomy	Respect	Social Power
Relatedness	Inclusion	Affiliation
I pay attention to my inner signals and rely on them to guide my behaviour. (Being.)	I pay attention to the quality/safety of the 'space' as a means of deciding my level of participation. (Being and doing.)	I pay attention to the signals around me and rely on them to guide my behaviour. (Doing and performing.)

As we grow, we begin to notice how we are perceived in the broader community, what impact we have, and how we can exercise influence to get what we want. We expand our awareness and begin to seek external validation for our accomplishments. The related extrinsic motivators of achievement, social power, and affiliation in column 3 lead us to pay more attention to what others consider as achievements, appropriate displays of power, and desirable social image and relationships. Relatedness broadens into a desire to be affiliated with or 'belong' to social groups or organizations well beyond our network of close relationships. We behave this way in order to gain influence and status. We want to attain a degree of social power and be recognized by others for our achievements.

Our individual patterns of how we pay attention to our inner experience, to the impact and influence we have on others, and to the outcomes we achieve, including the desirability of these outcomes in the eyes of others, is only part of the motivation story. If we are driven only by intrinsic or extrinsic motivators, we may limit our experience and feel less connected with the world. Fortunately, other motivators influence us. These motivators are associated with the middle column of Table 2-1; what we call inter-subjective motivation or 'shared space' – our need to feel included, respected, and recognized as unique and valuable beings.

In shared space, which we will return to later in this chapter, we feel no need to prove our competence to ourselves or to others. We don't have to display evidence of our achievements because we feel recognized through active engagement and appreciation. Similarly, we don't have to assert our power because opportunities and resources are equally shared. In terms of relationships, we can be authentically open, secure in a felt sense of belonging because inclusion and authenticity are the norm in shared space. Our greatest risk of being inauthentic lies in column 3, where we may feel pressure to behave in accordance with how we want others to perceive us in that particular environment.

In some respects the transition across the columns is akin to being alone with our private thoughts, sharing our true thoughts with close friends, and being in social space where the talk rarely turns deep. If you belong to a group, pay attention to whether the discussion stays in social space or takes occasional forays into shared space. The latter only happens if someone is willing to self-reveal and bring their authentic self (column 1) into the discussion. A group lucky enough to have a few members who can do that consistently and naturally is indeed fortunate. The same is true for organizations of any type, because such people stimulate true learning.

> ### *Why motivation matters to organizations*
>
> Motivation is essential to the commitment, mobilization, productivity and follow-through of the organization's members. Management system developers need to ensure that practices, processes, and structures are designed to motivate rather than demotivate performers, taking into account the diverse motivational preferences that drive engagement and performance.
>
> ***Theory in action:*** Not everyone or every group has the same motivational needs. Make a conscious effort to confirm that a practice is consistent with motivators that will lead to the desired outcome.

PROPENSITIES

Meaning systems refer to the sense-making and response formulating strategies that form unique world views. Propensities are natural inclinations or tendencies in individuals or groups to relate or behave in particular ways. Propensities are intrinsically connected with individual meaning systems and are the primary determinant of conscious and unconscious habitual ways of thinking, feeling, and acting.

Propensities are different from learned competencies. A propensity is a natural, in-born preference to reason, relate, and act in a particular way or be drawn to and succeed at particular activities. A learned competency is a developed skill that may be enhanced through training or experience. The distinction between propensities and competencies is important:

> ### DEFINITION: Propensity
>
> A ***propensity*** is a natural, in-born preference to reason, relate, and act in a particular way or be drawn to and succeed at particular activities.

> ### DEFINITION: Competency
>
> A ***competency*** is a developed skill that may be enhanced through training or experience.

An alignment of propensities and competencies enables the potential for high levels of performance, achievement, and satisfaction.

Propensities make individuals, teams, and whole organizations more likely to pursue, and succeed at, some activities rather than others. Because propensities are deeply ingrained preferences and patterns of behaviour, they have a profound impact on individual and shared world views, reasoning styles, and the ability of individuals to share space with those who hold different viewpoints. Propensities reflect operative meaning systems and deeply felt senses of 'who am I' and 'who are we' in relation to others and the world at large. They are a significant determinant of organizational culture.

Ongoing psychometric research spanning 30 years and involving 30,000+ individuals in 500 distinct jobs ranging from CEOs to labourers has mapped propensities across 35 broad occupational themes and 26 behavioural competencies (Cash 2011). The study identified and measured 85 statistically distinct behavioural and psychological attributes demonstrated in the workplace and in general life. While typically used to predict on-the-job behaviors for incumbents and select high-potential candidates for roles, the research provides compelling evidence that measures of aggregate propensity can predict success and satisfaction prior to role assignment for individuals, teams, and organizations.

Table 2-2 provides a sample of the rank-ordered behavioral preferences within 6 of the 35 occupational themes. Appendix B provides a complete list of the 26 behavioral competencies, 35 occupational themes, and 6 behavioural-based leadership styles.

The senior executive sample included over 1500 successful Chief Executive Officers, Vice-Presidents, and Senior Managers/Directors who were consistently rated as 'high' performers in their respective functions. This occupational theme includes executives from small, medium, and large organizations, including multi-national profit and not-for-profit organizations. The other themes in Table 2-2 include occupational titles typically associated with that grouping (e.g., medical encompasses physicians, nurses, dental hygienists, optometrists, chiropractors, etc.).

Table 2-2: Aggregate Propensities Related to Success in Selected Occupational Themes (Cash 2011)

Senior Executive	Engineering	Finance	Law and Politics	Medical Services	Education
Good to Excellent	**Good to Excellent**	**Good to Excellent**	**Good to Excellent**	**Good to Excellent**	**Good to Excellent**
• Leads decisively • Seeks innovation • Focuses on results • Initiates independently • Thrives on chaos • Demonstrates social charisma • Sustains profitability • Maintains accountability • Manages stress • Reasons critically • Exercises political influence	• Reasons critically • Builds consensus • Demonstrates character • Thinks conceptually • Strives for excellence • Overcomes adversity • Maintains accountability	• Reasons critically • Demonstrates character • Maintains accountability • Leads decisively • Builds consensus	• Communicates clarity • Leads decisively • Thinks conceptually • Demonstrates strategic vision • Utilizes humor • Reasons critically • Strives for excellence • Maintains accountability	• Demonstrates character • Thinks conceptually • Demonstrates strategic vision • Communicates clarity • Demonstrates community consciousness • Focuses on results	• Communicates clarity • Thinks conceptually • Demonstrates community consciousness • Builds consensus • Demonstrates character • Maintains accountability • Establishes alliances
Low	**Low**	**Low**	**Low**	**Low**	**Low**
• Communicates clarity • Manages self • Builds consensus • Demonstrates community consciousness • Demonstrates character • Thinks conceptually • Demonstrates strategic vision • Establishes alliances • Utilizes humour • Strives for excellence • Establishes order	• Manages self • Establishes order • Communicates clarity • Sustains profitability • Demonstrates social charisma • Demonstrates community consciousness • Seeks innovation • Exercises political influence • Drives achievement	• Manages self • Initiates independently • Responsive to change • Demonstrates community consciousness • Utilizes humor • Seeks innovation • Exercises political influence • Drives achievement	• Builds consensus • Responsive to change • Seeks innovation • Demonstrates community consciousness • Exercises political influence • Sustains profitability • Drives achievement	• Manages stress • Manages self • Demonstrates social charisma • Overcomes adversity • Initiates independently • Responsive to change • Demonstrates energetic enthusiasm • Seeks innovation • Exercises political influence • Sustains profitability • Drives achievement	• Focus on results • Manages self • Initiates independently • Demonstrates energetic enthusiasm • Reasons critically • Utilizes humor • Exercises political influence • Thrives on chaos • Overcomes adversity • Drives achievement • Sustains profitability

From the career themes in Table 2-2, it becomes apparent that the propensities of senior executives are significantly different from those of the other themes. This holds for comparisons across all 35 occupational themes.

Successful senior executives, as a group, demonstrate a strong focus on innovation and sustaining profitability. They achieve impact through opportunism, decisiveness, initiative, and demonstrating ease in rapidly changing and even chaotic circumstances. At the same time, preferences such as conceptual thinking and strategic vision are lower than average, suggesting that the effectiveness of senior executives derives from charting a near-term course and working systematically through managing and controlling rather than engaging in more systemic and integrative approaches.

Sustaining profitability, exercising political influence, seeking innovation, and demonstrating social charisma are all high in the senior executive profile, and at the same time are the most predominant lows across the other 34 occupational themes. Driving achievement, which is an average predictor of success for senior executives, is consistently very low across the other occupational themes. Senior executives tend to be more opportunistic, compete to win, and measure success and work monetarily.

As an example, senior executives are instinctively concerned with financial viability, whereas the majority of their workforce, including financial staff, typically do not focus on financial viability issues. The workforce concern may be with individual financial security, or control of resources for their function, but not the long-term financial needs of the organization. Senior executives need to pay attention to whether people with propensities for sustaining profitability are seeded into key spending areas such as production and marketing.

Table 2-2 reveals other differences among occupational themes. For example, the preference for improving the quality of life in communities, including respect for the environment (i.e., 'demonstrates community consciousness' in Table 2-2) suggests that such considerations are not important for success in senior executive, financial, engineering, legal and political occupations. In contrast, success in medical services and education demands a higher level of community consciousness. Such observations do not mean that the former groups are anti-community or anti-environment. It simply suggests that community and environmental concerns don't naturally occupy their attentional or intentional fields, and as such are less likely to be given significant weight in decision-making. Multi-stakeholder engagement is generally needed to insert these alternative perspectives.

Table 2-2 illustrates the importance of having the right propensity alignment between the individual, their role, and organizational needs. Individual suitability for a role determines success, satisfaction, and willingness to put forth discretionary effort. A balance between job challenge and individual skill contributes to a 'flow' state that represents optimal performance for the individual. A flow state maximizes an individual's contribution while maintaining their wellbeing. Seeding the right person and the right role into a team supports team functionality. For example, a financial person on a production team needs to have enough understanding of production to ensure his or her presence doesn't impede the team. One or more members of the team also require the propensity to bridge the difference between the engineering and financial worldviews and ways of working.

For obvious reasons, management system development teams need to be more versatile than most. They require significant diversity of reasoning and relating to be able to bridge and engage stakeholders from all areas and levels as they map processes across the organization. Key attributes are discussed in Chapter 5.

Propensities also shape power dynamics within a room. The degree of conflict in any interaction will be determined by the relative strengths of the preferences, the maturity of awareness of those who possess the strengths, and their capacity for strategic self-management.

The capacity to be effective in particular ways has long been understood to be the product of skills acquired through learning, plus talent or innate propensities. For example, to be able to reason critically at a highly competent level requires both a propensity to be analytical and advanced training in analytical techniques. It makes little sense to educate people to be lawyers, engineers, or financiers if their innate propensity is more intuitive, aesthetic or theoretical than critically rational. No one would ask their lawyer or banker to develop their international marketing campaign or fire protection strategy. Propensities have other implications for teams (see next sidebar).

A common bias in organizations is to presume that success at lower levels of leadership predicts success at higher levels. Different levels of leadership require distinctly different functionalities and therefore distinctly different competencies and propensities.

> ***Teams are stronger than individuals unless propensities interfere***
>
> If my dominant propensity is to drive achievement, and I am weak in your strength of political influence, two things are likely to happen. I will tend to force issues; while you attempt to negotiate. I will consider your manoeuvring as a weakness; while you consider my approach as domineering and lacking finesse. If our team doesn't include others who are good at bridging diverse meaning systems, solutions will be less robust, and relationships will become strained.

Propensities cannot be simply skilled in, willed in, or summoned for temporary duty through techniques such as attempting to be creative through brainstorming. Such methods cannot substitute for the creative capabilities of individuals for whom this is a natural talent. As stated by Larry Cash of Cash Lehman and Associates, "only individuals who are well suited for what they do, coupled with an intense love of what they do, produce exceptional results".

Propensities form the essence of the human system: propensities underlie meaning systems, and meaning systems underlie cultures. Surprisingly, people rarely think about the impact of their innate propensities on behaviour, relationships, performance and culture. Consequently, organizations mistakenly believe that education, training, background, and experience can provide sufficient information to select new recruits and assign people to teams. As Samuel Johnson quipped: "Almost every man wastes part of his life in attempts to display qualities he does not possess."

The good news is that propensities can be measured through validated psychometric tests that are simple to administer. Understanding propensities improves the ability to select new recruits, balance teams, and identify leadership potential for succession planning. It also allows individuals to self-select educational and career paths best suited to their natural talents.

> ### *Why propensities matter to organizations*
>
> Propensities represent the natural strengths and blind spots of individuals, teams, and leaders. They are a dominant force in shaping the meaning system and culture of an organization. They influence reasoning styles, external receptivity, adaptability, foresight, and many other dimensions that are critical to successful performance.
>
> Management system developers, in conjunction with organizational specialists, need to define for each process, structure, or team the required match between tasks and propensities for successful performance. This includes leadership styles appropriate for the activities and outcomes. The management system has to provide coherence between activities and performers.
>
> ***Theory in action:*** Stop thinking of people as worker bees who can be trained to do anything. Make a conscious effort to help people find a role in which their natural propensities can make a difference to them, their team, and the organization.

DIVERSITY

Propensities help clarify an important, yet often under-appreciated, aspect of diversity. Most people think of diversity in terms of gender, race, religion, culture, country of origin, sexual orientation, or membership in a visible minority such as the physically or mentally challenged. Equal opportunity employment practices often focus on these elements.

A deeper view of diversity involves an appreciation of different reasoning and relating styles, world views, patterns of behavior, and action logics that derive from differences in <u>individual</u> meaning systems and propensities. Mining this diversity can provide true strength to organizations. Organizations that fail to understand the value of diversity of propensities tend to clone themselves, and build in weaknesses that make them less resilient and adaptable.

For example, as suggested in the previous section, executive teams may not always have sufficient diversity for creative problem-solving, bridging different viewpoints, and systemic integration. For similar reasons, management systems are better developed by teams with diverse capacity rather than by monofunctional groups such as Quality Assurance departments. In Chapter 5 and Part B we will spend time matching propensities with the roles needed for developing and implementing a management system. A management system, because it is designed and driven by the human system, needs to accommodate diversity of reasoning and relating in order to be effective.

> ### *Why diversity matters to organizations*
>
> Diversity of reasoning and relating styles associated with individual meaning systems and propensities breathe life into an organization's ability to innovate, solve messy problems, and foresee risks. Organizations need to consciously overcome their tendency to clone themselves (and thus their weaknesses) by continuing to hire and promote only those who fit the comfort zone of their own world views.
>
> ***Theory in action:*** Assign individuals to positions and teams based on their ability to fill propensity gaps.

SOCIAL DYNAMICS AND SHARED SPACE

Most organizations are based on a power structure and roles and responsibilities. While these can facilitate the orderly execution of work, they can also inhibit productivity and the ability to mine the intelligence of the organization if the leadership does not promote and model a spirit of engagement and teamwork.

Let's examine what happens when we have to collaborate with others. How do our unique motivation patterns create the social dynamics we see around us every day? Our willingness to engage with others depends on how we value ourselves and value what we bring; and the trust we have in others and our belief about how they will treat us. If we bring trust and openness, and share ourselves, we create the possibility of safe emotional space for those around us. We create an opportunity for genuine exchange of thoughts and feelings, collaboration and learning. We can help build a shared meaning system from which we can formulate coherent responses. Without shared meaning, trust wanes and the desire for individual security begins to create separation, doubt, and defensive responses.

Shared space is not 'groupthink' where everyone buys into and embraces the same point of view. It is about being willing to hear different ideas and opinions, and to see the value inherent in diverse styles of thinking and reasoning, in ways of relating and prioritizing, and in exploring what is deeply meaningful to us. Since our personal motivational patterns are unique, questioning others' motives is less productive than trying to understand the basis for them. The concept of shared space is important enough to warrant a definition (see box).

DEFINITION: Shared Space

Shared space is a state of mutual, sincere receptiveness to diverse viewpoints, motivations, and desires with the aim of enhancing mutual growth, creativity, and understanding. Shared space embodies authentic engagement with others.

Creating shared space is not about giving up our sense of self and identity. While increasing the permeability of our thought/feeling/perception boundaries is conducive to authentic communication and sharing, we need to be mindful about honouring our inner conscience, intrinsic needs, and capacity.

We can help create shared space by bringing our authentic self into the space, keeping our permeability to new ideas open, and willingly entertaining the contributions of others. We can encourage self-reflection and curiosity, empower each other, consciously include others, and be willing to show vulnerability by expressing our true feelings and asking sincere questions.

Shared space is diminished through inappropriate power dynamics whereby one person either consciously or without awareness, uses personal or positional power to unduly influence others or control the agenda. This typically manifests as managing information flow, using alliances to exclude other, bullying, ignoring individuals or topics, or various forms of self-aggrandizement.

Figure 2-6 presents an image of the relationship between our inner selves, others, and the world at large.

How we choose to 'be' in the presence of others has the potential to create confusion and tension, or a clean and healthy space that is welcoming for all. Our awareness of the nuances of clean, shared space allows us to be authentic and effective. With mindfulness, we can become conscious of whether we are helping to create or disrupt this space. Management systems, because they are collaborative in nature, need to support the creation of shared space within organizations.

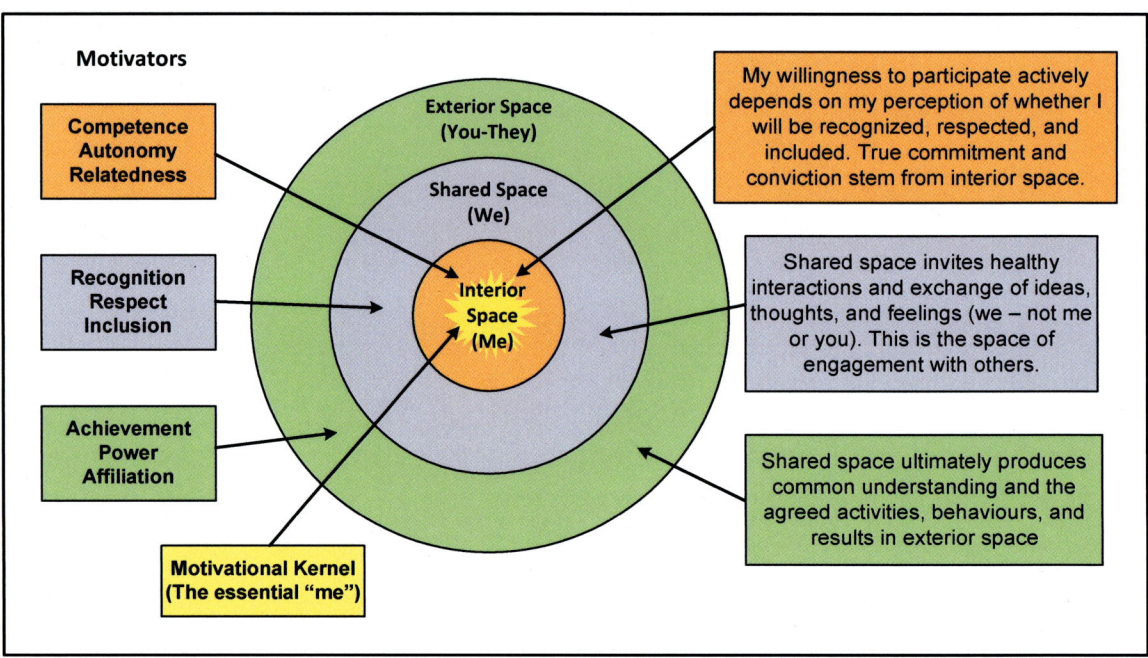

Figure 2-6: Personal motivation and shared space

Management system developers can promote shared space by helping ensure that cross-boundary interfaces, ownership, information sharing, and decision-making promote collaboration and inter-dependence rather than silos. Some of the approaches may seem subtle. For example, at first sight, a swim-lane approach to flow-charting seems attractive because it highlights the activities of individual departments and clarifies accountabilities. However, focus on 'my department's role' can also lead to ambivalence towards optimizing the functionality of the overall process or, worse, support a tendency to inflate the importance of the department's role by adding more activities such as reviews and approvals. Management systems empower people by making process knowledge accessible to everyone in the organization. This helps break down power structures associated with hoarded expertise and information.

FLOW

Now we can turn to another important question – What makes people feel energized and so totally absorbed that they skip lunch? What conditions enhance willingness and discretionary effort?

Figure 2-7 (Csikszentmihalyi 1990) illustrates the relationship between challenge and skill. When our capabilities match the challenges inherent in any situation, we have an increased likelihood of experiencing a state of 'flow' wherein our attention becomes totally absorbed in executing our activity without interference from noisy thoughts-felts, distractions, or even bodily needs and concerns. In contrast, when the challenges we confront exceed our capability, a growing sense of dis-ease happens until active worry takes over our awareness. Anxious thinking and feeling diminishes our attentiveness and increases the likelihood of misperceptions, misunderstandings, and mistakes. At the other end of the spectrum, when our capacity exceeds what is being asked of us, our sense of confidence and relaxation can gradually fade into boredom, disinterest, and complacency.

Management system specialists should consider whether the design of processes and structures contribute to flow through an appropriate balance between challenge and skill for the typical performer.

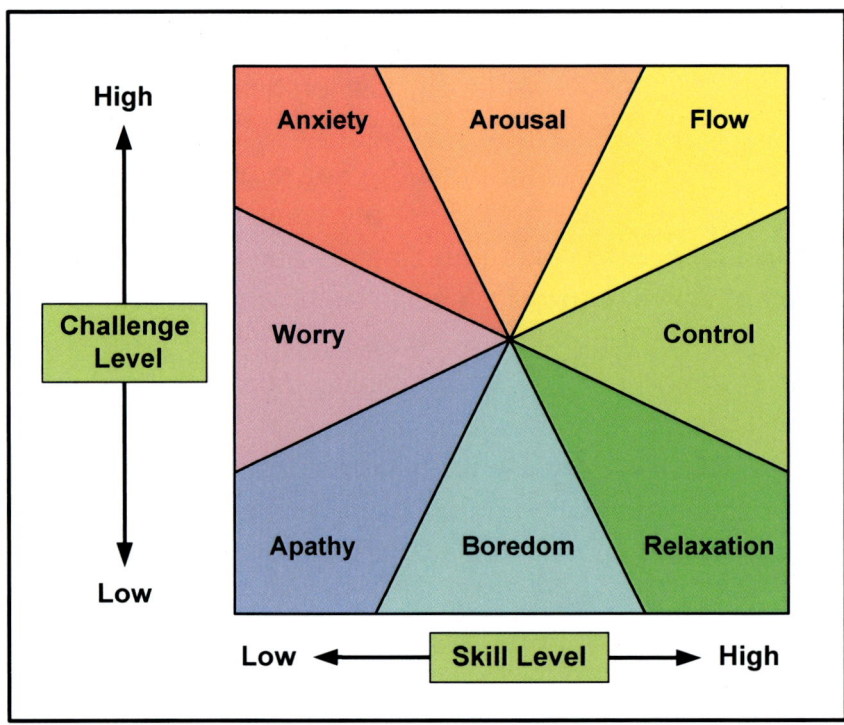

Figure 2-7: Challenge versus skill

Working in shared space lessens the likelihood that concerns for personal safety, status or outcomes will distract our focus and diminish flow in ourselves or others. Shared flow is aided by:

- Challenges appropriate to the capacity of each individual and the collective
- Clear roles and goals that help members know what they are doing and why
- Control over decisions and resources so members can easily and freely exchange what is needed to accomplish tasks
- Freedom from distractions
- Direct and immediate feedback that helps individuals know how they are doing so they can adjust course accordingly, and
- Activities that are intrinsically rewarding so there is an effortlessness of action.

Shared flow in shared space is possible when everyone believes that what they are doing is meaningful and of value materially, emotionally, and spiritually.

Organizations can contribute to employee flow by taking steps to place the right person, in the right job, on the right team, with the right leadership, in the right organizational culture and climate. Central to this is having individuals contribute to the way in which their work is structured, performed, and managed.

Organizations can also help to increase flow by understanding and shaping the different dimensions that support the creation of shared space. Figure 2-8 shows the elements that need to be considered in designing a human system that supports optimal human performance, to harness collective intelligence, agency, and productivity. Figure 2-8 shows these elements.

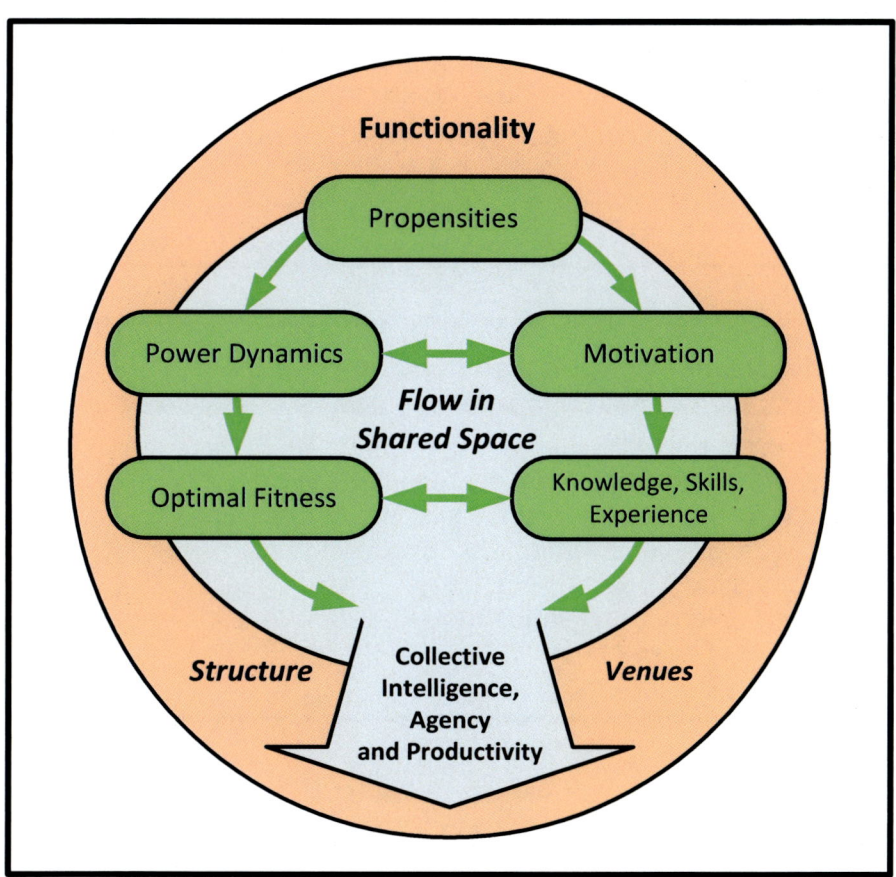

Figure 2-8: Creating shared space and flow in human systems

These elements are:

- the creation of balanced power dynamics necessary to support effective, productive interactions
- satisfaction of individual and team motivational needs and preferences
- alignment of individual propensities, knowledge, skills, and experience
- a work climate that respects and supports optimal fitness in terms of an individual's physical health, emotional health, and well-being
- alignment of functionalities and structure, and
- venues (meetings and work spaces) that promote connectivity.

Balanced power dynamics, in which leaders mitigate their tendency to be the voice of authority, helps prevent groupthink, jockeying for position, and suppression of ideas [Schein 2013].

Individuals can improve their own well-being and performance by increasing self-understanding and consciously choosing circumstances that honour intrinsic motivational needs and foster flow (see following sidebars).

What can I do to increase personal flow?

1. Define a clear purpose for myself.
2. Identify a compelling motive that is meaningful to me.
3. Take on a worthy challenge aligned with my propensities.
4. Establish or choose an environment conducive to my needs.
5. Allocate committed blocks of time.
6. Prevent interruptions and distractions.
7. Master the tools I need to use.

> ### *Why flow matters to organizations*
>
> Flow enhances productivity, performance, and job satisfaction. Willing, self-motivated effort occurs when circumstances align to support flow. This requires organizational leaders to engage participants to identify what constitutes flow in the context of their activities.
>
> ***Theory in action:*** Actively engage participants to design elements of the management system to promote flow.

SELF IN ACTION

It's useful to take a look at a model for how we as individuals operationalize, or fail to operationalize, actions we believe have value. In Chapter 5 and Part B we'll use similar models derived from the work of Drexler, Sibbet and Forrester [2011] to understand what makes teams and organizations effective.

Figure 2-9 provides a picture of how intention turns into mindful action. The 'V' shape suggests the arc of a bouncing ball. The left side shows the initial momentum associated with envisioning some aspect of our lives based on what has meaning to us, building connections with others who share that vision, and clarifying our intentions and goals. The turning point is the commitment of time, resources, and effort to achieve specific outcomes. The upward arc is transition into action where we organize our effort, leap in, and course correct as needed.

An alternative way to see this model is working from the top layer downward. The first layer is about what has meaning for us. When things are meaningful, we have energy and a sense of directedness. The second layer is about relationship. Both during formulation of direction and execution of our plans, engagement with the people and world around us allows it to happen. The third level looks at tasks; the specific actions that are needing to be executed using right processes, procedures and controls. Finally, the last layer is about choice.

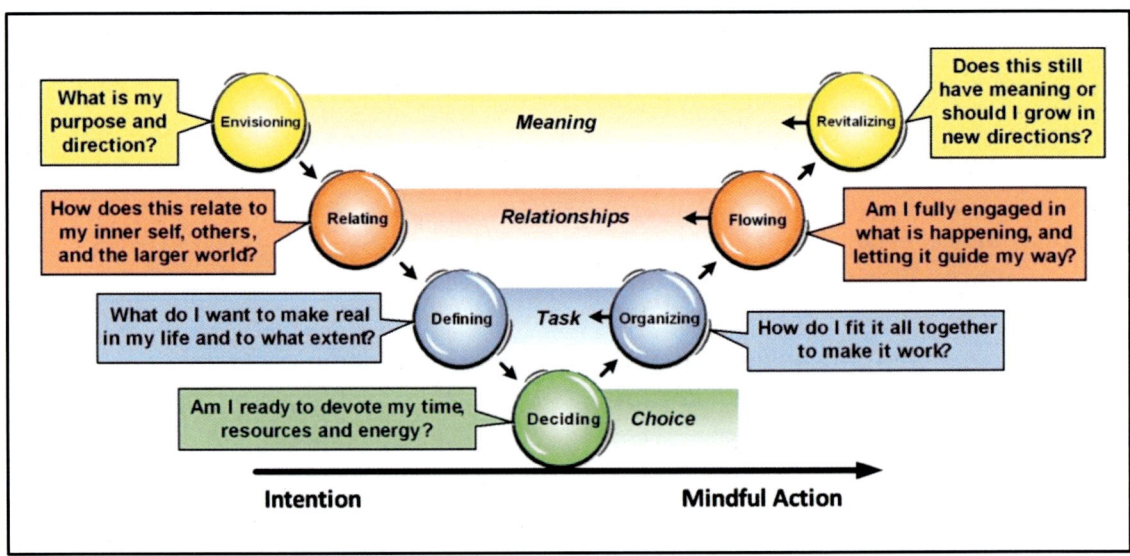

Figure 2-9: Individual Performance Model – Self in action

This arc of manifesting what we want to be and do starts with imagining what is wanted and possible. We answer questions such as how do I personally want to contribute to the world? Past successes or failures may temper or inspire our reasoning as we discern what we deem realistic and doable. This includes setting goals that sometimes reflect our willingness to let go of the need to control, to believe that we can trust ourselves and others, and to depend on situations being workable.

Eventually we settle on a course of action and begin to connect, control and contribute in order to create what we want. Based on feedback from our experiences we learn and adjust our course, building new capabilities as we progress. In time, as we achieve our goals, questions arise as to whether what we are doing is still meaningful to us, and we consider new directions that may spark a whole new cycle from envisioning through to commitment and action. The tiers of the model operate at the meaning, relationship, task, and choice levels.

Depending on where our personal strengths are in this cycle, different aspects will be easy or difficult for us. In other words, we are unlikely to be adept in every bubble of Figure 2-9. Some of us will find it more exciting to envision and articulate than to enact and accomplish what we set out to do. Others will be proficient at making things happen, but may struggle to define a clear vision of what they want to create that would be truly meaningful to them. This is one of the reasons why diversity on teams is so important.

Figure 2-9 can be expressed directly in terms of the behavioural factors or propensities that help propel action in each sphere. Figure 2-10 represents these behavioural factors, which are also listed in Appendix B with an explanation of each factor.

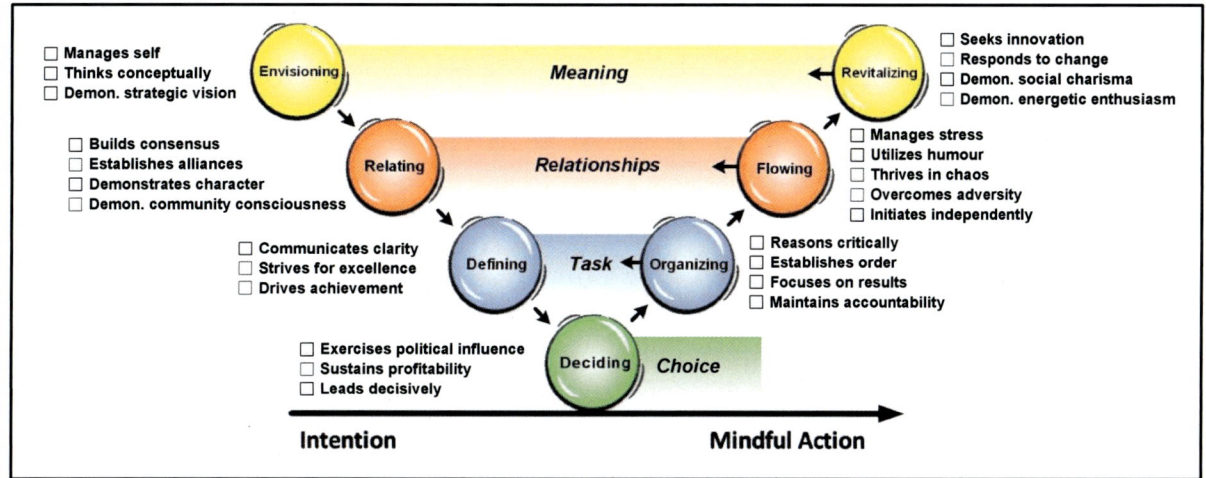

Figure 2-10: Behavioral factors that support the Individual Performance Model

It isn't our intent in this handbook to explore every dimension of this model, but it may be of value to illustrate its power by using the first bubble on 'envisioning' as an example.

The behavioural attributes that support envisioning are:

Manages self: I seek to deepen understanding of myself and sustain healthy self-acceptance without guilt and self-criticism.

Thinks Conceptually: I comprehend theoretical concepts and am curious about the broader 'why'. I use a holistic perspective to understand things inside and outside myself.

Demonstrates Strategic Vision: I take a longer-term and purposeful approach to finding solutions in order to actualize more meaningful or worthwhile strategic goals.

Combined, these propensities lead individuals to invest in creating a mental picture that links personal identity, meaningful engagement, and purposeful plans and activities into a coherent whole, thereby building their own sense of orientation and alignment, as well as that of others, if they are members of a team.

Validated psychometric assessments can provide specific information on an individual's propensities. Our intent here is merely to use the language of such behavioural models to ensure consistency throughout this handbook. As we deepen our understanding of our own propensities, we can look for more ways to give expression to what is most meaningful to us. We can decide what works for us and what patterns we might be better off changing. We can look for ways to increase our effectiveness, such as paying closer attention to what we are likely to overlook, or tapping into the talents of others who can help us along our way or provide perspectives that we are less likely to consider on our own.

One might wonder why this deep-dive into self-in-action and the other topics in this chapter are relevant to developing process-based management systems. The simple answer is that *everything is done by or through people, and we can't create a management system that will support high performance and achievement of desired outcomes without understanding something about how human beings perceive reality, create meaning within themselves and with others, and take purposeful right action.*

Our innate propensities, when exposed to interactions with our environment and others, create our individual meaning system. Individual meaning systems combine into a collective meaning system (a.k.a. culture). To the extent that individual meaning systems are aligned within a collective, they create an integrated/shared meaning system that is a vastly more powerful force than strategies, plans, procedures or any management action.

A model of self-in-action (Figure 2-10) grounded in propensities, and meaning systems is the building block for designing more effective teams and organizations. This approach combines and operationalizes the best of what has been learned from the full range of business/organization management theories which can loosely be categorized as:

- Theory X Management [McGregor, 1960] – managers and supervisors assume almost complete control of the work of

subordinates, thereby producing more systematic and uniform products or work flow
- Theory Y Management [McGregor, 1960]– managers and supervisors assume that workers are internally motivated, and relate to workers on a more personal level, as opposed to a more conductive and teaching based relationship
- Culture Management [Deal & Kennedy, 1982]– managers focus on understanding and shaping meaning that underlies behavior, thereby honouring autonomy while promoting conformity to acceptable norms of behaviour
- System Management [Senge, 1990] – managers focus on understanding and managing the relationships and interdependencies within the social system internal to and across organizations.

Each of these approaches are good at achieving some 'ends' – for example, Theory X Management focuses on greater consistency and variance reduction than do the other theories. However, it also brings with it the very real risk of worker disengagement. Each approach on its own leads to incomplete views of the management reality and can have unwanted side effects.

With the elements outlined in this chapter, we are proposing an integrative approach that will ensure that the management system helps the organization function as a self-conscious, self-motivating, self-actualizing entity that taps into the full intelligence and potential resident within its members. This will become even more evident when we look at the practicalities of organizational success in Part B.

Why self-in-action matters to organizations

Everything that organizations accomplish is done through people. Individuals have different capacities and interests in contributing to the chain of activities that move them (and their organizations) from intention to action. Failure to recognize all four dimensions that contribute to this human process:

- Individual inner experience and needs
- Individual talents
- Interpersonal relationships and shared meaning
- Systemic inter-connections and interdependencies

makes it harder for organizations to make conscious choices about resourcing teams that are adept at envisioning outcomes and proceeding to action.

Theory in action: In the management system, ensure that the organization is committed to working with a comprehensive perspective regarding these elements that drive high performance, and ensure that the process design and implementation teams form a balanced 'V' that provides both vision and action.

SUMMARY OF KEY POINTS

Foundational elements from this chapter will resurface in Part B. Key points related to the human system are summarized in the following box.

Key Points from this chapter on the roots of high performance

1. Alignment between individual and organizational meaning systems drives desired outcomes.
2. Since people are motivated by different things, motivation must be considered when designing teams, systems, processes and structures.
3. Individual, team, and organizational propensities fundamentally determine the capacity, culture, and sustainability of an organization.
4. Active creation and promotion of shared space enables organizations to mine the intelligence and productivity of participants.
5. Establishing conditions that support flow will enhance willingness and discretionary effort.
6. Staffing positions and teams for diversity of reasoning and relating gives better results and mitigates risk.
7. Understanding the self-in-action 'V' enables a conscious balance between envisioning what is needed and implementation through action.

Chapter 3
Organizational Evolution and Design

IN THIS CHAPTER

This chapter explores organizational development and maturity, and the value of rethinking hierarchical organizations. The sections cover:

- Organizational Evolution – Four stages
- Organizational Design – Creative chains, functionality, performance, and structural diversity.

ORGANIZATIONAL EVOLUTION

The stage of evolution and the predominant propensities that drive organizational culture determine its capacity to be effective and to change. Figure 3-1 shows a four stage model of organizational evolution [Watts and Paciga 2011]. Each stage has distinct attributes that influence organizational culture, resourcing strategies, management system design, and capacity for change.

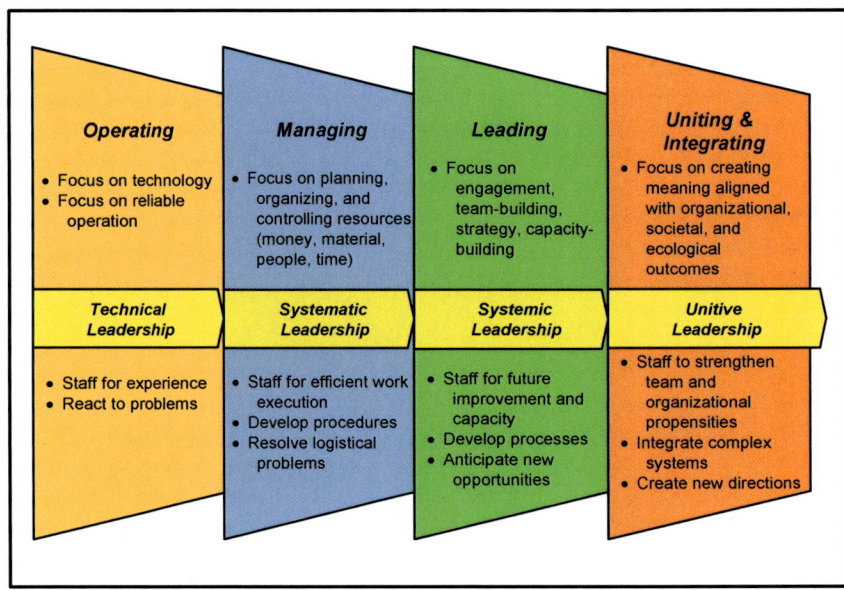

Figure 3-1: Organizational Evolution Model

Stage 1 – Operating*:* At the core of every organization is a hard or soft technology that defines the nature of its business. In the early phases, organizations focus on operating and enhancing their technology. Expert knowledge is prized for its ability to solve technical problems. Leadership becomes synonymous with technical competence and such individuals typically rise to positions of power and influence. Outcomes are viewed in concrete product terms, and employees are used to react to technical issues. Risk management tends to focus on the consequences of technical failures. The overall emphasis is on keeping the technology functioning. At this stage, the leadership propensity distribution reflects the primary occupational theme for the organization with relatively little diversity.

> ***Stage 1 Perceptions of Management Systems***
>
> We rely on technical competence, skills of the trade, and experience. We only need the management system to provide drawings, flow sheets, manuals, and procedures for specialized activities.

Stage 2 – Managing: As organizations grow, they begin to experience challenges in quality and productivity that require enhanced controls. Procedures, planning, and resource management become more formalized. Emphasis expands from technical aspects to logistical thinking aimed at improving resource utilization and work execution. Clear expectations for performance are used to improve productivity and reliability. Outcomes are viewed in financial and production terms, and employees are used to resolve operating challenges. Risk management expands to encompass financial concerns and assure minimal regulatory compliance. The overall emphasis is on achieving business results. At this stage, the leadership propensity distribution emphasizes productivity and reliability in terms of organizational and human performance.

> **Stage 2 Perceptions of Management Systems**
>
> We need good procedures and systems for work planning, prioritization, scheduling, procurement, cost control, etc. to improve logistics and efficiency.

Stage 3 – Leading: Stricter management controls enhance viability; however, these eventually give rise to issues related to employee motivation, satisfaction, and even loyalty. In response, emphasis shifts to include leadership development, team building, empowerment and similar efforts to boost morale and discretionary effort. Vision, mission, values, organizational culture, and strategic planning become a focus for enhancing organizational effectiveness. Processes and procedures become integrated into formal management systems. Employees are perceived as the means by which the organization distinguishes itself from its competitors, and their willingness to actively promote the organization's interests becomes important. Risk management expands to include safety culture and issues related to organizational capacity and sustainability. The overall emphasis is on capitalizing on new opportunities within and outside the organization. At this stage, the leadership propensity profile begins to value relatedness, consensus building, and human development. Leaders use socialization as the means to enhance cooperative effort.

> **Stage 3 Perceptions of Management Systems**
>
> Interdependencies among groups require us to develop standardized processes and systems to improve organizational interactions and efficiency.

Stage 4 – Integrating-Uniting: Advanced organizations recognize that long term sustainability requires them to pay attention to building and sustaining their capacity to anticipate, innovate and initiate changes on a societal and global level. The focus is on long term strategies, citizenship, contribution to society, and integration across organizational, (inter)national, political, and social lines. Employees are perceived as active participants in shaping the fabric and direction of the organization. Emphasis is placed on developing conditions that enable the full creativity and intelligence of the human system to flourish. These leading edge organizations continually shape and transform the nature of society itself through their exploration of new thought systems and new technologies. To achieve this level of performance, these organizations align meaning, propensities, and systems to create new directions. Possibly the world's best known example of a predominantly stage 4 organization is Microsoft with its encompassing reach and integration into all facets of our modern world. Tesla Corporation is similarly a good example of an organization devoting its efforts to realizing stage 4 priorities.

Leaders who operate at Stage 4 focus on the functioning of complex systems and their interfaces. They look beyond the constraints of existing systems to create transformative solutions. At this stage, the propensity distribution emphasizes visioning, optimism, enthusiasm, shared decision-making and problem solving, and a willingness to provide new learning opportunities in a supportive climate.

Stage 4 Perceptions of Management Systems

The management system enables knowledge management, promotes organizational coherence, and conveys organizational meaning. It enables disciplined oversight.

A more detailed discussion of leadership style by stage of evolution is provided in Appendix C.

The stage of organizational evolution has a significant impact on how an organization deals with issues. Different stages give rise to different management system designs, processes, and organizational structures. Each stage also anticipates and manages different types of risk:

- Stage 1 - Equipment failures
- Stage 2 - Schedule, coordination, logistics
- Stage 3 - Human engagement and motivation
- Stage 4 - External, long-term, context and systemic changes.

Each stage prioritizes different outcomes and cultivates different functionalities:

- Stage 1 - Expert problem solving
- Stage 2 - Operational risk management
- Stage 3 - Leadership and team development
- Stage 4 - Meaning-making and inter-connectedness.

Each stage integrates structure, processes, and procedures differently:

- Stage 1 - Discipline or specialty
- Stage 2 - Program or department
- Stage 3 - Productive chains and interdependent teams
- Stage 4 - Systemic formation of outcome focused process groupings.

We will return to these aspects and introduce others in later chapters. For the moment, it is worth looking at some of the human system dimensions associated with each stage of evolution. Each stage has preferred approaches to management and leadership style, staffing and talent management, and reasoning and acting in particular ways (prioritizing, problem solving, decision-making, influencing, etc.). These preferences have a direct impact on the:

- ability to envision, develop, and sustain coherent management systems
- predominant organizational and safety culture
- appetite and capacity for change
- investment strategies for learning and development.

Figures 3-2 and 3-3 illustrate the reasoning preferences associated with each stage. It is immediately apparent that 'doing and managing' emphasize operational and tactical decisions and results, whereas 'leading and uniting' emphasize longer term strategies. The reasoning and relating styles, focus, and action logics differ, with the former favouring pragmatism and immediate concrete action, and the latter favouring exploration, visioning, and engagement.

In essence, they represent distinct meaning systems, each of which are essential to successful organizational performance in entirely different ways.

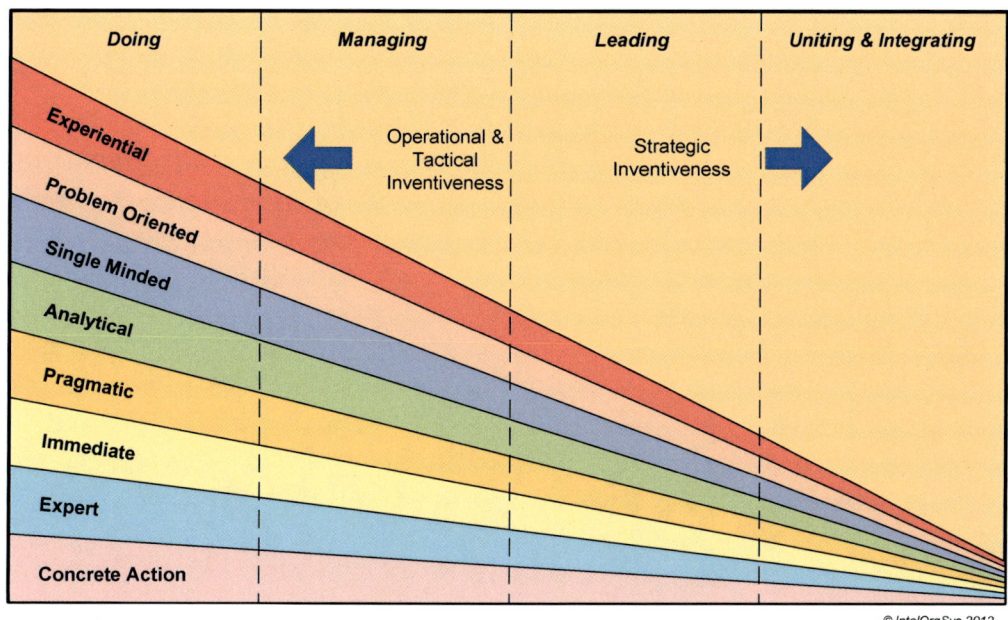

Figure 3-2: Doing (Technical) and Managing Propensities by Stage

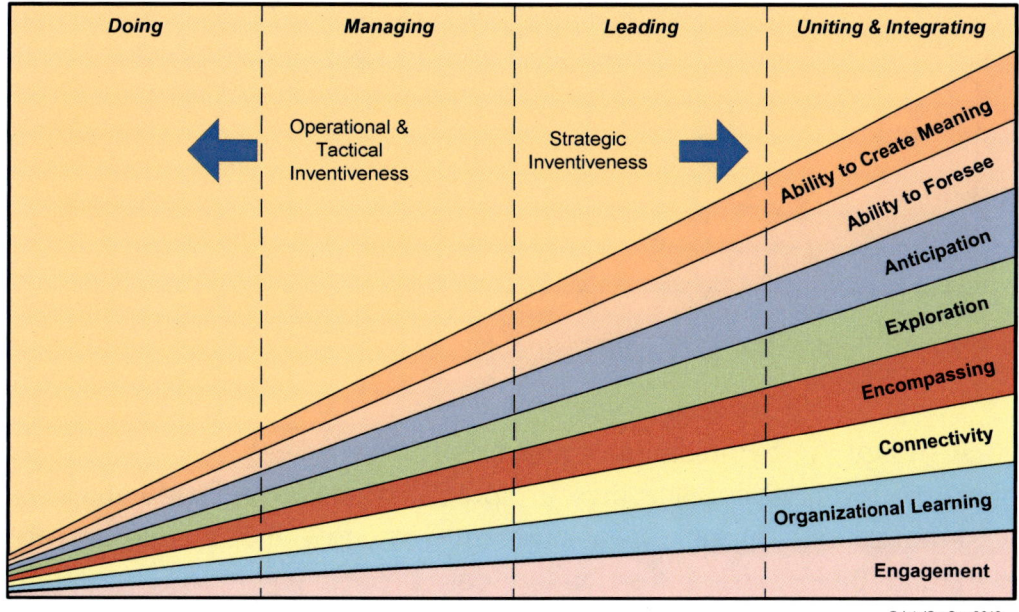

Figure 3-3: Leading and Uniting Propensities by Stage

Despite the different styles of reasoning, relating, and decision-making approaches that predominate at each stage, an organization's profile is typically distributed across stages rather than limited to a discrete stage (Figure 3-4). The propensity distribution is influenced by the operating context and technology. Each stage is essential to organizational functioning, with successive stages encompassing and addressing unresolved issues and risks of earlier stages. Different talent sets find their niche in different stages. *The desired state is to have a distribution so that all the different ways of managing risk, learning and adapting are present and active in supporting the work of the organization.*

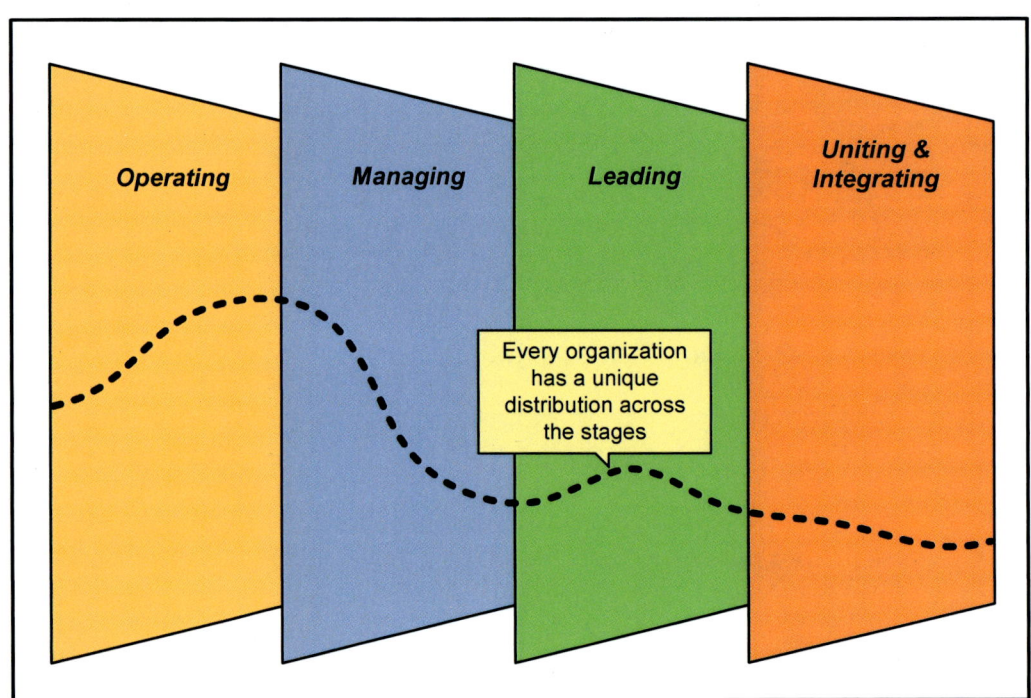

Figure 3-4: Example distribution of predominant propensities

A Stage 1 organization cannot transform itself into a Stage 2 or 3 organization without seeding different propensity sets and meaning systems into the organization through reassignment or new hires. Organizations that understand their current distribution can proactively manage propensities to strategically shape their evolution. As we will see in Part B, the stage of evolution has an impact on organizational readiness to develop an integrated management system.

ORGANIZATIONAL DESIGN

Organizations as creative chains

Organizations are creative chains that turn inputs into outputs [Watts, Paciga, and Whitcher 2013]. Depending on the stage of evolution, the creative chain is capable of a wide range of adaptive processes as illustrated in Figure 3-5. The chain essentially represents a productivity chain in which operational and tactical inventiveness increases towards the left and strategic inventiveness increases towards the right.

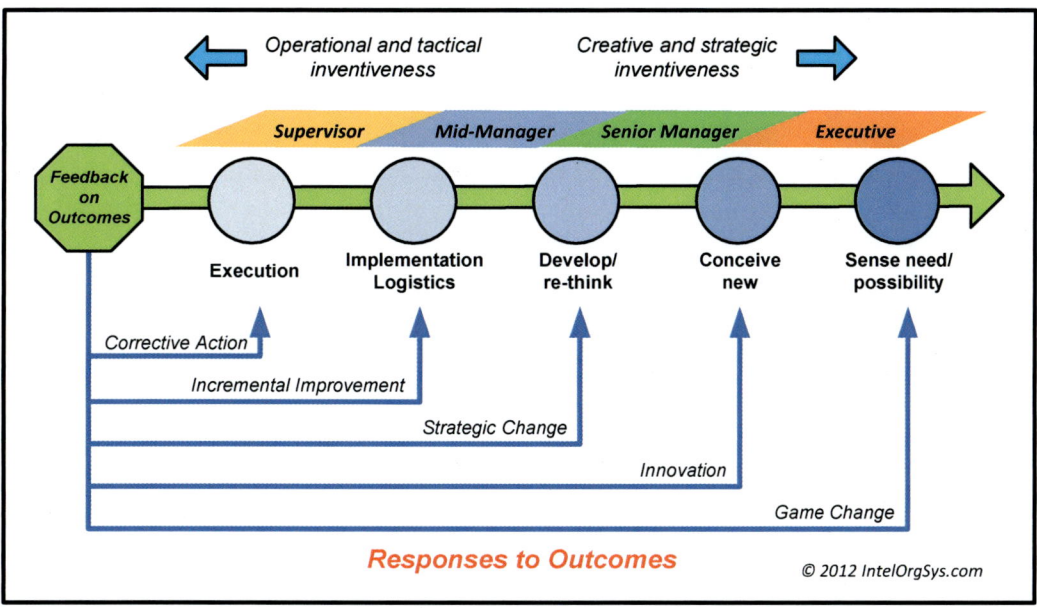

Figure 3-5: Organizations are creative chains

Figure 3-5 represents an organization with four formal leadership levels (supervisor, mid-manager, senior manager, and executive), each of which serves a distinct purpose. The type and level of functionality at each point along this creative chain involves different management and leadership activities and propensities. The nature and magnitude of change is also different at each point.

Organizations that understand this chain and clearly define and resource required functionalities can align innate workforce propensities with required organizational capacity to enhance sustainable performance. The extent of reliance on operational-tactical versus creative-strategic inventiveness depends on the context. If the environment and method of production is stable, a predictive structure is appropriate. If the environment is unpredictable and requires continual change in production to compete, then an adaptive, resilient structure is more appropriate. This is true for the organizational creative chain overall, as well as sub-sets of the organization which may require different functionalities.

Functionality versus Department Function

Different parts of an organization generally have different functionalities where functionality is the capacity to perform a task or fulfill an intended purpose. At the team or organizational level, functionalities reflect the extent to which people are able to align and integrate propensities to produce desired team outputs or achieve desired system outcomes (see box).

> ### *DEFINITION: Functionality*
>
> **Functionality** is the capacity to perform a task or fulfill an intended purpose. Functionality relies on the alignment of organizational structure, management system processes, and human propensities.

Functionality should not be confused with group function such as design, fabrication, maintenance, finance, or health and safety. For example, a maintenance department performs maintenance functions, but they are only one contributor to the key functionality of 'equipment reliability', which requires a broader spectrum of input and coordination (design, operations, planning, system health specialists, etc.). Other organizational functionalities that reflect important organizational capacities and desired outcomes include business excellence, innovation, and strategy. These can rarely be fulfilled by a single department or role.

For this reason, a design objective in aligning process systems with organizational structure is to group functionalities to enable efficient exchange of information and effort. Understanding the difference between the 'integrated' desired functionality and departmental function avoids getting trapped in the traditional approach which tends to simply bucket roles into departmental silos. Functionalities happen at the intersection of organizational structure, management system processes, and human propensities that breathe life into the activities of the organization. Figure 3-6 illustrates the importance of coherence among all three contributors.

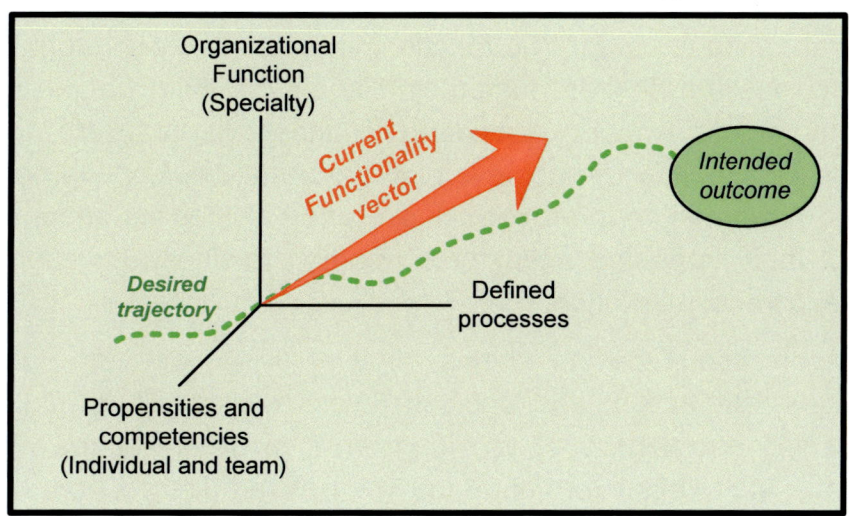

Figure 3-6: The three axes of organizational functionality

An example that illustrates Figure 3-6 is air travel, where the pilot (specialty) flies the plane using standard practices and procedures (defined processes), and brings personal competency and aptitude to the task along with other members of the flight crew. If the desired "trajectory" is well established, then the specialty, process, and competency requirements can also be well established. In cases where there is a need to manage the unexpected, for example, the 'trajectory' is less evident (e.g., navigation equipment failure), or circumstances are beyond the normal operating or design envelope (e.g., severe wind shear), there is heavier reliance on the skills and propensities of the pilot and flight crew. Passengers hope that the people in the cockpit have propensities related to responsiveness, managing ambiguity, decisiveness, and resilience to stress.

Although contingency processes are part of the management system, individual capacities come into play beyond what can be provided through training [Roberts and Bea 2001].

Organizational functionalities are best derived from a clear understanding of the core processes through which the organization performs its work, as well as the key executive and support processes that guide and enable the organization. Processes define, among other things, the logic of how work is organized, key interdependencies, and the authorities required for appropriate controls. High-level functionalities are the product of synergies between processes.

In practice the talent, process, information, communication, and organizational needs for a specific functionality have to be thought through and aligned to achieve the desired outcomes. Simply grouping people in traditional organizational charts without considering connectivity aspects that underlie effectiveness isn't sufficient to achieve high performance. For example, business planning and performance improvement are often treated as separate functions when in fact their combined intent of supporting business excellence requires cross-pollination and integration.

An organization design basis that clearly defines functionalities, accountabilities, authorities, and position level responsibilities can be used to guide resourcing decisions over the long term. In organizations with a formal management system, this information may be derived directly from management system processes. The purpose of an organization design basis aligned with a high-level management system model is to outline the way in which the organization is intended to function.

Organizational Performance

Drexler, Sibbet, and Forrester [2011] have developed organizational and team performance models that illustrate key attributes for achieving high performance. Figure 3-7 provides an adaptation of their organizational performance model. As indicated previously for the individual effectiveness or performance model (Figure 2-8), the 'V' shape suggests the arc of a bouncing ball. The left side shows the initial momentum associated with defining what needs to be done. The turning point is the commitment of time, resources, and effort to achieve specific desired outcomes. The upward arc is transition into action where we organize, act, and correct course as needed.

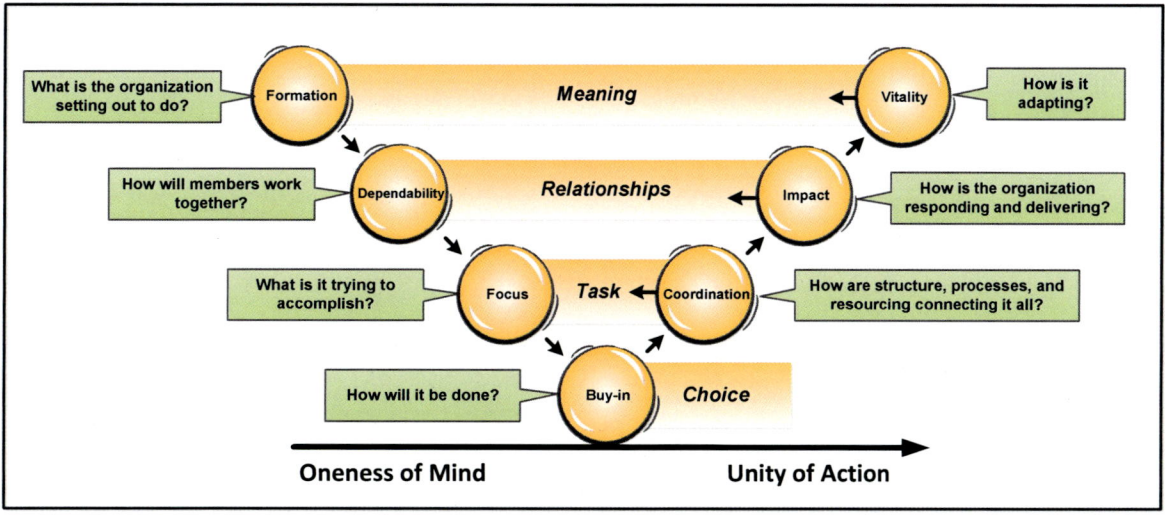

Figure 3-7: Organizational Performance Model

The organizational performance model provides a way of thinking about the functionalities and aggregate propensities required to support organizational effectiveness. For example, an organization striving to create new directions requires more strength in the areas of formation, focus, and vitality than does an organization intent on maintaining longstanding traditions and relationships.

Answers to the questions identified on Figure 3-7 help define part of the organization's functionality description and inform staff selection decisions.

The organizational performance model can be extended in terms of behavioural propensities shown in Figure 3-8. These behavioural factors are the same set for all three performance models we will use in this handbook – individual, team, and organizational.

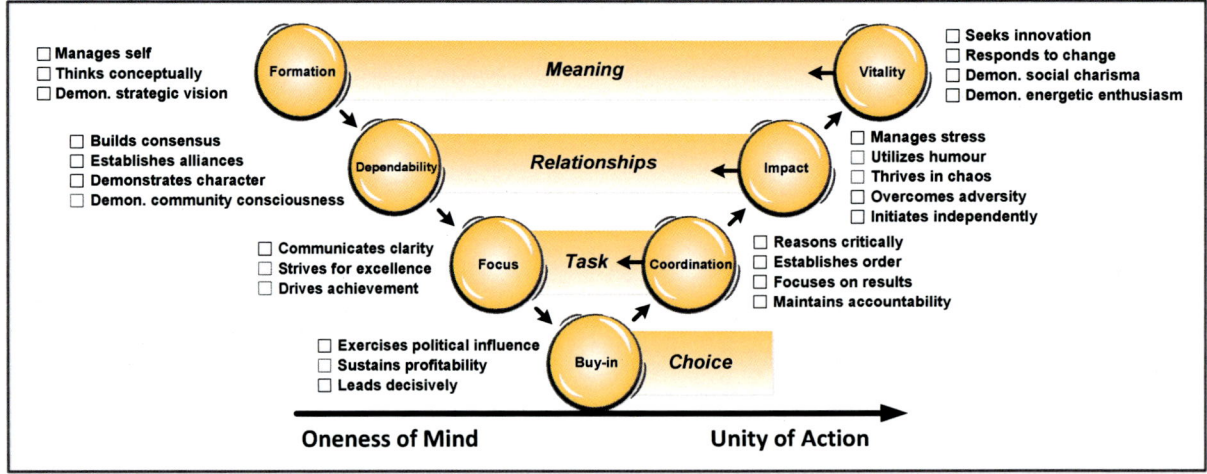

Figure 3-8: Behavioural factors associated with the Organizational Performance Model

Different combinations of aggregate propensities for teams and organizations not only influence organizational functioning, they also shape deep drivers of culture. For example, an organization that is high in critical reasoning, strives for excellence, demonstrates character, maintains accountability and builds consensus will be highly data-, stability-, and task-focused. This lends itself well to a stable environment that requires the rigorous controls typical of high reliability organizations. In the absence of infusing other strengths to supplement these preferences, the organization may struggle to demonstrate foresight, adaptability to changing demands, and a willingness to meet the safety, growth and development needs of its members.

Structural Diversity

Most people are too familiar with the hierarchical box-like organization chart. It is rarely the most effective way to structure an organization from top-to-bottom yet it remains imprinted in organizational consciousness. Rather than thinking of organizations as pyramids we should think of them as circles of cooperation. What if organizations replaced their traditional organization chart software with a full toolset of design options that best suit the functionality requirements and aggregate propensities of teams? If you revisit Figure 1-1, you will notice that it doesn't take a lot of imagination to see how this would work. The same structure can rarely be applied in cookie-cutter fashion across the organization. Mintzberg [1992] and others have pointed out that the structure should vary depending on the degree of control versus influence that management wishes to apply.

Let's look at a few options:

- Hierarchies work well when a clear chain of command is required, such as situations requiring 24-hour shift coverage in nuclear power plants, military units, and police or fire departments.
- Matrix organizations work well where there is a high need for cooperation, coordination, and efficient information sharing.
- Hubs work well when coordination is required among a number of functions or processes, e.g., planning and operations.
- Self-directed or self-organizing teams work well when the outcomes are clear but methods and responsibilities shift depending on evolving circumstances.
- Project teams work well when a defined outcome can be scoped, segmented, and coordinated as specific activities. Schedule and cost are project elements, but are not the primary drivers for an effective project team.

Each of these approaches works best if the team leadership and members are selected for propensities that support working relationships and functionality.

The point is that one can mix and match: an organization's design can include several structures depending on what different parts of the oganization are trying to accomplish. It is good practice to keep in mind a few basic design principles related to organizational structure. Appendix D summarizes ten important organizational design principles.

Returning to the concept of functionality, one can use process groupings to construct outcome focused process groupings or 'mobilizing constellations' around a specific functionality such as business excellence, innovation, performance, oversight, and so forth. Such mobilizing constellations help focus the organization on critical outcomes. The composition depends on the organization's self-defined critical success factors, e.g., operational excellence, safety, organizational effectiveness, customer engagement, research and innovation. Constellations may become permanent groupings within the structure or simply constitute key meeting venues that bring the right minds and processes to one table.

For example, Figure 3-9 shows how processes for business planning, finance, human system development, external relationships, and performance assessment and improvement can provide an organization with responsive, improvement-oriented decision-making for business excellence. 'Bubbles' outside the main circle attend or provide input on an as-needed basis. The construct of Figure 3-9 is based on a process view in which the designated process owners assemble to focus on the defined functionality. Although the concept can be applied to organizations driven by organizational functions rather than processes, the overall alignment is unlikely to be as powerful since functionally based leaders tend to have multiple agendas in any venue.

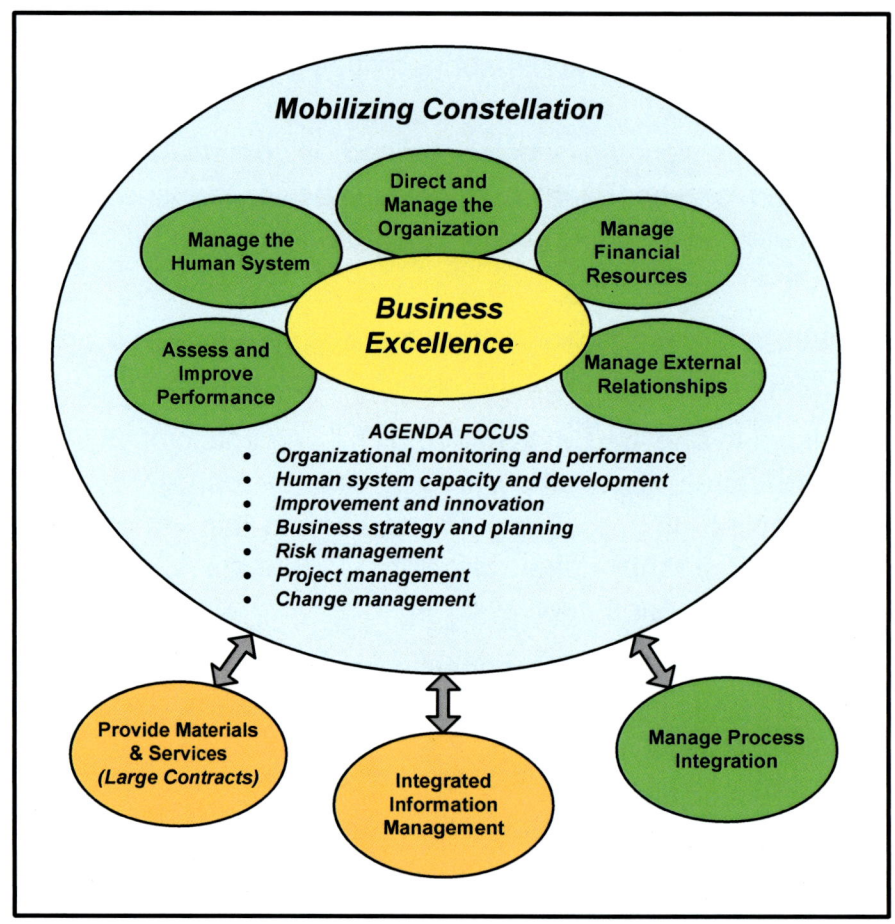

Figure 3-9: Example mobilizing constellation for business excellence

The clustering of processes with significant interfaces increases the ease of oversight, and assists process owners in making improvements across departmental boundaries and identifying important areas for self-assessments. It can also help organizational members recognize how larger pieces of the system are intended to work together, thereby fostering self-directed integration activities. Importantly, mobilizing constellations, when formed, can consciously develop a collective meaning system consistent with their vision of success. Instead of simply grouping like-with-like into common functions, mindful clustering of processes helps organizations align the focus, activities and outputs with intended organizational outcomes. In other words, this approach changes the interconnections and logic of the organizational structure since higher order goals become more important than individual departmental or process goals. This, in turn, requires a different approach to leadership (see box).

> ### *Leadership for Mobilizing Constellations*
>
> 'Mobilizing constellations', or outcome-focused process groupings, require a broader approach to management and leadership. The groupings cross organizational boundaries and process boundaries, hence a collaborative, bridging approach to managing such structures is essential.

A significant advantage of clustering is that it enables very rapid transitions to alternative structures when the need arises, for example, in crisis situations where a hierarchical structure may be too cumbersome for rapid sense-making and response to changing situations.

The organizational structure and its relationship with the process system should be documented in an organizational design basis (see following box) to ensure that significant changes to the organization or its processes take into account the design intent. This will be discussed in more detail in Part B.

Documenting the organization design basis

The documented organization design basis should include:

- organizational principles
- meaning system and desired operating culture
- rationale for key aspects of the structure, levels, and organizational groupings
- key leadership roles
- key mobilizing constellations, venues, and relationships
- how the design integrates the human system, management system processes, and technology
- responsibility, accountability and authority framework
- critical propensities at the team and leadership levels, and
- a glossary of organizational terms.

The design basis serves as a baseline for managing risks inherent in significant organizational and process changes.

SUMMARY OF KEY POINTS

In this chapter we discussed four stages of organizational evolution and basic elements of organizational design that we will be using in Part B. The key points are summarized in the following box.

Key Points from this chapter on organizational evolution and design

1. The predominant stage of evolution of an organization has a profound impact on its:
   - Reasoning, relating, and decision-making preferences
   - Preferred leadership styles
   - Meaning system and culture
   - Management system design
   - Staffing strategies
   - Approach to risk management
   - Priority setting practices
   - Change willingness and capacity.
2. Organizations can evolve or change by seeding the requisite propensities at key locations and levels within the organization.
3. Organizational structure should take into account and align processes, functionalities, team propensities and leadership styles.
4. Organizational structure should fit the context, desired interactions, and functionality rather than simply follow a traditional hierarchical model. Structure may vary across the organization.
5. Using mobilizing constellations clustered around desired outcomes, key functionalities and process groupings enables better communication and decision-making, and enables rapid changes in configuration when required.

Chapter 4

Leadership, Teams and Culture

IN THIS CHAPTER

This chapter explores leadership, teams and the impact of leadership on organizational culture. The specific sections cover:

- Leadership and meaning
- Unitive leadership
- Team leadership
- Management
- Organizational culture
- Power Dynamics.

High reliability organizations need leadership that anticipates like crazy and at the same time can shift rapidly to response mode in crisis situations. The traditional management-executive team typically brings strength to tactical aspects but is often challenged to exhibit the strength needed for the organization's long-term navigation and piloting system. Ensuring the inclusion of strengths in meaning-making, culture-building, and organizational formation, substantially broadens an organization's ability to move up the maturity model, improve its management system, and develop the ambidextrous leadership-management qualities necessary for resilience and response in challenging situations.

Organizations sometimes face an internal dilemma. Who recognizes the need for talents that are not resident within an organization and takes steps to include them? This is where theory, research, and best practice can help. Organizations are meaning-making systems comprised of many people. Leadership is the process whereby ideas and relationships are connected to enable aligned and focused action. Before we discuss the team profiles needed to develop, implement and sustain management systems, we will explore some general aspects of leadership.

LEADERSHIP AND MEANING

There are two dimensions of leading. The first involves envisioning, and the second involves engaging:

1. ***Envisioning***—Identifying opportunities and risk, and visioning into a field of near and long term possibilities requires:

    - Intuition and innovation
    - Strategic vision and conceptual/systemic reasoning
    - Focus on purpose and learning

2. ***Engaging***—Emotional engagement of people, meaningful integration of ideas, and logistical execution requires:

    - Relationship building: empathy, tact, expressiveness, humour
    - Task execution: analysis, decisiveness, stamina, discipline and determination.

Both dimensions are required for meaning-making (see next two boxes).

Why meaning-making matters to leaders

Leaders help create collective meaning to align members within an organization. The process system and organizational structure manifest the collective meaning system of leadership and are a means of enculturation within the organization. In the absence of collective meaning, both the organization and its leaders will have difficulty accomplishing desired outcomes.

For example, leaders may tell employees to report near misses and incidents, but when they do and are at fault, they are often criticized. This creates an internal conflict for the employee who wants to meet expectations but also wants to avoid negative consequences. In this case the leadership is not aligning messages for both physical and emotional safety of the employee. Since the employee can't easily integrate the conflicting messages into coherent meaning, he or she will opt for the emotionally safer route, which is not to report.

> ### *The illusion of shared meaning*
>
> Many leaders operate under the illusion that their associates think the same way they do. A fruitful eye-opener is to assemble a group of 'like-minded' people and ask them to use their non-writing hand (this levels the playing field) to draw a picture of a relevant subject, for example, 'leadership', 'customer service', 'safety', or 'quality'.
>
> The resulting pictures give remarkable insights into the variety of perspectives on the same topic within a seemingly homogeneous group. People describe their pictures and related thought processes in a way that gives a glimpse into how they process the world around them. In one workshop with a group of safety experts from a dozen countries, pictures of a 'healthy safety culture' ranged from a flower being watered to a rigorous flowchart showing the steps to achieve safety. Such pictures provide insight into intrinsic motivators and what will 'reach' people. This, in turn, has implications for evolving shared understanding and commitment.

There are countless pithy quotes about leadership, endless definitions, and a growing list of styles ranging from classical command-and-control to the cult appeal of charisma. Whatever the definition, leadership shapes meaning.

Without any pretense of adding anything profound to such lists, our working definition of leadership is in the following box.

> ### *DEFINITION: Leadership*
>
> ***Leadership*** is a willingness to take the initiative to build momentum for an idea, direction, or way of being or doing that has meaning and value to yourself and others.

There is nothing hierarchical in this definition. Astute readers will notice that throughout this handbook we prefer the term leadership rather than leader. Distributed safety leadership that permeates the organization is the best, and perhaps only, way to achieve a healthy safety culture in high reliability organizations. Key behaviours such as risk-informed conservative decision-making and a continual improvement mindset thrive in organizations that adopt a strategy of 'permeated' leadership.

For consistency in this handbook we use 7 behavioural-based leadership styles described in more detail in Appendix B and summarized in Table 4-1.

Table 4-1: Leadership styles

Leadership Style	Description
Administrative	Manages by rules and procedures; enforces order and predictability
Collegial	Participatory, hands off style that gives freedom to capable, motivated employees who require little direct supervision
Directive	Classical authoritarian who provides close supervision, makes key decisions, and expects others to follow orders
Entrepreneurial	Focuses on innovation, competition, change, and taking calculated risks
Transformational	Engages, mentors, and motivates people to create significant changes in thought and action to realize a different future
Utilitarian	Maximizes productivity and output; focuses on efficiency, effectiveness, action, and results
Unitive	Focuses on how complex systems can interact to create new meaning and higher good in a universal context

Smircich and Morgan [1982] equate leadership to the management of meaning, and state that "a formal organization is premised upon shared meanings that define roles and authority relationships that institutionalize a pattern of leadership". Alvesson [2012] also suggests that leadership is the management of meaning and learning, including organizational learning, is the re-definition of meaning. In short, effective leaders create meaning. This is sometimes attempted by establishing organizational positions with titles intended to convey meaning, such as Microsoft's VP of People and Organizational Capability, Yahoo's VP of Audience and Cloud Computing, eBay's Senior VP of Trust and Safety. Titles alone are insufficient since fulfillment of intent requires integration within the entire organizational system.

Anyone can provide leadership in the right situation. No single 'style' or 'type' is right for every circumstance. Nevertheless, the right leadership propensity in the right position at the right time will make any organization more effective. Different stages of evolution generally favour leadership with different styles of reasoning and relating. Appendix C examines the influence of leadership across the four stages. For management system development, we will focus on important dimensions of unitive leadership and team leadership. These are related to the envisioning and relating aspects discussed at the start of this section. We will also briefly discuss the implementation role of management.

UNITIVE LEADERSHIP – LEADERS AS WAYFARERS

Leaders are more effective when they actively explore the meaning systems of participants to seek win-win opportunities through respecting diversity. The most influential leaders in history have created or built on meaning systems that resonated with their followers. In essence, leaders are explorers, adventurers, and wayfarers who establish integrated meaning systems consistent with their vision and strategies. Managers are navigators and pilots who help communicate and integrate the organization's meaning system into daily activities. Management is a control process whereas leadership requires envisioning and synthesizing. Both leaders and managers are required in organizations.

Unitive leaders help people who are immersed or stuck in their own meaning systems to understand and value diversity and alternate ways of looking at the world. They seek meaning as a road to discovery. They assign staff not simply on knowledge, credentials, or experience but also for consistency with natural propensities and meaning systems in order to strengthen organizational capacity and promote healthy human systems.

Leadership can be classed broadly as people leadership, task leadership, and thought leadership. Unitive leadership encompasses all three, embodies the best of integrative and systems thinking, and focuses on creating meaning by synthesizing all elements of the organizational system in the context of its environment. Unitive leadership focuses on how complex systems can interact to create meaning and higher good. Such leadership is able to see the organization from outside the constraints of its own systems.

Unitive leaders instinctively consider the human system, process system, technological system, and external factors as an integrated whole. They consider the demands of technology in risk-sensitive industries such as the airline industry, nuclear power, or deep sea oil. They also consider the implications of rapidly changing technologies such as global interconnectivity in communications. Their long-term view helps ensure that the organization and the demands of society are not at odds.

Unitive leaders are often iconoclastic thinkers who tap into ideas and talent sets beyond traditional leadership models. They look for cues in the human system that others miss. They focus on the realities of the organization rather than the key performance indicators that are the realm of management. Their interest lies in knowing:

- how the organization knits into its context and environment
- how systems and people acquire and share information
- how systems function and integrate to accomplish goals
- how to place the required mix of leadership talent in each area to achieve results across the organization
- how to enliven and evolve the organization
- how the organization functions in relation to the larger world, and
- how to create higher good in a universal context.

Unitive leadership is required not only at the senior level, but needs to be cultivated as an organizational propensity within each sub-system to build coherence and maintain momentum towards the desired human, organizational, business, and societal outcomes.

The *attentional* field of unitive leaders focuses on the functioning of the entire system and its interfaces, and long-term, adaptive strategies. The *intentional* field of unitive leaders extends beyond 'me and my direct reports' to the broader organization and social responsibilities. Their focus is not about the leader and power, but about functioning, healthy human systems. It's about growth, learning, conscience, and contribution to a larger ideal. Unitive leaders have the ability to think beyond 'what is' to 'what wants to be', and 'what needs to be'.

Neither the latest leadership guru bestseller nor the Harvard School of Business tome on unitive leadership has yet been published, but our guess is that they are forming somewhere. Perhaps the closest approximation is the bridging approach of the International Integral Leadership Collaborative [2014].

TEAM LEADERSHIP

Teams exist at all levels of an organization. They bring diversity of reasoning and action. Individual meaning systems represent the unique gifts that people bring to teams. Such differences can create conflict and confusion, but they also provide expanded capacities to support team function, provided the differences are visible, understood, and respected by all members of the team. Team leadership involves focusing and coordinating diverse talents to accomplish specific tasks.

The power of teams is loosely reflected in the relationship:

Power of Teams (coherent effort) = Diversity x Integration x Momentum

Effective team leaders balance all three elements on the right side of the equation. They understand that productivity and desired outcomes are directly contingent on the integration of meaning.

Many organizations use simple tools such as Myers-Briggs [Briggs Myers et al. 1998] or various forms of the DISC model [Marston 2012] to help teams understand interpersonal differences. More informative behavioural tools such as the Pathfinder Career System [Cash 2013] are available to identify individual propensities and career suitability. Regardless of the tools applied, team functionality and performance can be systematically enhanced if individual meaning systems are considered when assigning staff. At the time of formation, teams can create pictures, develop meaning system diagrams such as the molecular spray diagrams used in Appendix C, or use mind maps to help understand and integrate their relationships and roles. Importantly, they can use such methods to self-identify missing propensities, potential rub points, and opportunities to leverage strengths. One often has to add both capability and meaning in order to fill holes in the fabric of team comprehension and capacity.

MANAGEMENT

Compared with leadership, management is often considered a discipline or profession, since the action path is generally known and the focus is on optimizing control systems rather than systemic change. This is not to denigrate the essential role of management, its leadership function, or its daily front-line challenges. In the wake of pioneering work by Peter Drucker, many excellent books have been written about management. Other than identifying behavioural attributes in the next chapter we will not discuss management in depth. Effective managers are essential for bridging organizational interfaces, allocating resources and resolving problems. They must be adept at planning, focused execution, maintaining relationships, and coordinating change.

ORGANIZATIONAL CULTURE

We made the point in Chapter 2 that culture and meaning are linked. What may be less evident is that the management system design is a direct product of the propensity profile and culture of the organization. Figure 4-1 shows the relationship between stages of evolution of any organization and influence on culture.

The left side of Figure 4-1 shows a modified version of the iceberg model of culture developed by Edgar Schein [2010]. The top level consists of the observable manifestations or artifacts of the culture. The second level includes the espoused values intended to serve as guiding principles for the culture. The third level consists of the underlying assumptions related to how the culture perceives reality. This layer represents the deepest drivers of culture or meaning system on which people base their reasoning and actions. It forms the root of intention. For this reason, change at this level often requires significant effort and time. The iceberg model operates at the group, organizational, community, and societal levels, further adding to the complexity of any culture change initiative.

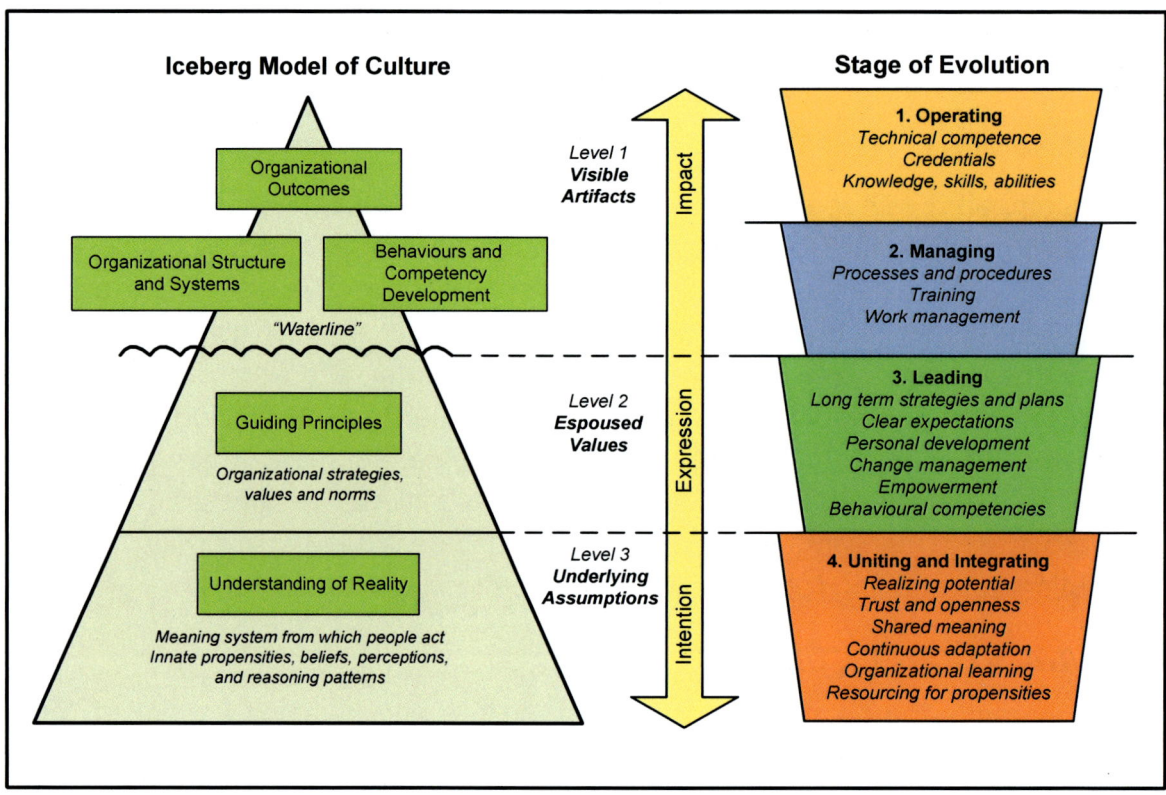

Figure 4-1: Iceberg model of culture, organizational evolution and leadership

On the right side of Figure 4-1, we show the influence of the leadership focus related to each of the four stages of organizational evolution. Leadership at the uniting and integrating stage (Stage 4) pays the greatest attention to how others understand reality. This approach has the greatest potential to influence culture. Many of the cultural assessment tools currently in use tend to focus on the artifact and espoused value levels in the mistaken belief that anything at the bottom level is too fuzzy, ingrained, and individualistic to be of value. There are effective ways to assess the impact of culture on safety [IAEA 2014] and although they are beyond the scope of this handbook, they are important for senior management to consider.

Behaviour and culture change are known to be difficult and can't be accomplished solely by leadership trying to exert influence on others. An organization that attempts to mandate required behaviours but is not aligned in meaning is unlikely to achieve its full potential. Dominance and preaching merely submerge meaning systems and promote the intelligence of the few rather than the many. Regulating behaviors through processes is also challenging because the human system tends to rely heavily on informal networks and always defaults to such networks when organizational systems are weak. **Organizations often believe that 'communication' is the problem when it is actually a breakdown in meaning that is the barrier.** Unitive leadership works with meaning systems to integrate organizational design, the human system, process system, and technology into a coherent organizational system. Smart organizations cultivate meaning, grow the required propensities, and seed unitive-oriented leadership in key areas to achieve desired organizational and societal outcomes.

POWER DYNAMICS

No matter whether you are a team member or formal organizational leader, your toolkit should include an understanding of how power dynamics affects team performance.

Power dynamics significantly influence whether the interactive space is functional or dysfunctional. Dominance by some members may make the creation of true shared space discussed in Chapter 2 virtually impossible. Situations with unhealthy power dynamics will make some individuals reluctant to participate. They will typically exert the minimum effort required to avoid trouble.

Some researchers suggest that power and culture are intertwined, and that power dynamics must be considered when discussing topics such as safety, particularly because of the competition for scarce resources. Culture is not always shared or harmonious. Every organization includes sub-cultures, and these sub-cultures may have different values, attitudes, perceptions, or patterns of behaviour. Antonsen [2009] identifies three dimensions of power:

1. The ability of 'A' to get 'B' to do something that 'B' would not otherwise do. This may be based on:

    - Positional power
    - Information and expertise, i.e., 'know what' and 'know how'
    - Control of rewards and resources
    - Coercive power, i.e., the ability to constrain, interfere, or block
    - Alliances and networks, i.e., 'know who', and
    - Personal power (charisma, energy, reputation).

2. The ability to keep potential issues out of decision-making processes by controlling the agenda.

3. The bias of social systems to reflect the values of a few dominant groups at the expense of other groups.

Power dynamics have a significant impact on the ability of an organization to create the shared space needed to enable continual improvement. Leadership plays a significant role in ensuring that power dynamics do not interfere with effective interactions. The following box provides suggestions on how leadership can help compensate for power dynamics.

Compensating for power dynamics

Savvy leaders and teams are attentive to and strive to overcome the potentially negative impact of power dynamics.

Equalizers that encourage participation:

- Inclusion, respect, team focus
- Delegation, willingness to share power, shared accountability
- Visible support, empathy for people's emotional states and concerns
- Sincere listening, considering and questioning
- Self-reflection, shared 'beginner-hood'
- Objectivity
- Flexibility

Differentiators that inhibit participation:

- Position, title, seniority, expertise, physical arrangements
- Ego, self-interest, self-importance
- Withholding information, hidden agendas
- Ignoring or excluding individuals or topics
- Controlling or micro-managing
- Preserving the status quo
- Humiliating or criticizing others, even with humour.

CORE VALUES

Most large organizations have developed vision and mission statements and a list of values to help guide organizational culture. Are values of real benefit in shaping culture or mitigating unhealthy power dynamics?

The Aspen Institute and Booz Allen Hamilton [2010] surveyed 365 people holding senior positions in companies from Europe, Asia/Pacific (China, Japan, Australia), and North America to identify core values. Seventy-five percent of the respondent companies had annual revenues over $500M. Figure 4-2 shows the percentage of respondents who identified a specific espoused value for their organization. The expression of core values is so similar across organizations that one could almost use Figure 4-2 as a checklist. High reliability organizations often add values related to safety.

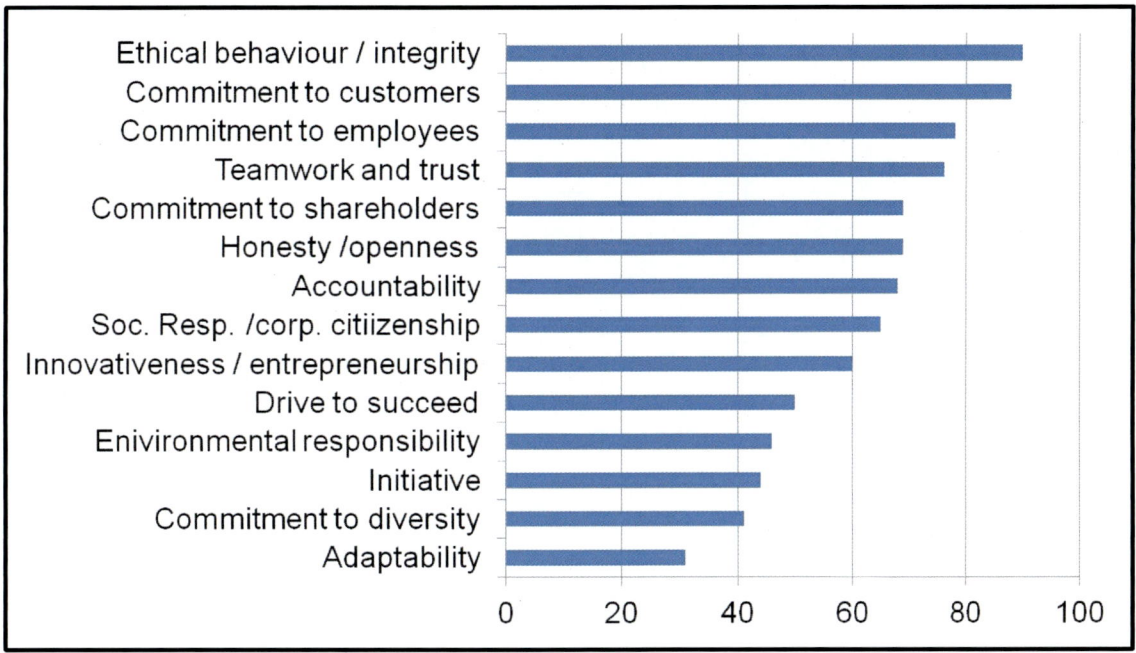

Figure 4-2: Commonly expressed organizational values

The value statements for two different organizations are provided in the box on the following page. What do the value statements reveal about each of the organizations? What type of organization might each set of values represent? After you examine the values in the box, follow the cue to find the organizations they represent. The values themselves are laudable in each case. The nature of the culture is rather different, as are the people who would be likely to succeed in one organization versus the other.

Espoused values within two organizations

The following are abbreviated versions of the values espoused by two organizations. Examine them carefully. Can you identify which one represents high reliability organizations? The answer is at the bottom of this page.

Organization 1	Organization 2
• **Trust** – people won't disappoint • **Respect** – brings out full potential • **Belief** – believe in someone and they will move mountains to prove you're right • **Humility** – we're not afraid to ask • **Integrity** – set the highest ethical standards	• **Excellence** – make it better • **Perseverance** – there is no finish line • **Leadership** – make things happen • **Relationships** – knock down walls and build bridges • **Integrity** – we are what we say and do

---

To move beyond 'feel good' statements, values must emerge directly from the collective meaning system of the organization at the base level of the Iceberg model in Figure 4-1. We will return to values in Part B.

ANSWER: In the espoused values box Organization 1 is Avon and Organization 2 is the Institute of Nuclear Power Operators.

SUMMARY OF KEY POINTS

This chapter focused on leadership and culture. Elements from this chapter will resurface in Part B.

Key Points from this Chapter on Leadership, Teams, and Culture

1. A key role of leadership is to help create collective meaning to align people within an organization.
2. Unitive leadership focuses on organizational envisioning, alignment, integration, meaning, and context.
3. Management focuses on operational planning, resource allocation, organizational interfaces, and achieving results.
4. Team leadership focuses on engaging and coordinating diverse talent to accomplish specific tasks.
5. An understanding of power dynamics can prevent it from inhibiting the performance of individuals and teams.
6. A management system is a manifestation of an organization's culture, hence an understanding of the underlying drivers of an organization's culture is required for the successful implementation of a management system.

Chapter 5
Team Selection, Performance and Propensities

IN THIS CHAPTER

This chapter explores team selection in terms of the attributes and propensities that contribute to the development, implementation and sustainability of an integrated management system.

The sections cover:

- Leadership structure
- Team design and selection
    - Management Team
    - Management System Owner-Architect
    - Project Manager
    - Development Team
    - Process Owner.

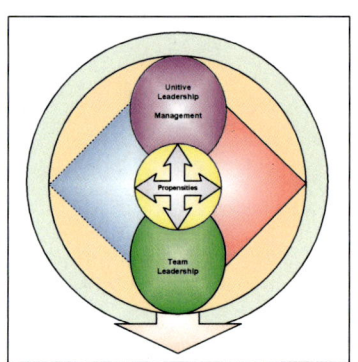

Each team requires a somewhat different profile of strengths that enable the team to accomplish its specific role. We will begin with some general attributes of typical leadership structures.

LEADERSHIP STRUCTURE – Right Person, Right Leadership, Right Position

The leadership structure from frontline supervisor to chief executive officer plays a pivotal role in shaping how an organization functions and the effectiveness of its systems. A well-defined and appropriately resourced leadership structure will provide the direction, resources, integration and support required for frontline employees to be able to function at their best. Table 5-1 identifies strengths and blind spots at typical leadership levels in organizations.

Each level in Table 5-1 contributes a different focus and functionality to overall organizational effectiveness by identifying opportunities and mitigating risks in different aspects of operations. Common strengths represent the propensities associated with patterns of high performance that enable the individuals to function well at a specific level. Common blind spots refer to propensities that are often missing or undervalued by each level. The strategic and conceptual blind spots in senior executives may seem counter-intuitive, but except for a few notable exceptions such as Bill Gates of Microsoft and Jeff Bezos of Amazon, those aren't the skills that typically get people into executive roles.

Table 5-1: Leadership Focus, Strengths, and Blind Spots

Organization Level	Focus/ Functionality	Common Strengths	Common Blind spots
Executive	Organizational direction, results and culture	<ul><li>Leads decisively</li><li>Seeks innovation</li><li>Focuses on results</li><li>Initiates independently</li><li>Thrives in chaos</li><li>Demonstrates social charisma</li><li>Sustains profitability</li><li>Maintains accountability</li><li>Manages stress</li><li>Reasons critically</li><li>Exercises political influence</li></ul>	<ul><li>Demonstrates strategic vision</li><li>Thinks conceptually</li><li>Communicates clarity</li><li>Demonstrates community consciousness</li><li>Demonstrates character</li></ul>
Senior manager	Functional operations	<ul><li>Leads decisively</li><li>Focuses on results</li><li>Maintains accountability</li><li>Demonstrates energetic enthusiasm</li><li>Reasons critically</li><li>Initiates independently</li><li>Sustains profitability</li><li>Thrives in chaos</li></ul>	<ul><li>Thinks conceptually</li><li>Demonstrates community consciousness</li><li>Demonstrates character</li><li>Establishes alliances</li><li>Demonstrates strategic vision</li></ul>
Mid-manager	Process or department execution	<ul><li>Reasons critically</li><li>Builds consensus</li><li>Demonstrates character</li><li>Responds to change</li><li>Focuses on results</li><li>Strives for excellence</li></ul>	<ul><li>Thinks conceptually</li><li>Communicates clarity</li><li>Exercises political influence</li><li>Drives achievement</li><li>Establishes order</li></ul>
Supervisor	People	<ul><li>Demonstrates character</li><li>Leads decisively</li><li>Reasons critically</li><li>Maintains accountability</li></ul>	<ul><li>Utilizes humour</li><li>Establishes alliances</li><li>Overcomes adversity</li><li>Exercises political influence</li><li>Initiates independently</li></ul>

Organizations and employees often see the promotion path as a career driver and avenue to success. Unfortunately this belief is often perpetuated by Human Resource departments and stems from a failure to recognize four important points:

1. Different levels of the management structure require fundamentally different talent sets.
2. Individuals cannot simply flex their innate preferences to meet these differing needs, nor can they be trained into such roles, despite innumerable supervisory and management courses.
3. Discipline-specific talent does not assure management capability within the same discipline.
4. Past performance doesn't predict future success in a different job.

Exceptional performance results from an alignment of innate propensities, learned competencies (knowledge, skills, experience, and credentials) in the context of the job mandate and activities (Figure 5-1). Innate propensities are those natural talents and preferences that make us more likely to pursue and succeed at some tasks than others.

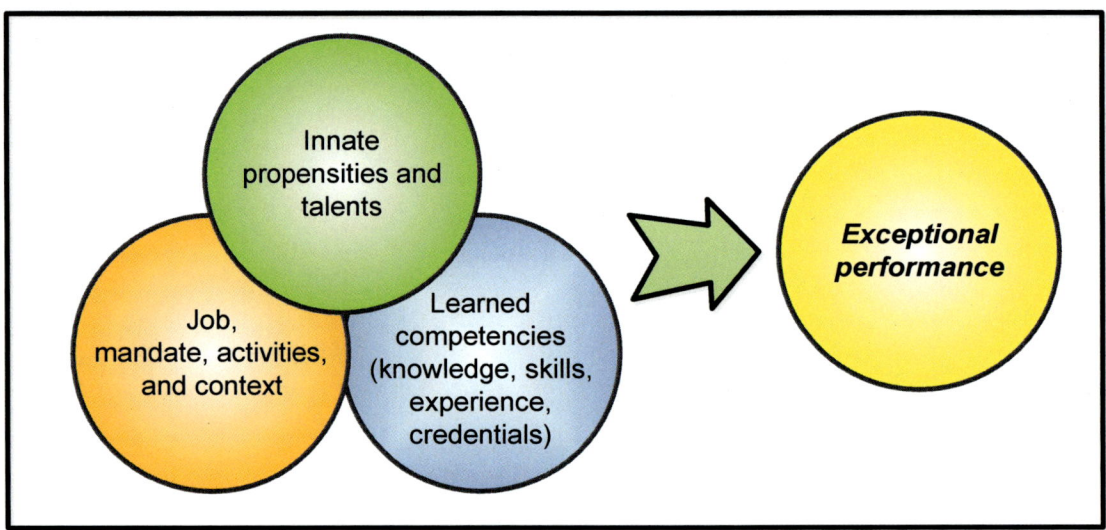

Figure 5-1: Elements of exceptional performance

For example, a supervisor may be very good at engaging and motivating her work group yet not have the strategic capacity to envision and lead the organization into the future. Similarly, a supervisor who is not oriented towards profitability will not demonstrate the financial-mindedness required to lead a successful commercial operation. Despite a wealth of technical talent and experience, the best IT professional may lack management competencies.

Simply put, managers need to focus inward and downward; CEOs need to focus outward and forward. The various levels of management involve different activities, mitigate different risks, and require distinctly different reasoning and relating patterns:

- Supervisors focus on organizing specific resources to accomplish tasks
- Managers focus on processes, projects, logistics, cost, and results
- Senior managers focus on organizational direction, integration and change
- Senior executives focus on stakeholders, way-finding and seeking new opportunities.

Sticking to traditional approaches for hiring and promoting may ultimately leave an organization without the breadth of leadership talent needed to operationalize a fully functional management system and achieve the desired outcomes. In addition, management may continue to focus on developing internal talent without recognizing that the return on investment in training poor-fit talent is marginal at best. Finally, and possibly most importantly, the talent pool for senior positions can become prematurely constrained by decisions made when promoting at the supervisory level, thereby eliminating talent with different skill sets that could be essential for success in more senior roles.

The way organizations fill positions has a significant impact on whether any type of management system will be effective, no matter how well conceived and pretty on paper. Since the human system is the primary driver of performance, it has to be carefully and intentionally resourced (see following box).

> ### *What CEOs can do to strengthen talent pools*
>
> Six strategic ways to strengthen talent pools:
>
> 1. Clearly articulate the key activities of mid and senior positions, not just their roles, responsibilities and accountabilities (not surprisingly, this requires an activity based management system to accomplish well)
> 2. Define the talents required for each position beyond knowledge, skills, experience and credentials by including the critical behavioural strengths needed to perform the activities effectively
> 3. Determine whether mid and senior level leadership teams have the aggregate propensities required to deliver on their mandates
> 4. Assess the entire leadership pool to determine whether there are at least three high-potential suitable successors for each mid-level and senior level position
> 5. Recognize that propensities cannot be trained in, coached in, or performance managed in, and align resourcing and development dollars accordingly
> 6. Ensure that predictors of future success, as well as team fit, form part of succession search criteria.

Traditional resourcing methods can result in overlooked talent, gaps in the requisite talent set at the management table, and a lack of sufficient talent in the succession pipeline. CEOs who insist that their Human Resource departments think more broadly and develop a more rigorous approach to staffing can develop stronger teams and more resilient, adaptable organizations. They will almost certainly discover hidden talent within their own organizations and reap the discretionary effort that comes from more engaged employees.

Different combinations of aggregate propensities not only influence organizational functioning, they also shape deep drivers to culture. For example, an organization high in critical reasoning, striving for excellence, demonstrating character, maintaining accountability and building consensus will be highly focused on data, stability, and tasks. This lends itself well to a rigorous environment needed in high reliability organizations. Depending on other strengths that accompany these preferences, the organization may struggle to demonstrate adaptiveness to changing demands or meet the growth and development needs of its members.

Figure 5-2 shows how different behavioural preferences contribute to specific dimensions of organizational performance. Combinations of strengths create cultural dynamics in much the same way as they create team dynamics and personality dynamics in individuals.

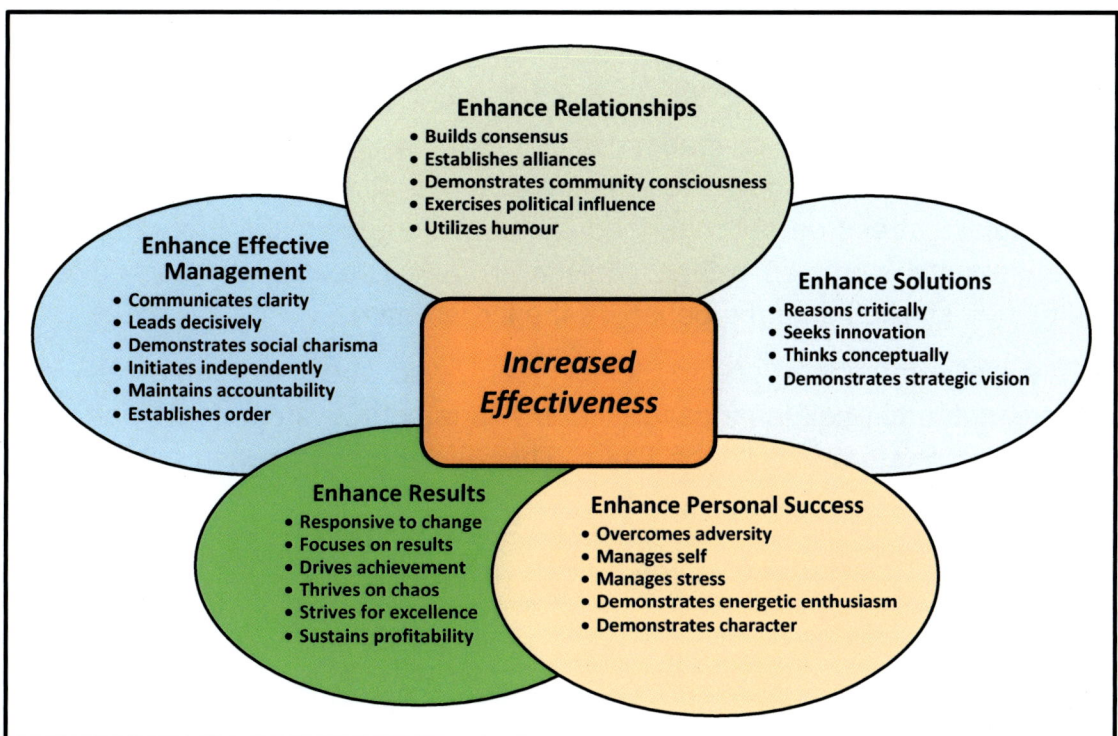

Figure 5-2: Behavioural enhancements for improving effectiveness

MANAGEMENT TEAM PROPENSITIES FOR SYSTEM SUSTAINABILITY

The following sections discuss specific team and individual requisites necessary to conceive, develop, sustain, and improve a management system. Success requires at least some members of the senior executive and management teams to have a clear understanding of the long term value of an integrated system, and the visioning capacity to understand how it can be built and maintained. The propensity profile to enable this is shown in Figure 5-3 based on the organizational performance model introduced in Chapter 3. Not surprisingly, the desired items in red cover nearly all the elements required for an organization to function effectively. It is a rare individual who is strong in all of these attributes, hence the senior team must rely on the collective strengths of the entire team. One of these is assigned as the champion of the management system. If important attributes are missing from the senior team, it is unlikely a change initiative to enhance the management system will succeed. The team must be aware of its propensity gaps, and take action to fill them. An element of unitive leadership is essential for the team to succeed at developing a management system since the journey is one of understanding how complex systems interact to accomplish goals.

We are big fans of co-leadership. Leaders who try to juggle all the balls often feel they have to know everything and make all the decisions, a state that puts needless stress on both the leader and the organization. It is preferable to pair leaders with complementary requisite propensities and let these co-leaders work to their strengths for the benefit of the larger team.

Typically members of the senior team who are most engaged in the development and maintenance of the management system form part of the Management System Excellence Team. This will be discussed in Part B.

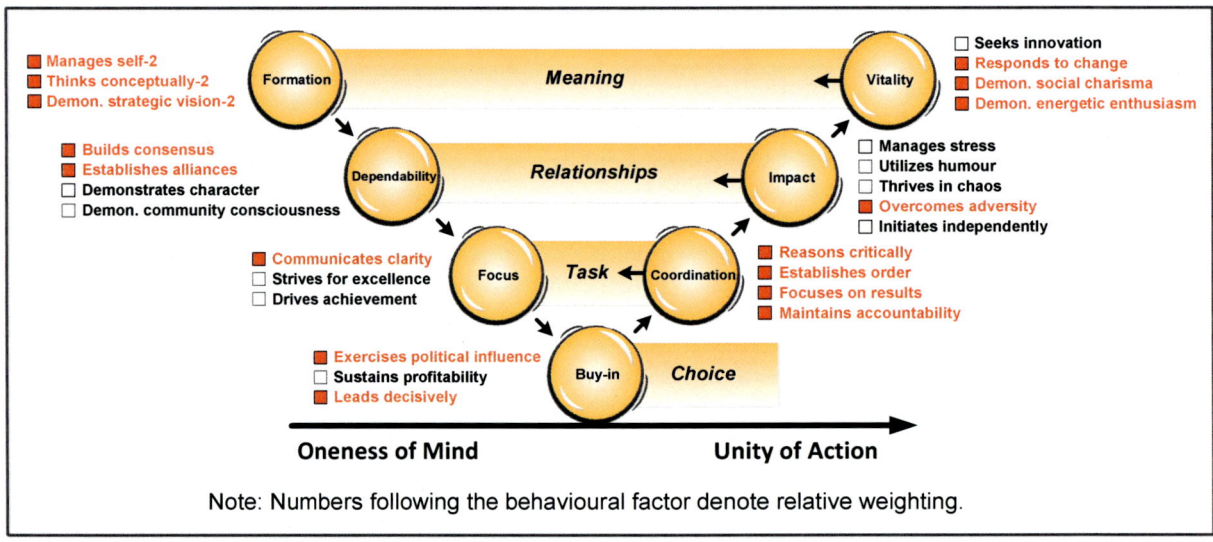

Figure 5-3: Management team selected propensities for system sustainability

Senior teams typically have more strengths on the right side of the V rather than the left side, since their orientation towards action is part of the reason they tend to rise to higher positions of authority within organizations. They often rely on consultants to supplement blind spots on the left side of the V, particularly in the areas of conceptual thinking and strategic vision. However, reliance on consultants without nurturing internal capacity can result in sustainability issues with any new initiative, including development of the management system which requires a long term comprehension and focus to enable continual improvement. Hence it is important that the requisites in Figure 5-3 reside within the senior team, and are seeded in other areas of the organization as noted in the following sections.

> ### *Counter-intuitive thinking?*
>
> The statement that executive teams may have blind spots in terms of conceptual and strategic thinking (see Table 5-1) is not the only thing that may seem counter-intuitive.
>
> A management system requires innovation, but too much strength in the behavioural factor 'seeks innovation' can be disruptive to the underlying intent of consistent, reliable performance. Similarly, management systems are a key to achieving excellence, however, a strong propensity towards 'strives for excellence' at the senior level can foster micro-management and stifle progress at the working level.
>
> Attributes that are desirable or even coveted in some roles may be counter-productive in others.

MANAGEMENT SYSTEM OWNER-ARCHITECT PROPENSITIES

The mandate or role of the owner-architect is to provide overall direction and focused guidance for the design and development of the management system architecture, documentation methods and controls, information gathering, facilitation approach, integration, and quality assurance. The individual also serves as a regulatory and corporate interface. In the case of large-scale transitions, this role works closely with a project manager described in the next section. The owner-architect role typically evolves into the long-term process owner for the management system following the project phase. In principle, the senior executive 'owns' the management system and is accountable for its effectiveness; however the management system process owner is the agent who devotes attention to its functioning and continual improvement.

The owner-architect role needs a strong creative component requiring vision and conceptualization in order to evolve a systematic, integrated picture of what is needed and to maintain focus on it throughout the development process. This unitive aspect helps ensure that development considers the interactions of the system as a whole. The role needs to include a strong focus on strategic change facilitation to help people adjust to a new way of thinking about the organization and its processes. The propensity profile is given in Figure 5-4, which is based on the individual model we introduced in Chapter 2.

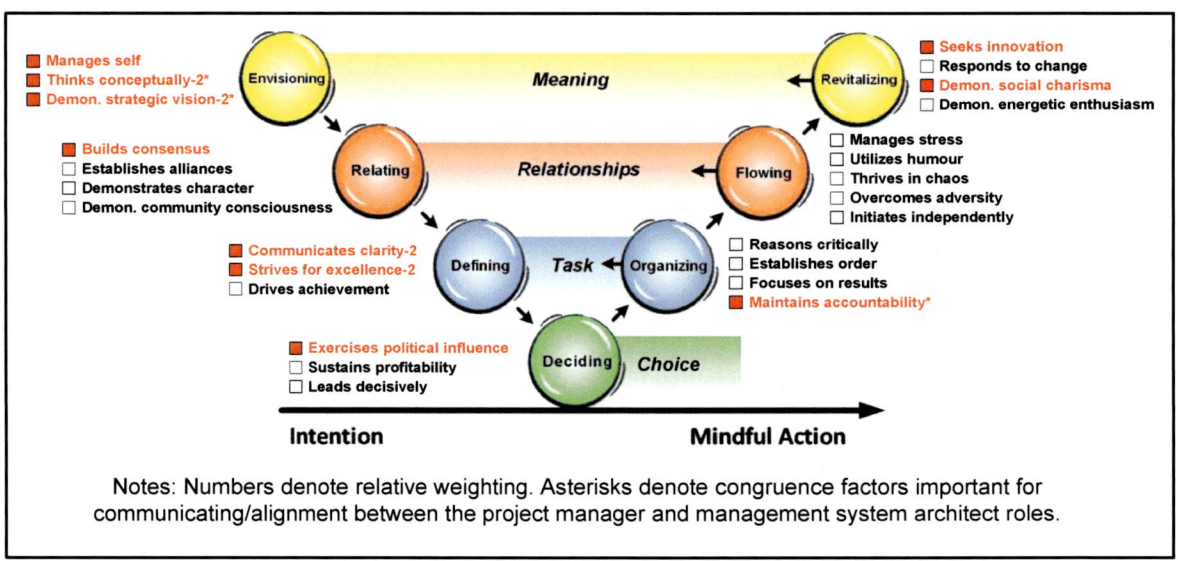

Figure 5-4: Management system owner-architect propensities

The numbers after the behavioural factors in Figure 5-4 indicate the relative importance or weight of the element when selecting candidates. Strategic vision, conceptualization and internalized accountability (indicated by the asterisks) are included to provide psychological congruence between the architect role and project lead role, enabling these individuals to clarify and hold a common mental framework that will allow them to self-organize within their respective roles. For the owner-architect role 'seeks innovation' is valued to avoid concretizing existing processes, and 'strives for excellence' is valued to avoid developing weak or flawed systems.

In assigning the role, it is desirable to seek a unitive-transformational-utilitarian style of leadership with experience in the following:

- A broad knowledge of the organization and its functionalities related to both the people and technology
- Familiarity with management systems
- Knowledge of the applicable regulatory and industry standards and expectations, and
- Previous management level experience.

Selecting candidates based on both the behavioural attributes in Figure 5-4 and the acquired knowledge, skills, and experience parameters is important. Selection on the basis of the latter elements alone is less likely to ensure a proper fit to the role. For example, some organizations assume that the senior quality assurance person is the logical position to take on the added role of management system architect. In fact, the two roles are significantly different and the propensity profiles for persons who self-select into quality assurance may be unsuited to the strategic and conceptual reasoning required of the owner-architect.

MANAGEMENT SYSTEM PROJECT MANAGER PROPENSITIES

In cases where the organization does not have a well-developed process-based management system, it is good practice to assign a project manager to lead the transition in conjunction with the owner-architect. This is an example where co-leadership is beneficial. The project manager role or mandate is to provide overall project control, including project planning, resource management, and serve as corporate and regulatory interface in conjunction with the Owner-Architect. Some organizations err in believing that they simply need to assign a competent individual from the planning organization to develop schedules, track activities, and monitor cost versus budget. Project management for an organization-wide collaborative change initiative requires both the order and results focus typical of project management and the human system and organizational skills required to facilitate culture change. The propensity distribution for a project manager in this context is given in Figure 5-5 which is also based on the individual performance model.

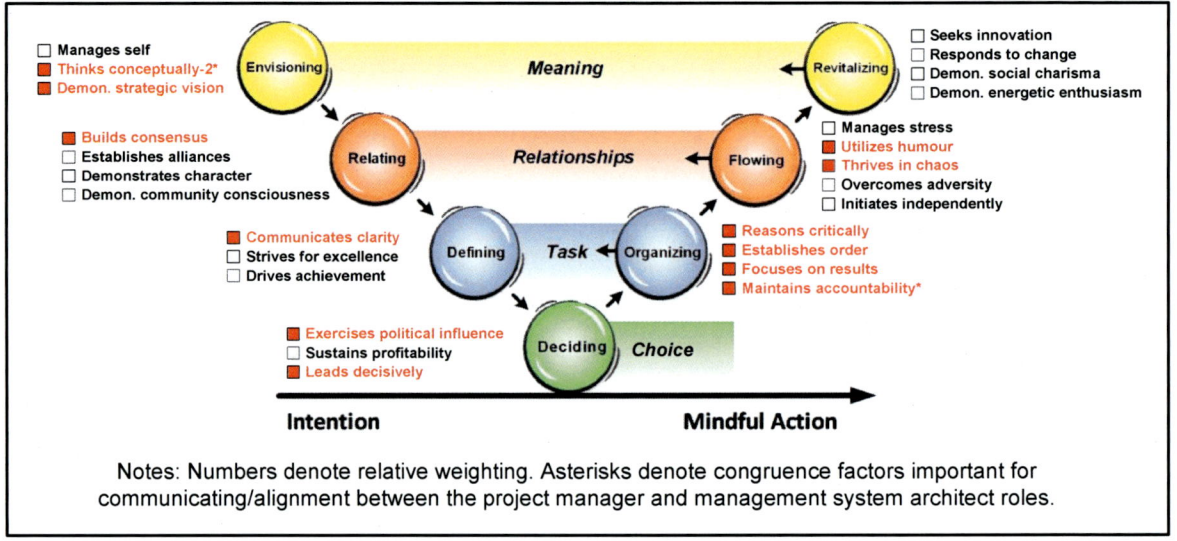

Figure 5-5: Management system project manager propensities

In Figure 5-5 the numbers after the behavioural factors represent weightings applicable for selecting candidates. The asterisks represent congruence factors between the owner-architect and project manager. Results focus and establishing order in the project manager contrast with innovation and detail focus in the owner-architect to maintain a balance between productivity and creativity. Utilizes humour, while not mandatory, brings relief from the tension that can easily accompany project environments.

For the project manager, a utilitarian leadership style provides focus on costs, streamlined activities, and determination to achieve timely follow-through. For the owner-architect the focus is more on change, engagement and creation opportunities through collaboration with others. The styles are complementary, with the relational style of the owner-architect role bridging the differences in approach. Organizations tempted to assign one individual to fill both roles should remember that it is rare to find the full combination of behavioural factors from Figures 5-4 and 5-5 in one individual.

Table 5-2 summarizes the role differences for the two key positions. The ability to relate to and influence key decision-makers is a function of the aggregate propensity distribution of the owner-architect, project manager, and other team members.

Table 5-2 Comparison of the Owner-Architect and Project Manager Roles

\multicolumn{2}{c}{*Team Mandate:* To develop and populate a process-based management system including training and implementation support.}	
Management System Owner-Architect	**Management System Project Manager**
Mandate: Provide overall direction and guidance to the design and development of the management system architecture, documentation methods and controls, information gathering, facilitation approach, and quality assurance.	Mandate: Provide overall project management, including project planning, and resource management. Jointly with the Owner-Architect serve as the regulatory and corporate interface.
Functionalities	**Functionalities**
• Concept innovation • Strategic change facilitation • Systemic and systematic integration	• Strategic project definition • Implementation logistics • Execution control
Key Activities	**Key Activities**
• Design management system model • Develop management system manual • Define process mapping methodology • Develop process controls • Define management system document hierarchy • Guide process owner selection and development • Organize process mapping teams • Facilitate collaboration • Identify process requirements • Identify process links and interactions • Determine process grading • Integrate processes and functional maps • Document and publish processes	• Establish project structure, processes and protocols • Establish information technology platform • Establish project plan, schedule and deliverables • Secure and allocate resources • Coordinate plan execution • Monitor progress against milestones • Provide project quality control • Maintain team and cross-functional communications • Provide regular reporting • Resolve emergent problems

DEVELOPMENT TEAM PROPENSITIES

We turn now to the desired composition of the team needed to support the owner-architect and project manager during the design, development and implementation phases before formal turn-over to the assigned process owner. The latter operationalizes the process and is responsible for on-going maintenance and continual improvement. We will focus only on the core team that forms a continuing part of the project rather than the temporary sub-teams that develop each process. Both will be addressed further in Part B.

The number on the core support team depends on the size of the initiative but should generally be about 6-12 people. The team will require broad representation across the organization, but not all departments need to assign a full time representative since every department will participate during the development of processes important to their functionality. The core development team has a broader purpose and is constituted for the duration of the project, which may be several years for a large change initiative. We will discuss the specific membership and skill set for the core team in Part B.

For now, we limit discussion to the propensity map for the team. To do this we introduce a team performance model, which is similar to the individual and organizational performance models except for the wording in the spheres. The relevant questions for any team are in Figure 5-6, based on the work of Drexler, Sibbet, and Forrester [2011]. The team-specific propensities for the development team are in Figure 5-7.

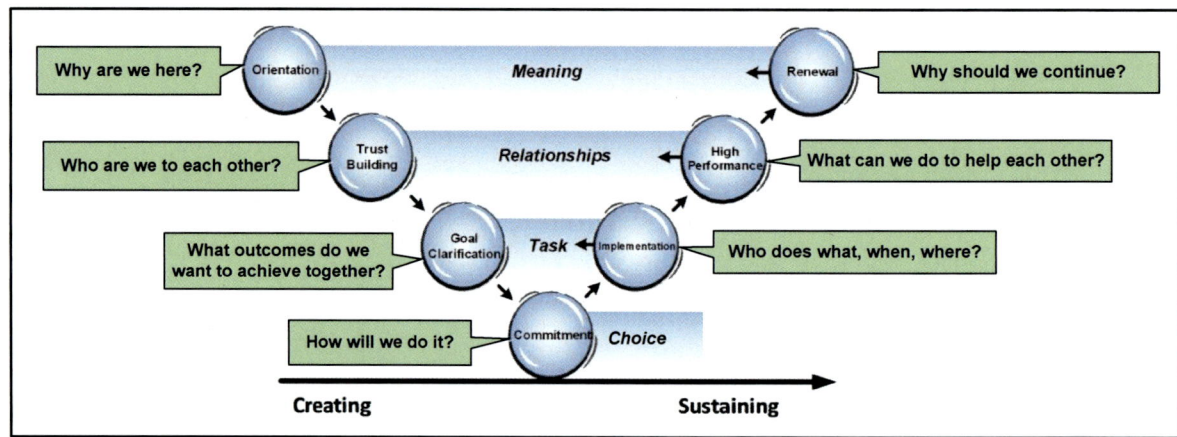

Figure 4-7: Team performance model

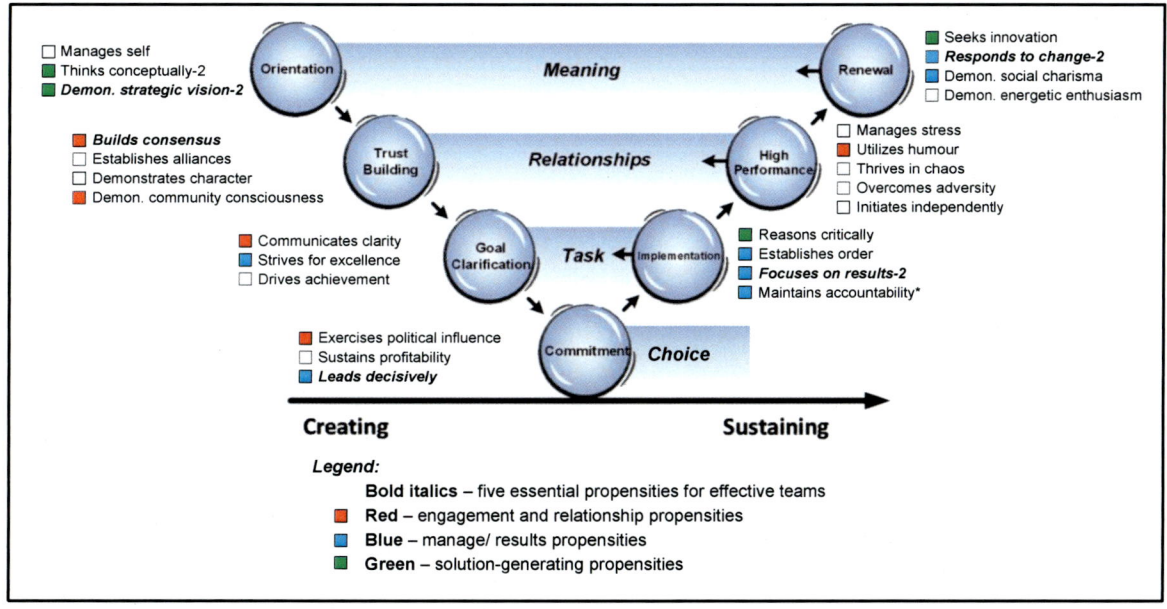

Figure 5-7: Development team propensities

The questions on the left side of the V in Figure 4-7 are a fruitful area for discussion during team formation since the responses help the team define their collective meaning system.

In Figure 5-7 we have changed the presentation somewhat. The bold text in the figure highlights the five essential propensities that contribute to effective functioning of any team; namely, demonstrates strategic vision, builds consensus, leads decisively, focuses on results, and responds to change. The coloured elements are all important aspects for the development team. As before, the numbers represent weighting for selecting the entire team, and the asterisks represent bridging elements for relationships with the owner-architect, project manager, and other stakeholders. As with the management case, not every team member has to have all attributes, but team members should be selected to ensure all attributes are present in the team.

Some, but not all, of the development team members may continue past the project phase to support the owner-architect in continually improving the management system and its interfaces.

PROCESS OWNER

Process owners for each of the individual processes are another important consideration when selecting team members for the management system. We will defer this discussion to Chapter 13.

SUMMARY OF KEY POINTS

We have barely scratched the surface of the power of the tools and methods identified in this chapter and their ability to diagnose management, team, and individual efficacy; however, our intent here is to focus on their use in relation to management system development. Elements from this chapter will resurface in Part B.

Key Points from this Chapter on Team Selection

1. Leaders at different levels in the organizational structure require different propensities from leaders at other levels, and these propensities cannot be gained through experience or training.

2. Successful implementation of a management system requires the staff selection process to consider the behavioural propensities of the:
   - senior management team
   - management system owner-architect
   - management system project manager
   - development team, and
   - process owners.

Chapter 6

Process-based Management Systems

IN THIS CHAPTER

This chapter explores key elements of process-based systems, management system standards, and high level models.

The specific sections cover:

- The evolution of quality
- Process building block
- Processes and organizational functions
- Integrated management systems
- Management system standards
- Applying standards
- Management system models
- A generic approach to process development.

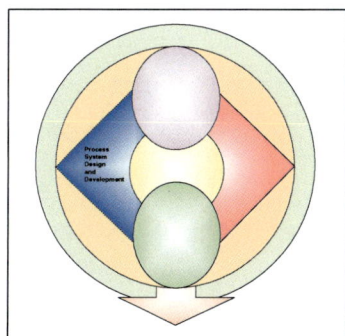

THE EVOLUTION OF QUALITY

Figure 6-1 illustrates the evolution from the concept of quality control in the 1950s to recent trends that focus on increased coherence among the human system, processes, and technology.

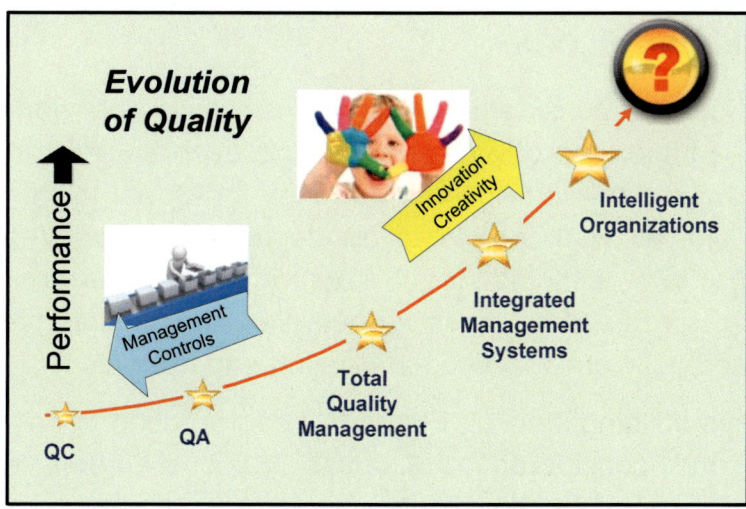

Figure 6-1: Evolution of quality

Associated with this historical trend has been a loosening of management controls to enable the emergence of the full intelligence of the organization's human system. Moves towards integration and beyond attempt to establish coherent resonance among the following elements:

- Human system and propensities of individuals and teams
- Processes and functionalities
- Organizational structure and functionalities
- Technology
- Information
- Outcomes
- Socio-sconomic-ecological context.

Some organizations stretch beyond mechanistic views of integrated management systems to a level of integration that utilizes the intelligence of the human system involved in developing and operating the processes and technology. What is apparent across industries is the added value of processes designed by people who do the actual work. Although high reliability organizations cannot employ the degree of innovation, flexibility, and creativity of the likes of Google or Apple, the ability to integrate systems is essential for safe operation. Although the future evolution represented by the question mark in Figure 6-1 is anyone's guess, ours would be that it will have something to do with unitive systems.

PROCESS BUILDING BLOCK

ALL work can be considered as a process, even the work of specialists, managers and leaders who often maintain (and even believe) their work is too variable, too complex, or too dependent on their individual talents to be mapped as a process. Not all work needs to be documented for every process, but analyzing the framework for how each category of work is done avoids many traps, including loose ends, missed activities, weak interfaces, poor risk management, and deficient knowledge retention and transfer.

The process building block in Figure 6-2 can be used to develop processes at any level, and consideration of these basic elements during process development will lead to better results. **A process is simply a set of linked activities that convert inputs to value-added outputs for an internal or**

external customer in accordance with defined requirements. We won't fuss over a more formal definition since the related elements in Figure 6-2 are relatively straightforward. The power of understanding this simple model should not be underestimated. For example, defining boundaries is key to avoiding process duplication and overlap. Similarly, it is important to understand the differences between process inputs and the process resources required to operate the process. Suppliers and customers may be internal or external to the organization, and primary or secondary.

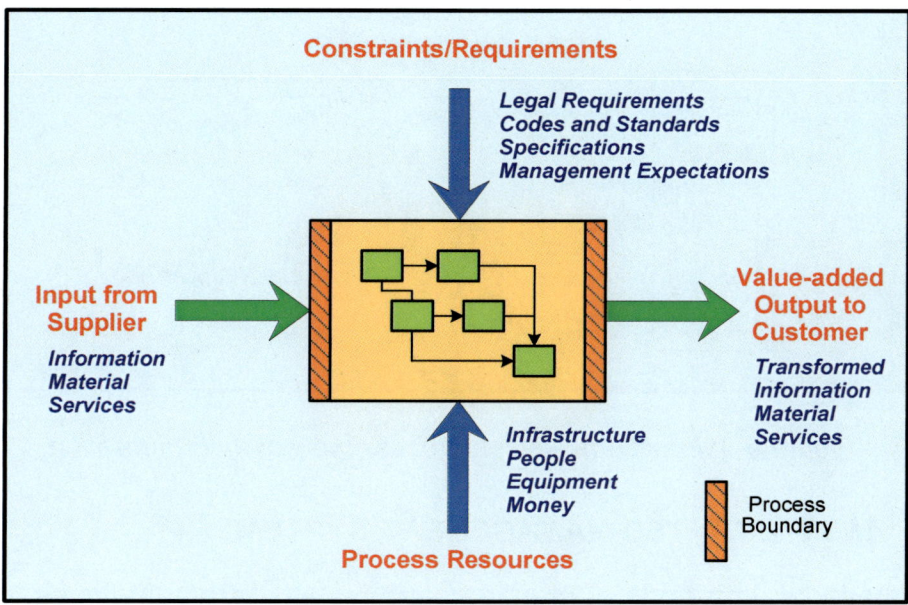

Figure 6-2: The process building block

PROCESSES AND ORGANIZATIONAL FUNCTIONS

Processes nearly always cross organizational boundaries between departments or functions (Figure 6-3). Process-based management has significant implications because it moves organizations away from the duplication and sub-optimization that occurs when departments or units develop processes in silos to carve out and protect their self-perceived role. A true process approach has huge capacity to enhance horizontal organizational communication, cooperation, and intelligence.

Implementing processes in organizations with a strong culture of functional silos is challenging because process owners require the authority to work cross-functionally for the overall benefit of the organization. For this reason, senior management needs a realistic understanding of their organization's culture and the propensities of individuals at management and supervisory levels. Such information is a key input to change management strategies.

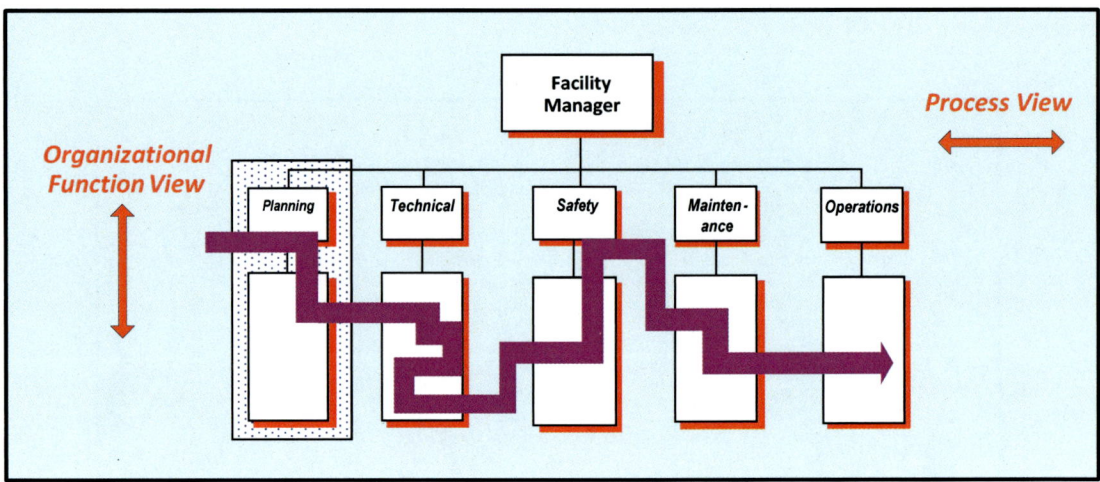

Figure 6-3: Functional versus process view of an organization

WHAT IS AN INTEGRATED MANAGEMENT SYSTEM?

International definitions of management systems are sometimes vague and often limit themselves to policy and process elements:

- ISO:
    - "The framework of processes and procedures used to ensure that an organization can fulfill all tasks required to achieve its objectives."
    - "A system to establish policy and objectives and to achieve those objectives."
- IAEA:
    - "The management system is a set of interrelated or interacting elements that establishes policies and objectives and which

enables those objectives to be achieved in a safe, efficient and effective manner."

For our purposes, such definitions are limited since they don't encompass the full dimensions of integrated management systems.

The Integrated Management Special Interest Group of the Chartered Quality Institute provides a definition based on a more holistic view of integrated management:

"An Integrated Management System is a single integrated system used by an organisation to manage the totality of its processes, in order to meet the organisation's objectives and equitably satisfy the stakeholders." [CQI 2007].

We'll get to our working definition after a brief explanation of its underlying components. Figure 6-4 is a simplified illustration of the various elements that impact the effectiveness of any organization. It is a variation of Figure 1-2. As indicated in the figure, organizations develop principles, processes and practices relevant to their specific operational and technological requirements. Their objective is to convert material, resources and information into value-added outcomes. Outcomes extend beyond products and business outcomes (profit, cost, market share, growth, risk, etc.) to include human (development, health, wellness, compensation, security, etc.), organizational (reputation, productivity, quality, diversity, locations, etc.), ecological (environmental impacts), and societal (contribution, value, job creation, etc.) outcomes.

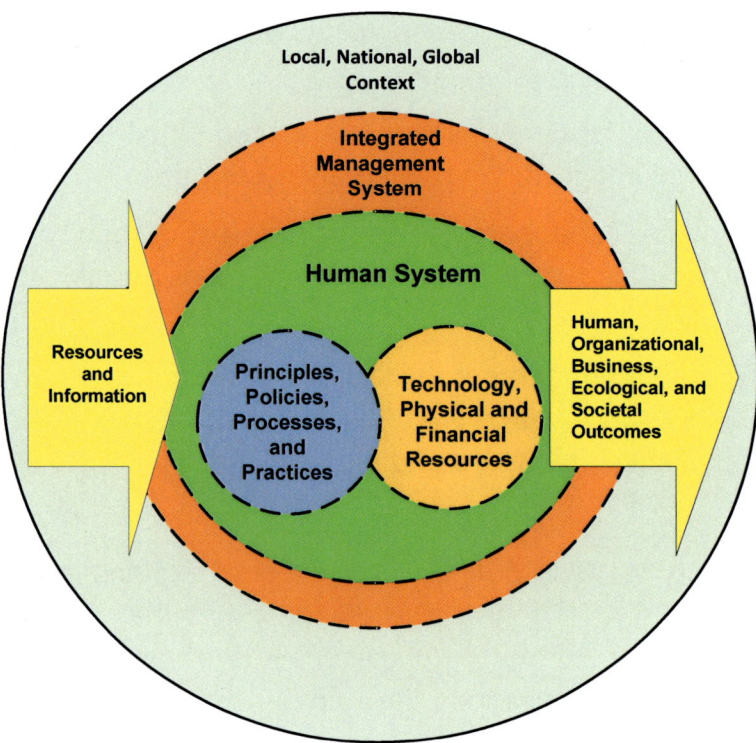

Figure 6-4: Integrated management system

All of this is enabled and enacted by the human system (see definition in Chapter 2 or Glossary). The human system includes culture, competencies, relationships, leadership, and the many other dimensions of human interactions.

Finally, the organization functions within a local, national, and global environmental context that includes regulations, requirements, public expectations, history, culture, and economic-market conditions.

Another way to look at organizations is as coupled systems (Figure 6-5) that are largely integrated through the elements of organizational design and management system design. It is important to create representations that suit your specific organization, and only use other models as sources of ideas.

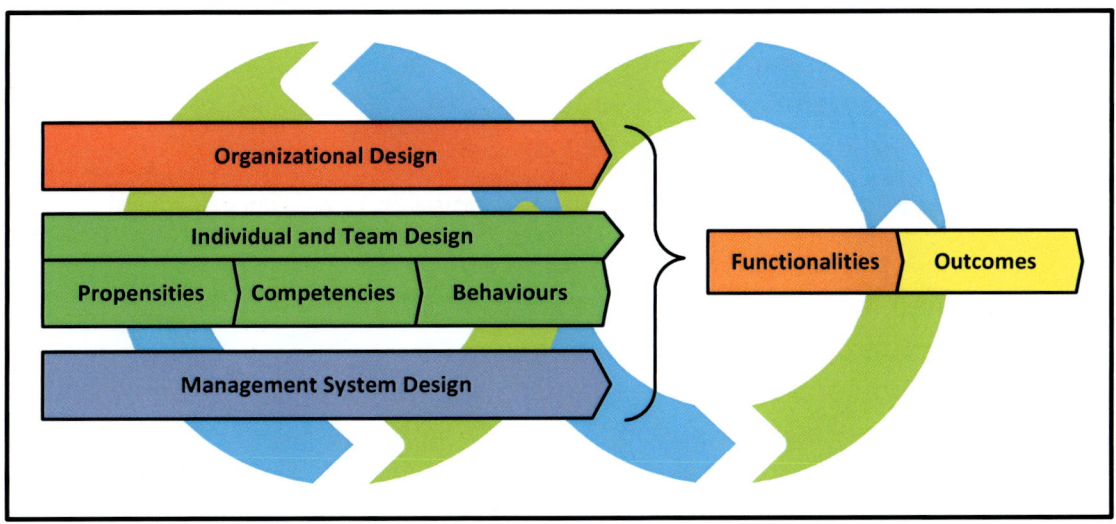

Figure 6-5: Organizations as coupled systems

Integration is sometimes considered to mean simply that all the requirements from codes and standards are integrated into a single management system. In order to broaden the perspective of the term 'integrated management system', we will use the working definition of an integrated management system shown in the box. QA specialists may be troubled that the definition doesn't use expressions such as "meeting requirements and customer expectations"; however, these are only a few of the desired outcomes of a management system.

DEFINITION: Integrated Management System

An ***integrated management system*** is the purposeful alignment and interaction of an organization's human system, process system, and technology with its external context to achieve desired organizational and societal outcomes.

This broader approach implies that integration includes the organization's structure, process system, human system, technology and operating context. In other words, all the elements in any of the Figures 1-1, 1-2, 6-4, or 6-5 have to be coherent for an organization to be effective.

Effective integration means that two key principles have to be applied:

1. Develop and implement ***systemically*** → All elements and interactions related to the functioning of the organization need to be considered as a complex interacting system.
2. Develop and implement ***systematically*** → the framework and practices need to support a systematic approach to development, implementation, and improvement.

Systems thinking (see box) considers complex systems in their entirety. It is based on the observation that the elements of a system are often best understood in the context of their relationships with each other and with other systems, rather than in isolation. Systems thinking considers the dynamic web of temporal, conceptual, social and logistical interactions rather than simple linear cause and effect relationships. Systematic thinking (see box) tends to be more sequential and involves a repeatable cycle of analyzing the entire system (systemically, of course), planning for integration, organizing across the system, implementing processes within the integrated system, monitoring system performance, and adjusting with attention to the impact on dynamic relationships within the overall system.

Once the systemic aspects are understood, systematic thinking can be applied to ensure that requirements are met efficiently and effectively through logical structures, interfaces and flow.

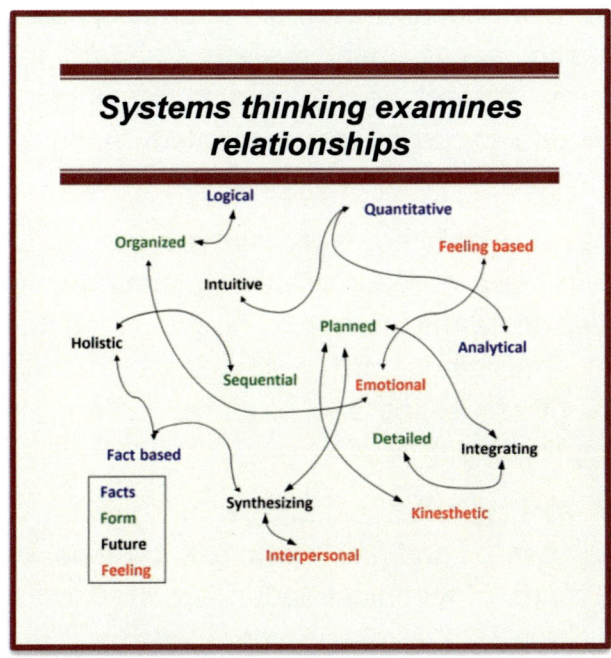
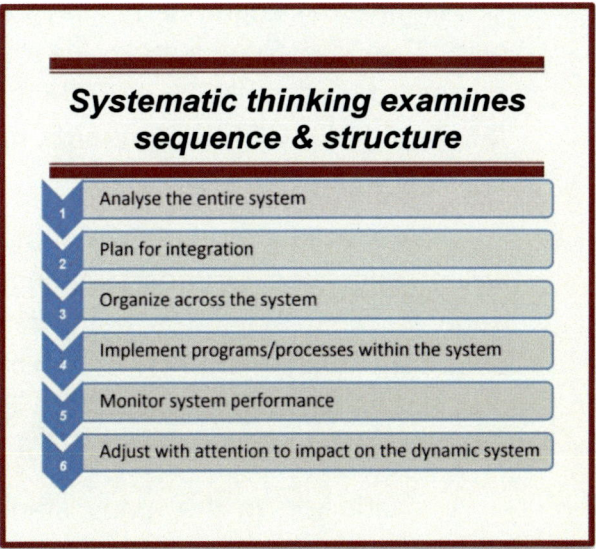

MANAGEMENT SYSTEM STANDARDS AND GUIDES

There are many management system standards. The most widely used are the International Organization for Standardization standards such as ISO 9001, "Quality management systems – Requirements" [ISO 2008]; and ISO 14001 "Environmental management systems – Requirements with guidance for use" [ISO 2004]. OHSAS 18001 "Occupational health and safety management systems – Requirements" [OHSAS 2004] is a widely-adopted British standard compatible with ISO.

The International Atomic Energy Agency has published standards for the nuclear industry, including GS-R-3, "The Management System for Facilities and Activities" [IAEA 2006a] as well as a number of supporting publications [IAEA 2006b, 2009, and 2015]. The European Foundation for Quality Management (EFQM) publishes an Excellence Model that can serve as a foundation for management system development [EFQM 2012].

Individual countries typically adopt international standards or develop their own. Canada, for example, has a specific management system standard for nuclear facilities N286-12, "Management system requirements for nuclear facilities" [CSA 2012]. Standards may be referenced as requirements in national legislation or regulations.

Most management system standards are updated every five years or so to reflect advances in understanding and to keep abreast of other standards. In general, most standards have similarities in terms of specifying the need for policies, management commitment, provision of resources, defined accountabilities, competent staff, control of processes and products, control of documents and records, and continual improvement.

In addition to the many standards and guides for management systems, high reliability organizations, including nuclear, oil and gas, chemical, aerospace, and pharmaceutical, are subject to thousands of technical codes and standards that must be accommodated in some fashion by the management system. This non-trivial problem can only be addressed through a systematic approach to management system design and development. A process based approach enables a direct tie between codes/standards and work instructions.

Despite the value of standards, there are several points that management system developers need to keep in mind:

- Standards don't provide sufficient information on <u>how</u> to develop a management system
- Standards are developed through consensus teams of experts who tend to focus on requirements rather than provide practical guidance on how to perform work or integrate systems
- Management system standards typically evolve from quality assurance standards, and are therefore developed through the lens of quality assurance experts rather than organizational or business experts
- The multiplicity of standards, with sometimes conflicting or vague requirements, means that one has to select the ones that best fit the activities of your organization
- Despite the existence of various management system standards for environment, safety, and specific industries, only <u>one</u> integrated management system is required for any organization.

APPLYING STANDARDS

Figure 6-6 shows our recommended approach to applying standards. This approach is intended to minimize the likelihood of developing processes that meet each clause of a specific standard but pay insufficient attention to how the process will meet the desired operational goals. Processes developed to meet standards often look great on paper, satisfy quality checklists that map requirements to documents, but are often problematic from an implementation perspective. A typical outcome is management's frustration that "people aren't following procedures" when the ability to follow them was simply assumed, not a primary design principle.

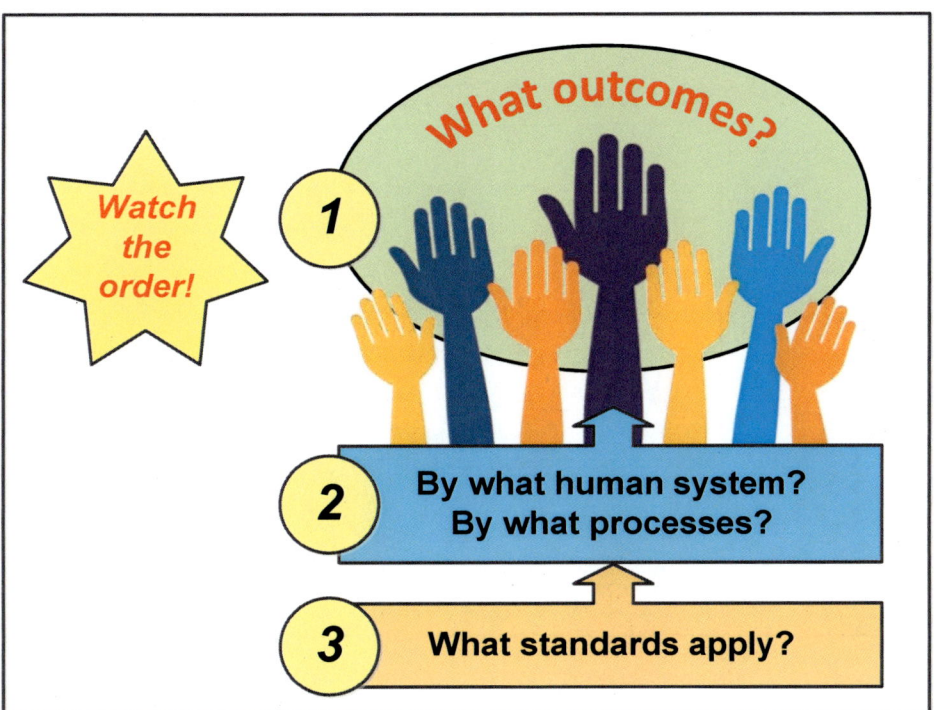

Figure 6-6: Approach to applying standards during process development

The sequence in Figure 6-6 is intended to focus attention on the desired outcomes before exploring what processes and human system elements (people and organization) are best suited to achieve those outcomes. The last step is to identify the standards that have to be met and how they should be applied. One has to have some information on all three aspects in the early stages but the trick is not to lock on to the standards prematurely.

MANAGEMENT SYSTEM MODELS

A high level model of the management system provides a framework for building the component elements. We will examine a few models to look at their basic construction, strengths, and weaknesses.

Figure 6-7 represents the ISO 9001 [2010] model for a management system. It is more conceptual than practical; however, it illustrates the importance of customer input related to requirements, and customer satisfaction with the outcomes. It also illustrates the quality improvement cycle. ISO has driven the customer satisfaction surveys that seem to follow every retail transaction from hardware purchases to online technical support.

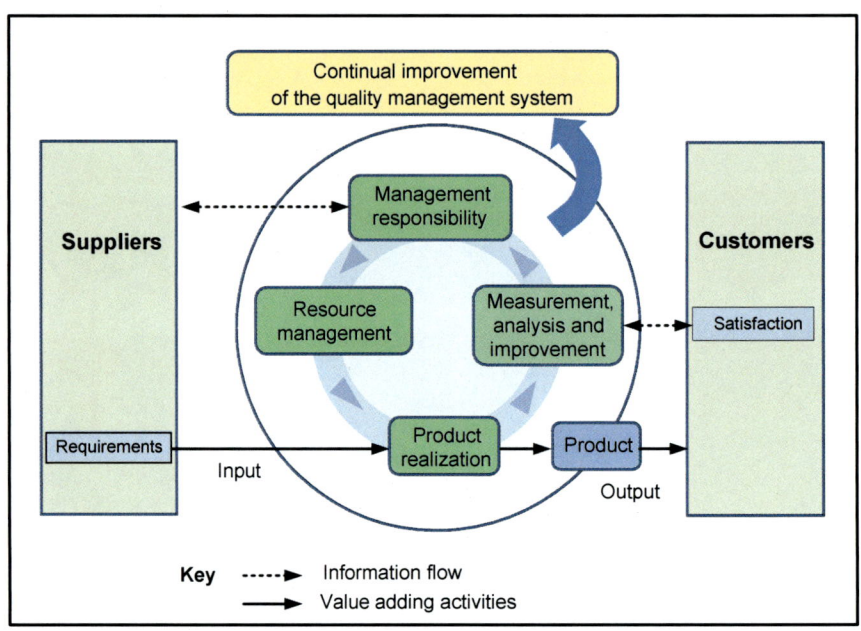

Figure 6-7: ISO 9001 Quality management system model

The ISO system contains many thousands of lower tier standards specific to a variety of industries and activities.

The EFQM Excellence Model [EQFM 2010] in Figure 6-8 provides another view of a management system framework. Each element is given a relative weighting in terms of its perceived contribution to effectiveness. The model explicitly recognizes the importance of a feedback loop related to learning, creativity, and innovation. Although still somewhat conceptual, the model conveys a message that leadership, people, and societal impact are important parts of the system.

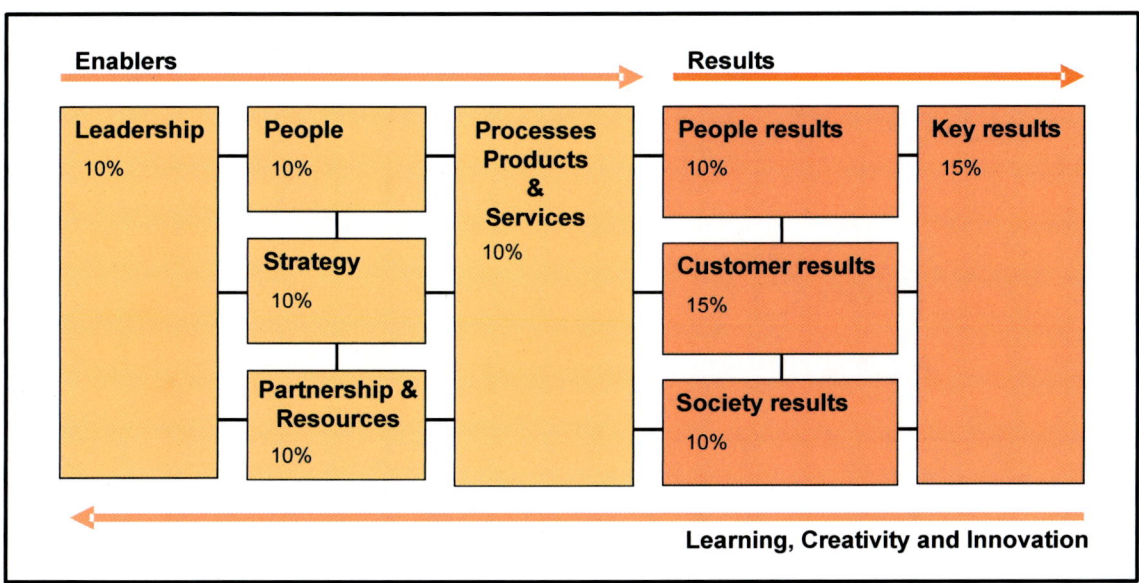

Figure 6-8: The EFQM Excellence Model

The model is based on eight fundamental concepts (Figure 6-9). These provide a useful framework for management system practitioners to view their role in the broader context of organizational effectiveness. It is evident from Figure 6-9 that the spectrum extends beyond traditional quality management.

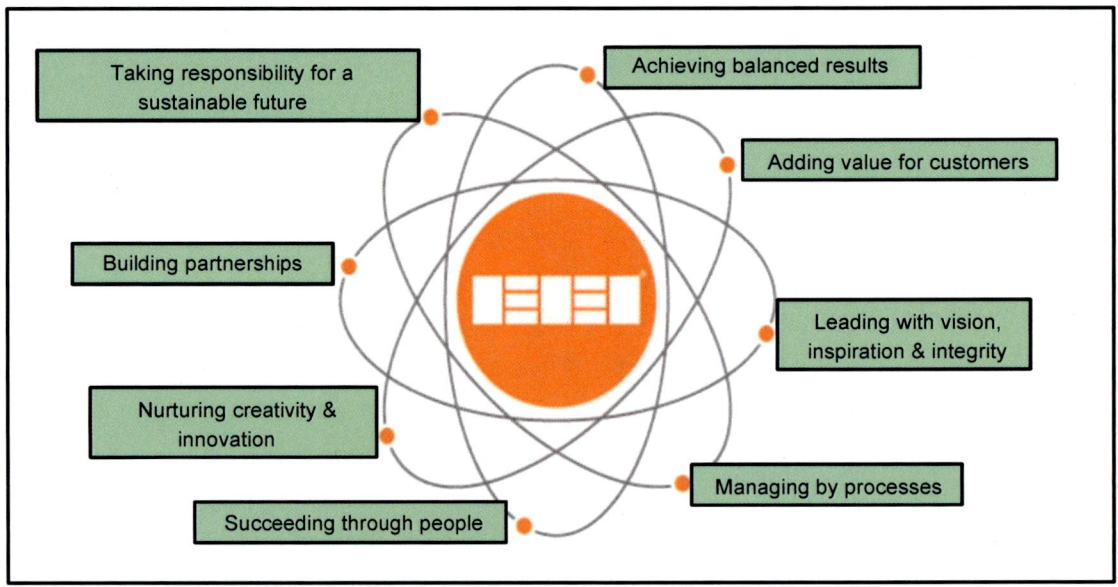

Figure 6-9: The EFQM Excellence Model is based on 8 fundamental concepts

Figure 6-10 is a representation of a model developed for the nuclear industry through the joint efforts of the Nuclear Electric Institute and Institute of Nuclear Power Operators in the U.S. In other words, it focuses on the left hand diamond of Figure 1-2 in Chapter 2 rather than all the elements. It illustrates a model that is more visibly process driven compared with the previous examples. The detailed model includes 46 sub-processes distributed across the top level processes shown in Figure 6-10. Although one has to be a member organization to get access to information, each process has a 'community of practice' to support and improve each process.

The NEI / INPO model [NEI 2004] was initially developed to support utility efforts to compare costs and resourcing effort for various processes, and is credited with significantly improving efficiency and performance within the U.S. nuclear industry. Although many plants use the model for guidance and benchmarking, few have adopted it in its entirety since each organization evolves its own approach to performing work. The model is a clear example of how such a framework can be used to improve performance.

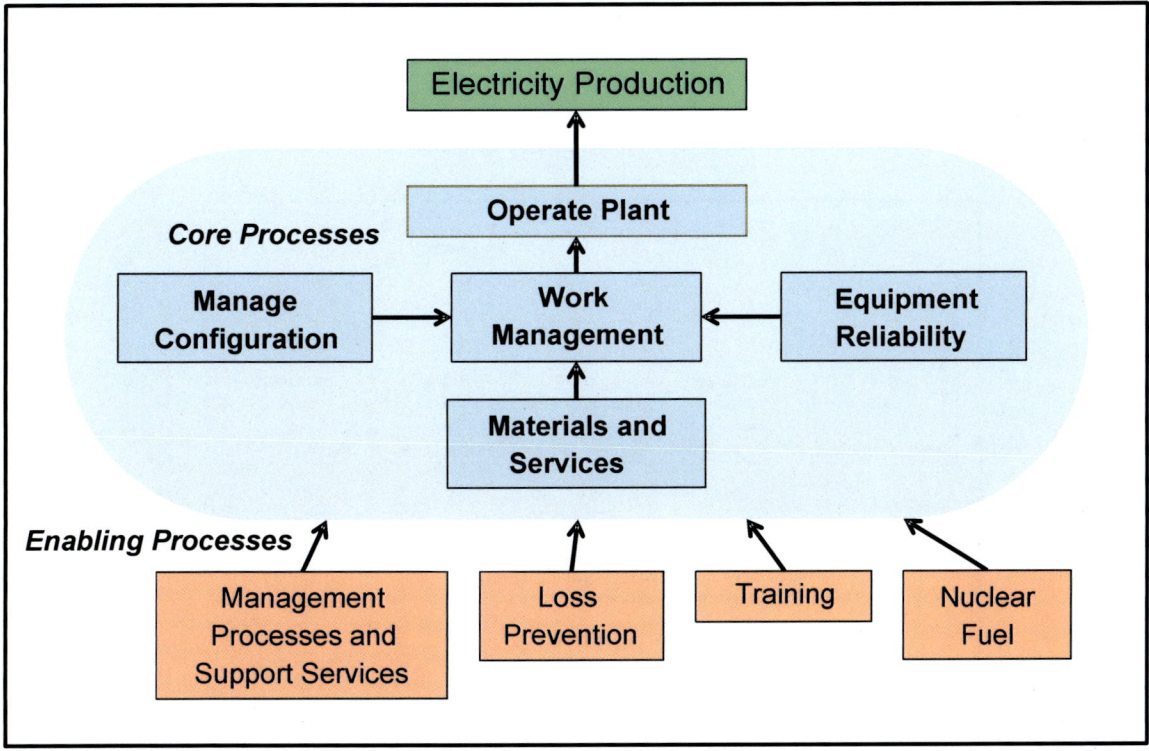

Figure 6-10: NEI / INPO management system model for nuclear power plants

The NEI / INPO model is relatively silent in the important area of processes related to directing and managing the organization. This has been attributed by some to the fact that the approach was developed by accountants (for activity-based-costing) and engineers (for controlling quality), whereas others suggest that different styles of management make such processes difficult to establish. As we will discuss later, processes for directing and managing the organization are an important contributor to organizational performance and leadership focus.

Figure 6-11 provides another example of a fully process-based approach to management systems applicable to a broad range of enterprises. The Process Classification Framework (Standard Model) or PCF [APQC 2014] was developed by non-profit APQC and its member companies as an open standard to facilitate improvement through process management and benchmarking, regardless of industry, size, or geography. The PCF organizes operating and management processes into 12 enterprise level categories and over 1,000 processes and associated activities. The full PCF and industry-specific versions of the PCF as well as associated measures and benchmarking are available at *www.apqc.org*. For process developers, the PCF provides a consistent language and approach that can leverage development; however, like similar products, they must be adapted to the organization's specific characteristics and needs.

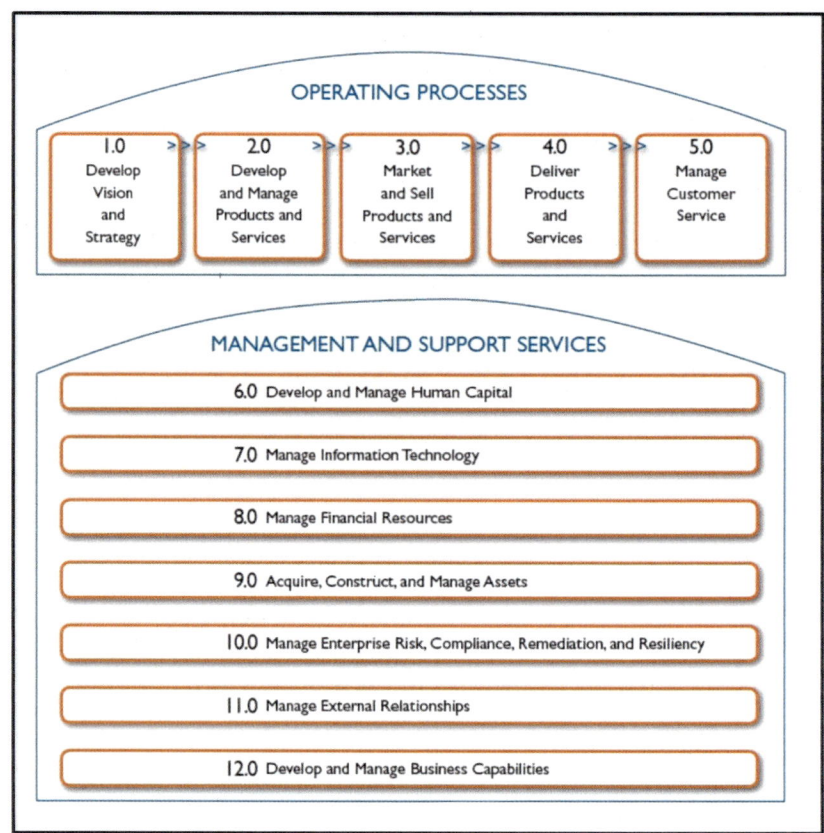

Figure 6-11: APQC Process Classification Framework^{SM}

The previous examples are but a few of the models that can be used as a framework for management system development. The intent of showing them is twofold:

- There are many ways to approach a top level model, and
- Trying to adopt someone else's model rather than adapt relevant features to your organization is a route to failure.

In brief, the management team and support staff must do considerable work to ensure the model they develop fits the specific needs of the organization. What others do is valuable for benchmarking and generating ideas, but importing something that simply looks like it will do the job will likely result in failure at the implementation stage. Your management system has to align with your organization's business model, strategies, plans, and activities, not with someone else's.

For this reason, we will illustrate a process-based approach that can be applied to any organization without preventing one from using experience from others as value-added input.

A GENERIC APPROACH TO PROCESS DEVELOPMENT

This section provides a process-based approach that can be applied to any organization without foregoing the opportunity to integrate useful features from alternative approaches. The left side of Figure 6-12 shows the process components of the management system. An important point is that everything on the right side of the figure is integrated into an enacting process somewhere on the left side of the figure.

Create, don't copy

A top level model is an act of creation, not duplication. Seeking the experience of others is important but insufficient. Although some aspects may be adapted to your situation, the unique nature of each organization requires senior management to invest time building a model they believe is right for their circumstances.

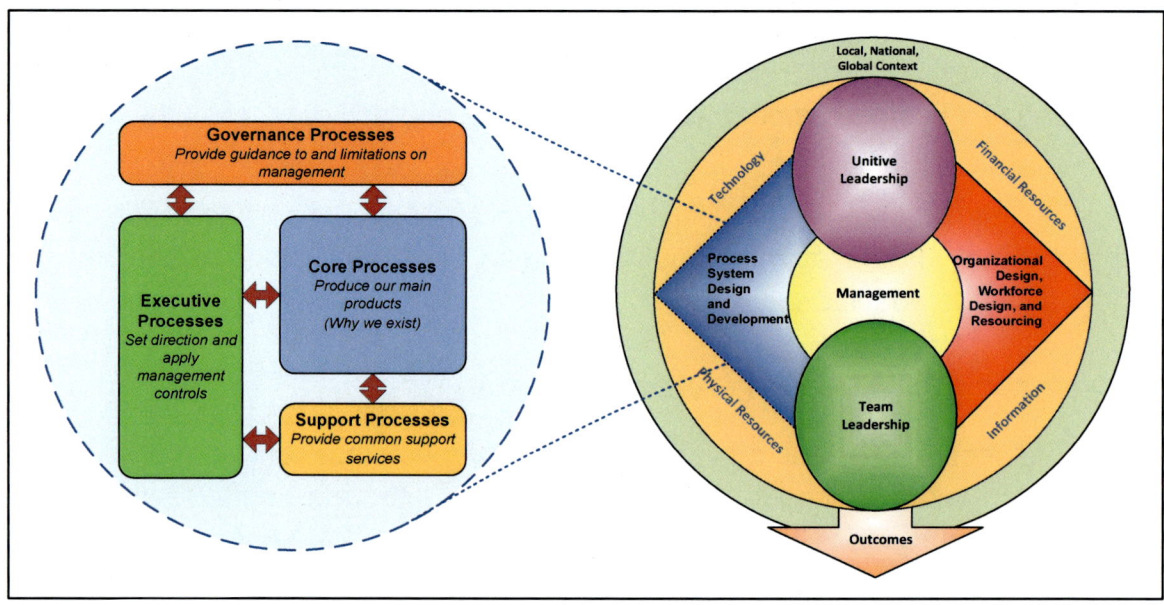

Figure 6-12: Process component of an integrated management system.

Management systems typically contain four types of process: governance, executive, core, and support, executive. These are described in the following sections.

Governance Processes

Governance processes (Figure 6-13) are typically established by a Board of Directors that provides oversight and guidance to the senior management team who are accountable for the day-to-day functioning of the organization. Governance processes set limits on management authority and establish rigorous stewardship and oversight practices. Participants at this level require broad capabilities for discerning organizational health, capacity, and risk in relation to the local, national, and global environment.

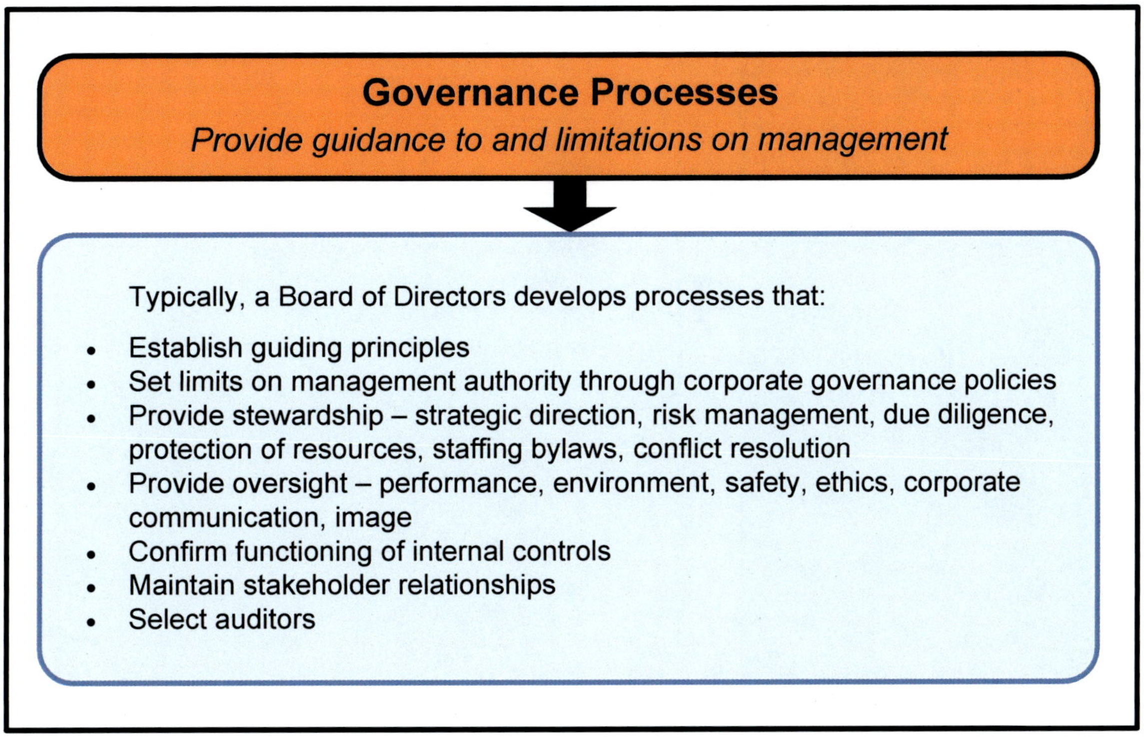

Figure 6-13: Governance Processes

Executive Processes

Executive processes (sometimes called Management Processes) in Figure 6-14 establish direction and management controls for the entire organization. Their primary role is in defining strategy, allocating resources and managing organizational risk. Direct and manage the organization is the primary process for providing organizational direction. As indicated in Figure 6-14, it includes key sub-processes related to plans, priorities, project management, risk management, and change management.

The propensity distributions for owners of executive processes require a high degree of systems and strategic thinking, the ability to translate concepts into action, and the ability to constructively engage stakeholders. In addition, diversity of reasoning is important since these processes address a broad range of issues beyond the financial and business workings of the organization.

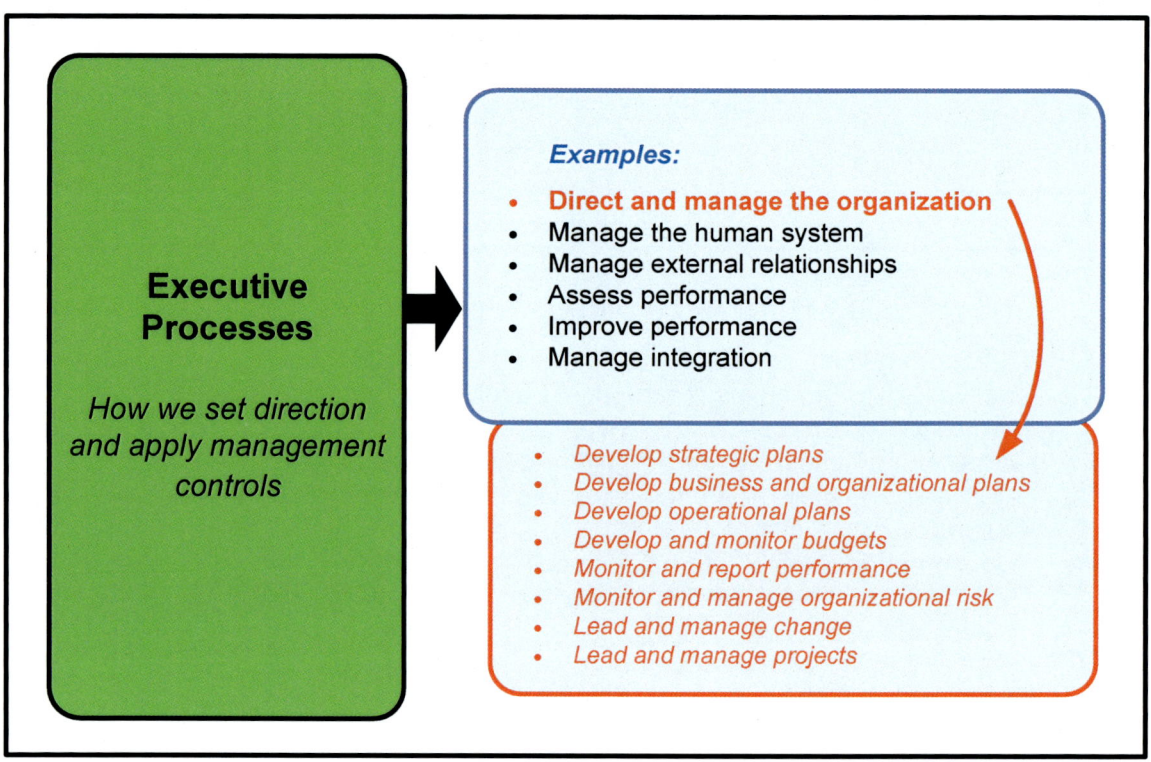

Figure 6-14: Executive processes

Processes within a category are not merely lists, but form part of a systematic design that ensures the interfaces between processes make sense. A sure route to excess complexity is to develop a process whenever one is needed, without regard for how it fits within the entire system.

Two Executive processes are worth mentioning specifically since they are not commonly understood. 'Manage the human system' provides integration of the organizational design basis, requisite propensities and competencies, and organizational functionalities or mobilizing constellations discussed in Chapters 2 and 3. This process operates in a broader organizational context than the support process 'Provide human resources' (Figure 6-13) which provides traditional HR functions such as staffing, payroll, and employee wellness programs. The second process worth mentioning is 'Manage integration' which establishes standard methods for process development, interfaces between processes, and assignment of requirements. It also ensures integration with other aspects of the management system through, for example, interfaces with 'Manage the human system'.

Figure 6-15 provides an example of how Executive processes interconnect to provide resources to any other process. The list of processes is a bit different from Figure 6-14. The reason is simply that we don't want anyone to lock into one of our lists as being the right fit for their organization. The beauty of the approach is that it can be applied to design an appropriate set for any organization.

Of particular note in Figure 6-15 are the loops from 'Direct and manage the organization' that provide resources based on process needs, and the role of 'Manage process integration' in assigning requirements to each process and establishing controls on process changes. In this respect, this process is more limited in scope than "Manage integration' in Figure 6-14. We will explore some of the Executive processes in more detail in Part B.

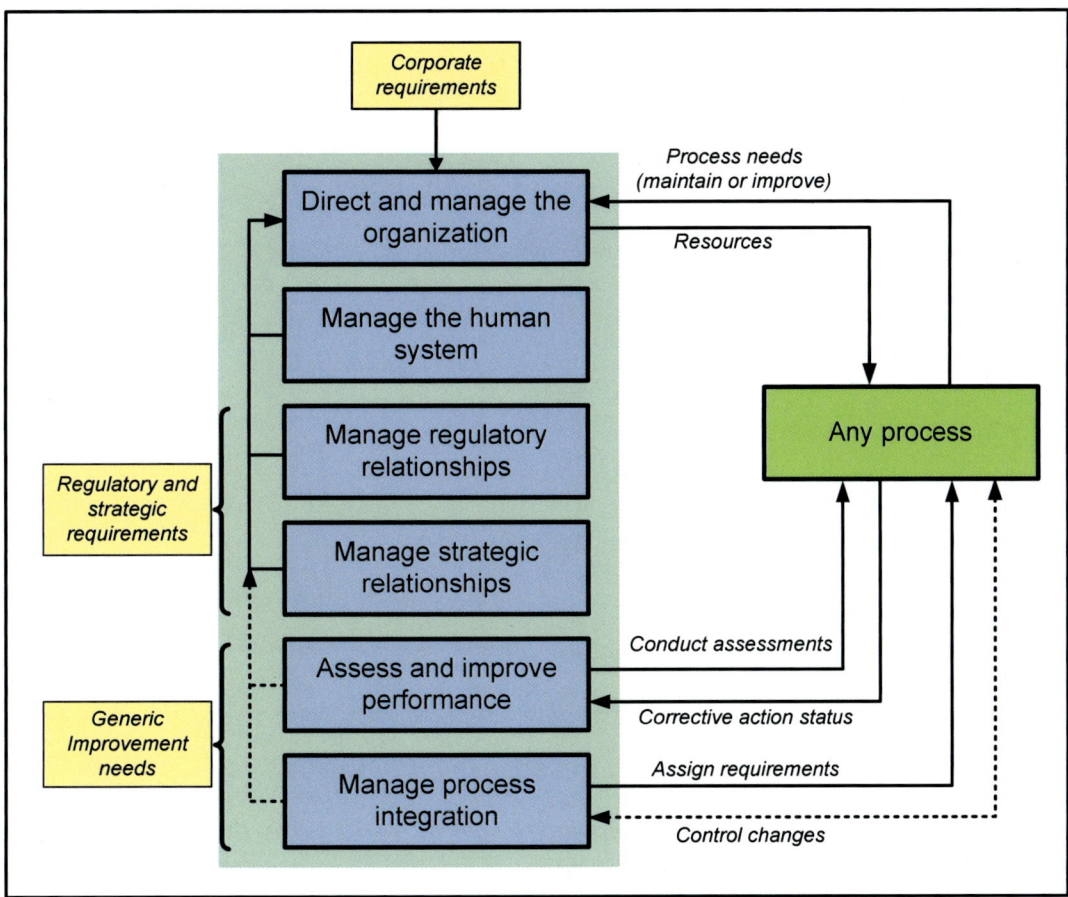

Figure 6-15: Interfaces of Executive processes with other processes

Core and Support Processes

Core processes (Figure 6-16) define functionalities the organization must excel at in order to flourish. Organizations as diverse as nuclear power plants, oil companies, banks, and shoe manufacturers differ primarily in their core processes.

Core processes are the primary driver of the organizational structure and the propensities, competencies, and experience requirements for senior managers and staff who work in core functions. These processes determine the minimum resourcing levels needed to produce organizational outcomes and manage short- to medium-term operational risks. For high reliability organizations, core processes may be grouped into broad categories such as design, operation, equipment reliability, etc. with specific processes assigned to each group.

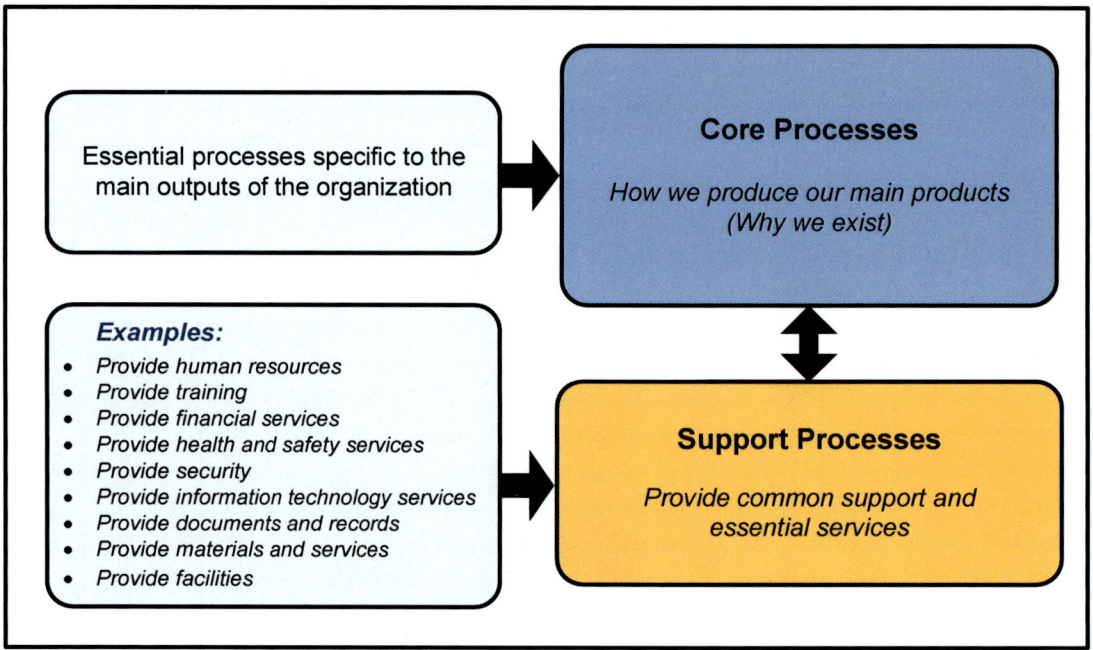

Figure 6-16: Core and support processes

Support processes provide essential services to core and other processes within the management system. These tend to be similar across different organizations, although in some cases a support process may warrant consideration as a core process. A construction company, for example, may regard *Provide materials and services* or its equivalent as a core process because of its critical role in meeting schedule.

Support processes require different propensities and competencies than core processes. It is important in staffing these functions to ensure a sufficient degree of propensity for proactivity so that issues such as staffing, training, procurement, and information management anticipate emerging organizational issues rather than simply react to existing needs and problems.

The four process categories (governance, executive, core, and support) described in the previous sections are useful groupings; however, the underlying processes are specific to each organization, and are named according to what makes most sense for that organization. You may notice a few conventions:

- Begin process names with an active verb. 'Documents and records' is just a collection. 'Provide documents and records' implies the act of production.
- Make process names unambiguous. 'Manage Information', or more infamously, 'Information management' is too encompassing. Information management is the job of the entire management system, not the IT system or documents and records system.
- Reserve 'manage' for the executive processes. Everyone likes their process to manage, and every process does manage some aspect of the organization, but the verb gets overused. For example, 'Manage' safety is a support process that 'provides' safety services. Safety is managed by embedding it in the processes where it is required. Even though the Safety Manager may wish to have the process titled 'Manage safety', it is wise not to confuse departmental roles with processes.

Leadership, Management, and Processes

Figure 6-17 shows the relationship between leadership, management, and management system processes. Leaders and managers use elements of the management system inherent in executive and other processes to perform their work. Clearly defined, transparent executive processes significantly assist in organizational alignment, communication, resource allocation, and decision-making.

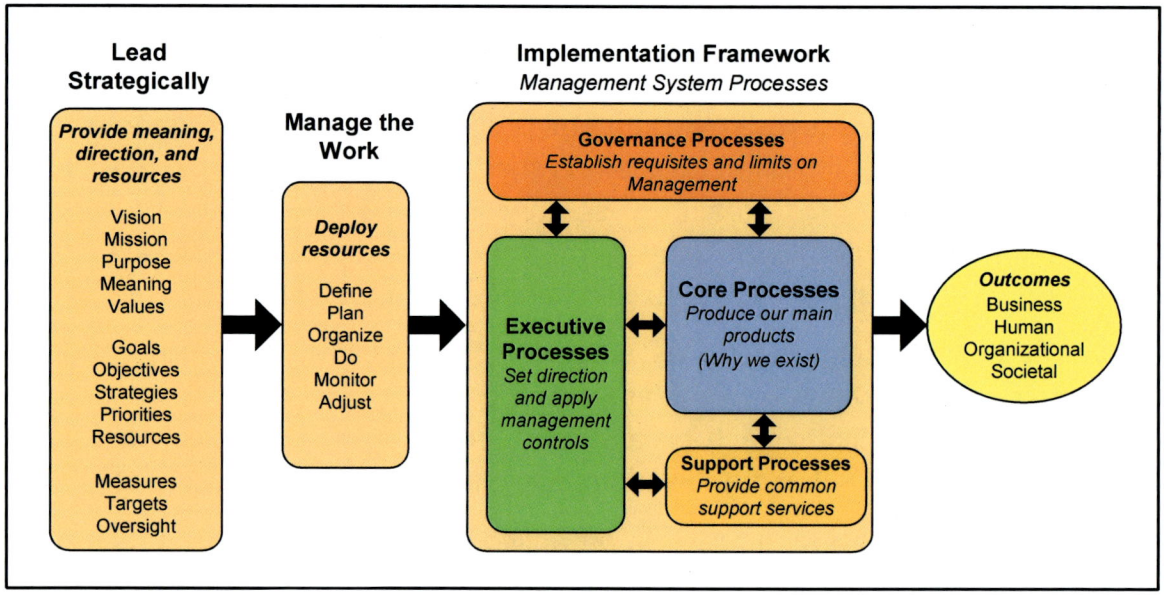

Figure 6-17: Relationship between leadership, management, and processes

Because senior leaders serve a different function than managers, their focus and aggregate propensities are different. Leaders and managers sometimes believe their work is too dynamic, people-driven, and problem-oriented to benefit from standardized executive processes; however, development of these processes can significantly improve leader and management alignment, efficiency, and effectiveness. They also serve as a basis for leadership development (see box on next page).

Examples of Management System Models

Appendix E provides sample models from high reliability organizations based on the general approaches described in this chapter.

> ### *Leadership training and development*
>
> A management system provides a specific framework for leadership, including behavioural expectations that apply to all employees. Process understanding supplements the interpersonal and motivational attributes associated with leadership at all levels of the organization.
>
> Processes for directing and managing the organization (e.g., planning, prioritization, decision-making, change management, risk management, project management, continual improvement, performance monitoring, communication, organizational development, and human resource management) provide a structure for identifying training and development needs for leaders and managers. Learning programs focus on the knowledge, skills, abilities, and behaviours necessary for effective implementation of processes. Familiarity with internal processes for accomplishing work builds bridges between departments, management, and employees. The ability to accomplish work is facilitated when people have confidence in the organization's processes.
>
> Although many organizations purchase external courses and instructors to teach elements of leadership from change management to communication, such training has a short half-life if it does not include relevant processes within the management system. External training can often give rise to new opportunities to improve internal processes, but it is no substitute for such processes.

In closing our discussion of management system models we stress once more the importance of senior management getting directly involved in management system design rather than delegating such development to support staff. A management team that takes hands-on action to develop the top level model based on their understanding of the organization and how they want it to work is more likely to own the result, and will certainly be able to communicate and monitor performance more effectively. Specialists such as process and process improvement staff, organizational development staff, and quality assurance staff will be required to support the work, but they will be unable to implement the requisite elements without the deep understanding, engagement, and active support of senior management.

SUMMARY OF KEY POINTS

The foundational elements from this chapter will resurface in Part B as practical considerations for developing an integrated management system.

Key Points from this Chapter on Process-based Management Systems

1. The process building block provides all the elements necessary to develop any process at any level.
2. All work can be usefully examined from a process perspective, even the work of leaders and managers.
3. Management systems do much more than control work. They enable senior management to understand how the work of the organization fits together, flows, and accomplishes desired outcomes.
4. The cross-functional nature of process management requires a different approach to managing than occurs in most hierarchical organizations.
5. Integration requires purposeful alignment of the process system, organizational design, human system, and technology with the external operating environment.
6. Many top level models exist, from conceptual to practical. The only one that has a reasonable probability of successful implementation is the one that senior management makes the effort to develop for the specific needs of the organization.
7. Successful development and implementation requires the organization to seed both systemic and systematic thinking from conception of the management system through to continual improvement.
8. An approach based on core, support, executive, and governance processes aids both systemic and systematic implementation.
9. Management systems provide an essential framework for learning, knowledge management, risk management, continual improvement, training, assigning accountabilities, and leadership development.

Part B

Application

Chapter 7

Assess Organizational Readiness and Capacity

IN THIS CHAPTER

This chapter introduces the flowchart for the systematic approach taken in the rest of the handbook. It also describes methods to assess organizational readiness and capacity. The topics include:

- A flowchart to enable a systematic approach to management system development
- Assessing organizational readiness and capacity
- Who should perform the assessment
- Details of the assessment
- Charting the way forward.

TAKE A SYSTEMATIC APPROACH TO DEVELEOPMENT

Since we stressed the importance of being systematic as well as systemic, we will follow a disciplined step-by-step process that makes no assumptions about the organizational systems already in place. An organization may be tempted to skip steps or areas in the belief that the requisite systems are already in place or that a particular aspect doesn't apply. This should be done only when performance data supports that position. Otherwise, development may lead to a patchwork approach akin to building a sky-scraper without including plans for electrical and water distribution systems.

Figure 7-1 identifies our suggested systematic approach with a key to each chapter containing the detailed discussion. In this chapter we will address the first block in the flowchart related to assessing organizational readiness and capacity. Other chapters will follow the schematic of Figure 7-1.

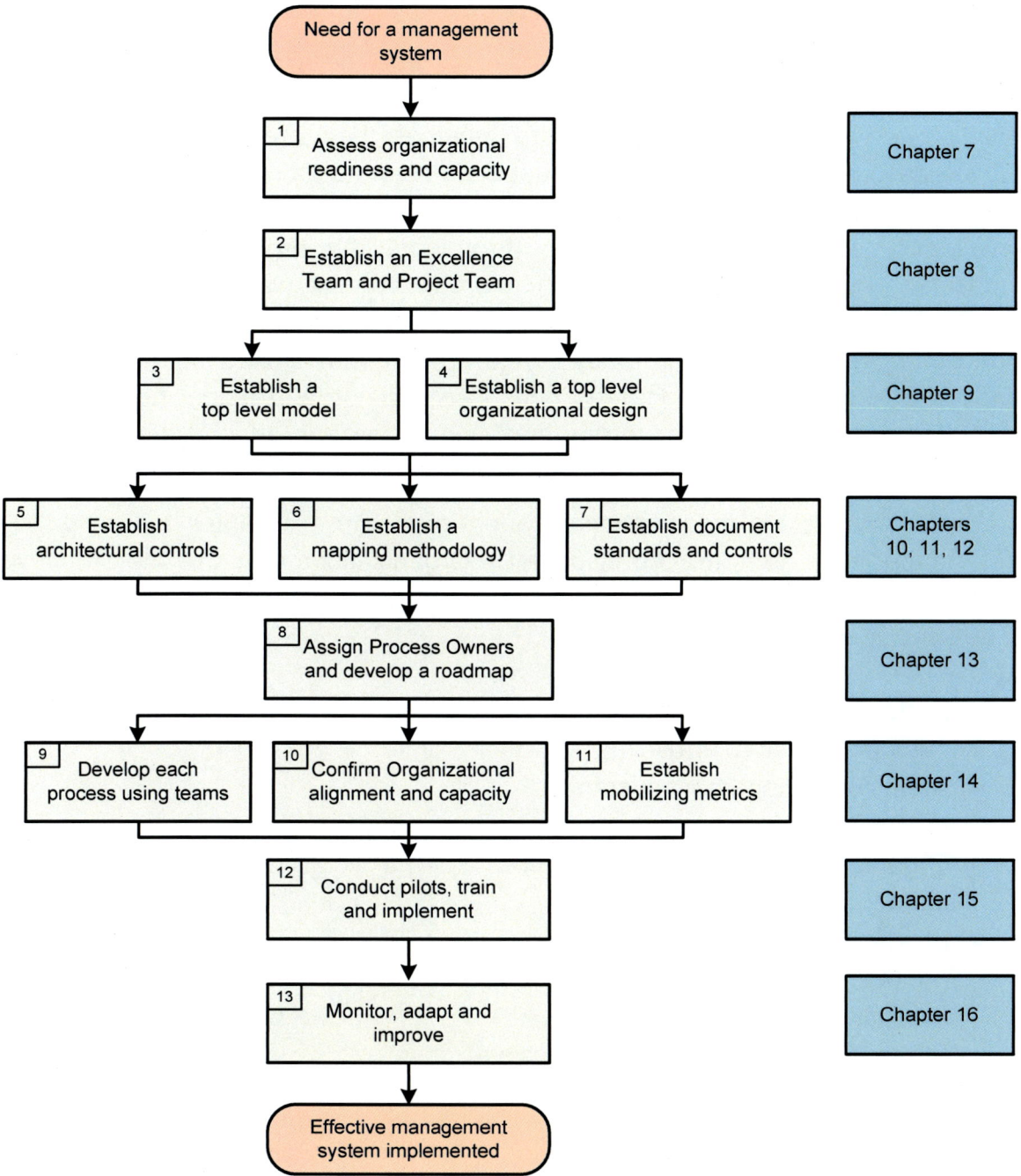

Figure 7-1: Process flowchart for management system implementation

ASSESS ORGANIZATIONAL READINESS AND CAPACITY

An assessment of organizational readiness identifies what needs to be changed and whether the organization is equipped to change. This goes beyond looking at what processes exist and whether they are working effectively. Organizational readiness for change depends on the current stage of evolution of the organization, the capacity of the senior management team, and the availability of requisite propensities throughout the organization. Failure to consider organizational readiness in a broad context will make it difficult to implement and sustain a fully integrated management system. For example, a function-oriented or program-based organization with limited change capacity may choose to develop processes consistent with organizational functions with some standardization across the organization rather than attempt a full transition to an integrated system.

We will use the organizational system model from Chapter 1 (Figure 1-2), reproduced here, to frame the discussion. Organizations may use their top level business model or management system model to supplement the assessment. The specific sections cover:

- Performance – achievement of desired outcomes (bottom arrow)
- Status of management system processes (left diamond)
- Organizational design status (right diamond)
- Leadership capacity and diversity (unitive, management, team, shared meaning and propensities)
- Status of financial resources, physical resources, technology, and information (circle)
- Context and climate (outer circle)

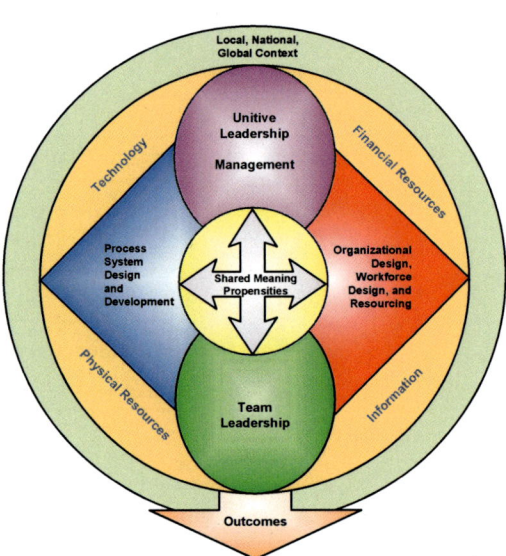

We will also include some additional aspects:

- Stage of evolution
- Current change initiatives.

Finally, we will consider strategies for planning the way forward, either through improving the existing systems or evolving a significantly different approach.

WHO SHOULD PERFORM THE ASSESSMENT

Although your organization may already have an assessment group or quality management group, the team performing the readiness and capacity assessment needs to have attributes that are broader than typical audit teams. The composition of the team also enables management to see a mix of talent in operation. The team will be temporary, although some members may transition into later phases depending on their interests and capabilities.

Some considerations include selecting individuals who:

- have a broad understanding of the organization, its people, processes, and what it is trying to accomplish
- are genuinely interested in how human systems organize to accomplish work
- are genuinely interested in organizational culture and its influence on individual, team, and organizational performance
- have a good understanding of the organization's propensity distribution and cultural stuck points
- enjoy thinking strategically and systemically
- are analytically inclined but don't get lost in the weeds
- are realists who are not afraid to think differently
- have organizational respect and credibility, not just positional power
- are trusted within the organization so that others will freely provide information, offer insights into potential issues, and volunteer suggestions regarding potential solutions
- take an unbiased approach towards information gathering and analysis, without jumping to conclusions about causes, solutions, or who to blame.

Obviously, this is not a one-person endeavor, but the team doesn't have to be larger than 5-7 people, nor does the task have to take more than 2-3 weeks spread over a reasonable period to allow for reflection and solicitation of views from outside the team. It should have one management level representative to serve as coach and mentor rather than team leader. Small teams, if selected with care, often don't need a formal leader since individual participants will naturally know when to move into the lead when it helps the team, and know when to let someone else to step in when another person's contribution better suits the team's current needs. Fluidity is important through all phases of development.

Although it may be democratically tempting to have every 'department' represented, this is generally unnecessary, and may inhibit a fluid ability to obtain information, since teams may feel constrained by protocols associated with a formal system of representation. Finally, the team is not expected to deliver a final answer. Its role is to develop a high-level picture of significant issues and the risks that the organization may face in moving forward.

Appendix F provides a detailed assessment approach based on a series of questions that complement the information in this chapter. Such tools can be useful for getting additional input beyond the team. Like all such tools, the information is useful for identifying and discussing issues to foster organizational understanding and alignment before prioritizing issues and applying resources to their resolution. Discussion in the following pages supplements the information gathered from an assessment such as in Appendix F.

ASSESS CURRENT PERFORMANCE OUTCOMES

Organizations need to determine where they are, how much they want to stretch, and what additional capacities are required to enable a desired shift. To do this effectively, one needs to examine current performance information in a consolidated and systematic fashion. The objective is to get an overall picture of how well the organization is achieving its outcomes. Information should include:

- Feedback from external stakeholders
- Feedback from management and staff
- Benchmarking against best practices
- Performance measurement data and trends
- Findings from internal audits and self-assessments

- Findings from external audits and assessments.

This information helps identify positive attributes and opportunities for improvement. It also aids in the prioritization of key performance issues.

IDENTIFY THE STAGE OF EVOLUTION AND PREDOMINANT CULTURE

Review the section on Organizational Evolution in Chapter 3. Determine the stage of evolution and key aspects of the culture by exploring the following questions related to the evolution model in Figure 3-1:

- What stage describes our predominant focus?
- What stage describes our predominant leadership style?
- What stage describes our general approach to staff?
- What stage describes our approach to anticipating and managing risk?
- What stage describes our approach to prioritization?
- What stage describes how we integrate structures and processes?
- What stage describes our perceptions on the value and use of the management system?
- Using Figures 3-2 and 3-3 from Chapter 3, what propensities are highly regarded in our organization? What stage would this suggest is predominant?

How does this compare with the assessment information obtained from completing Appendix F. How would you explain any discrepancies? These questions are important because they give an indication of how far and in what ways the organization might have to stretch. This has an impact on strategy since large stretches are less likely to succeed unless significant changes are made to the propensity distribution within the human system.

DETERMINE THE HEALTH OF THE PROCESS SYSTEM

Determine the health of management system policies, programs and processes by exploring questions such as:

- Are all important governance, executive, core, and support processes sufficiently well-defined and documented?
- What processes are performing well? Poorly? What insights can be gained from exploring the reasons for the differences in performance?

- Are the processes well integrated such that handoffs, information transfer, and interfaces are clear?
- If organizational responsibilities are assigned by program rather than process, are processes being used as the foundation of each program?
- Does each key process have a designated individual rather than a department as owner?
- Is duplication minimized throughout the organization, such that departments use common processes, particularly in the executive and support areas?
- Are all the program and policy documents necessary?
- Is process documentation activity-based and lean such that descriptive information, training material, and design basis information does not add unnecessary material to operational documentation.
- Are documents designed with human capabilities in mind and are they easy to find, use, and revise?
- Is there adequate oversight and a formal periodic review of the overall effectiveness of the management system?
- Are the processes necessary to undertake a significant change project sufficiently well-developed (e.g., project management, change management, communications)?

At this stage, a general understanding of overall status is all that is needed, since a detailed inventory can wait till later.

DETERMINE THE HEALTH OF ORGANIZATIONAL SYSTEMS

Determine the health of organizational systems by exploring the following questions:

- Does the organizational design and structure consciously take account of the processes used within the organization?
- Do positions at all levels have responsibilities, authorities, job descriptions, and development/ training needs tied directly to process activities?
- Does an organizational design basis exist to establish principles, structure, and positions to support processes and changes to the organization?

- How would a shift to a process-based management system affect organizational design and structure?

These questions should focus on whether the current organizational structure is amenable to management by process and whether the structure is flexible should changes be needed. The latter is highly dependent on the organization's history and culture, and willingness to change as evidenced by the success or failure of previous change initiatives.

DETERMINE THE CAPACITY OF THE HUMAN SYSTEM

Elements of the human system include unitive, management and management team leadership as well as the propensities, knowledge and experience of individuals and teams throughout the organization.

Determine leadership capacity by exploring questions such as:

- Is the senior leadership team unanimous on the need to improve or develop a management system?
- Is the senior team aligned on what type of management system is best suited to the needs of the organization?
- Is the senior leadership team willing to commit the necessary resources and time (including their own) to undertake a management system project?
- Does leadership at key levels of the organization possess the behavioural attributes that can facilitate the design, development, implementation, and sustainability of an integrated management system?
- Are managers sufficiently flexible to accept changes that might significantly affect their roles and responsibilities?
- Are team leaders likely to support the project when asked for resources to map processes related to their functionalities?

These questions help determine the visioning capacity and level of commitment of the leadership. Change always occurs for a reason. Sustainable change occurs when the reason is embraced by leadership and the organization at large. Consider whether the change driver stems from a genuine belief that it will improve outcomes and organizational performance, or whether it comes from external considerations such as regulatory requirements or market pressures.

Determine the capacity of the broader human system by exploring questions such as:

- Is there sufficient ground-level support in the organization to undertake such a project in terms of resources and change impact?
- Is the culture sufficiently forward thinking to be receptive to a change in the way the organization is structured and functions?
- Is there appropriate talent at all levels in the organization to undertake the management system initiative, including the project phase and the sustainability phase?
- Are there a sufficient number of individuals who have the attributes to assume the role of process owner for each of the key processes?
- Are there change agents and facilitators within the organization who will help facilitate the necessary changes?
- To what extent will external support be required during the initial phases?

Such questions are intended to determine whether appropriate talent exists to implement and sustain the desired change. External consultants are only of value if the work they do enables talent within the organization to develop, implement and continually improve the processes after the consultants and experts have moved to other projects. Work performers and process owners must have a key role in the step-by-step development. Success is unlikely if management believes that an off-the-shelf, turn-key management system can be purchased simply by identifying the software tools for project management, procurement, maintenance tracking, work control, timekeeping, and so forth.

DETERMINE THE ADEQUACY OF FINANCIAL SUPPORT

Developing management systems costs money, time, and organizational attention. Neither the benefits of a well-integrated system nor the hidden costs of a poorly integrated one can easily be quantified or monetized. The evidence appears only in the outcomes.

Determine the adequacy of financial support by exploring questions such as:

- Is there management willingness to devote financial and personnel resources to the development of the management system?

- Is management willing to devote financial resources that may be needed in terms of upgraded technology or information management systems to support the implementation of the management system?
- Where does the initiative rank in terms of overall priorities for the organization?
- Is there a reasonable understanding of the cost and effort needed, including external and infrastructure costs?

No one likes projects that spiral out of control in terms of cost and schedule. If the transition effort is significant, experience indicates that a properly planned initiative may take several years and millions of dollars.

DETERMINE THE ADEQUACY OF OTHER SUPPORT SYSTEMS

Determine the adequacy of other key support systems by exploring questions such as:

- Are the current technological systems adequate?
- Are the information management systems adequate?
- Is any new infrastructure required?

Such questions are intended to surface hidden costs, change management issues, and potential risks. It is not the intent here to consider the health of the underlying technology on which the organization is based, despite the importance of that question to the overall sustainability of the organization.

CONSIDER THE STATUS OF CURRENT CHANGE INITIATIVES

Consider the state of current and recent improvement initiatives:

- How many have been undertaken and how big in terms of scope?
- Did any of them involve significant cultural or organizational changes?
- What is the history of success in terms of completion and effectiveness?
- Are improvement initiatives successfully prioritized, resourced, and managed in relation to ongoing work?
- Is your organization suffering from change fatigue?

The objective is to determine how effectively the organization handles change that requires sustained focus and a potential cultural shift. Often, improvement initiatives falter because they have to compete with day-to-day operational and emerging issues, and this is amplified if there is not full buy-in to the desired change.

CHARTING THE WAY FORWARD

The overall intent of this chapter is to identify at a high level the most important issues related to the current state of the various systems that support the organization's functionality and outcomes. In turn, this provides an indication of the risks facing the organization in relation to its ability to embark on significant improvement initiatives to its organizational systems. Steps may have to be taken at the pre-project phase to ensure that the right talent is put in place to conceive, develop, implement, and sustain the desired changes.

There are many ways to capture the results of a preliminary assessment, and generally the simpler the better to avoid overwhelming the organization with data. The objective is to identify the main issues to help determine the scope of work. For example, the results may be in simple tabular form as shown in Table 7-1.

Table 7-1: Example Issues List

Number	Issue	Impact	Potential Solution	Priority
1.	Project management lacks discipline	Outcomes are overly dependent on the skill of the project leader	Develop a project management process	High
2.	Responsibilities and authorities are based on generic roles	Ownership of cross-cutting processes is unclear (e.g., change management, business planning)	Develop related processes and define ownership	High
3.	Etc.			

Depending on appetite, one may add columns to identify the owner of the issue, or bucket issues into categories such as process type (core, support, executive, governing) or area (infrastructure, technology, administration, leadership, competency, etc.). Often the appropriate bucketing strategy doesn't become clear until after all the issues are identified, so it isn't necessary to lock into a system too early. As the saying goes, hang loose until rigor counts.

At this stage of information gathering, it is often useful to summarize important information using such tools as a SWOT (Strengths-Weaknesses-Opportunities-Threats) analysis, gap analysis, causal analysis, or future state visioning.

Once a reasonable picture of the current state is available, it is worthwhile to construct a realistic yet vivid picture of the desired future state. Briefly, this includes revisiting key questions such as:

- What are the desired outcomes for our organization?
- What functionalities are needed to accomplish these outcomes?
- What business, management, or organizational models might be appropriate to support these functionalities?
- What organizational propensities are needed to support these functionalities?
- What leadership and team capacity is needed to conceive, develop, implement, and sustain any changes required to achieve our desired future state?

The vivid description and related questions will be explored in more detail in Chapter 9.

As we proceed into the next chapters we will make several assumptions:

- The organization has done a reasonable assessment of its current issues and capacity related to its organizational systems
- The improvements required are beyond the scope of normal operations and require a focused change initiative that will have impact throughout the organization
- The organization recognizes that changes must be considered from an integrated systems perspective – technology, processes, people, structure, and context.

Although the material in the following chapters assumes that the change initiative is significant and organization-wide, this does not preclude grading or selective application to suit the specific needs of the organization.

SUMMARY

The box below summarizes key points from this Chapter.

> ***Key Points from this Chapter on Assessing Readiness and Capacity***
>
> 1. Take a disciplined, systematic approach to management system development as suggested by Figure 7-1.
> 2. Assessing the current state of organizational systems is important to avoid under-estimating the work required or failing to recognize risks associated with either inaction or implementation.
> 3. Assessing the capacity of the human system to conceive, develop, implement, and sustain the desired change is critical to avoid performance mismatches and weak implementation.
> 4. Summarizing key issues in a succinct way makes it easier to determine scope and implications for the organization.
> 5. A clear picture of the desired future state is a necessary step for deciding what needs to be done and potential strategies for doing it.

Chapter 8

Establish an Excellence Team and Project Team

IN THIS CHAPTER

In accordance with Step 2 of the flowchart in Figure 7-1, this chapter describes criteria for selecting members of various teams involved in developing a management system. The topics are:

- Establishing an organizational structure
- Management team role
- Gaining management commitment
- Selecting a Management System Excellence Team
- Selecting a Management System Project Team
- Selecting individual Process Development Teams
- The role of existing Quality Assurance/ Performance Improvement Groups.

From the very beginning of the project, every decision should be weighed for its impact on organizational culture and motivation.

ESTABLISH AN ORGANIZATIONAL STRUCTURE

We begin with structure simply because it is easier to show a sample organization before describing each of the parts. In practice, a more logical approach is to determine the desired functions before deciding how to organize them, so we are in fact presenting the last step first simply for ease of discussion. Figure 8-1 shows a sample organization for a full-scale management system development project.

Other sections of this chapter will cover the specific elements of Figure 8-1, namely:

- The executive/management team role
- The Management System Excellence Committee composition and role
- The Management System Project Team composition and role
- Individual Process Development Team composition and role.

Individual roles within each team will be described as appropriate.

One of the first observations about Figure 8-1 is that it is not a typical hierarchical chart but more of a relationship map or mobilizing constellation described in Figure 3-9 of Chapter 3. Many of the positions have dual or interfacing roles as indicated by the dual colours in Figure 8-1. For example, the process facilitators help each process owner develop their specific process; however, they follow the disciplined methodology established by the Project Team to ensure consistent application to each process in the overall system. Similarly, although the Organizational Development and Communications Liaisons are formal members of the Project Team, their location on the chart reflects their unique bridging role across the organization.

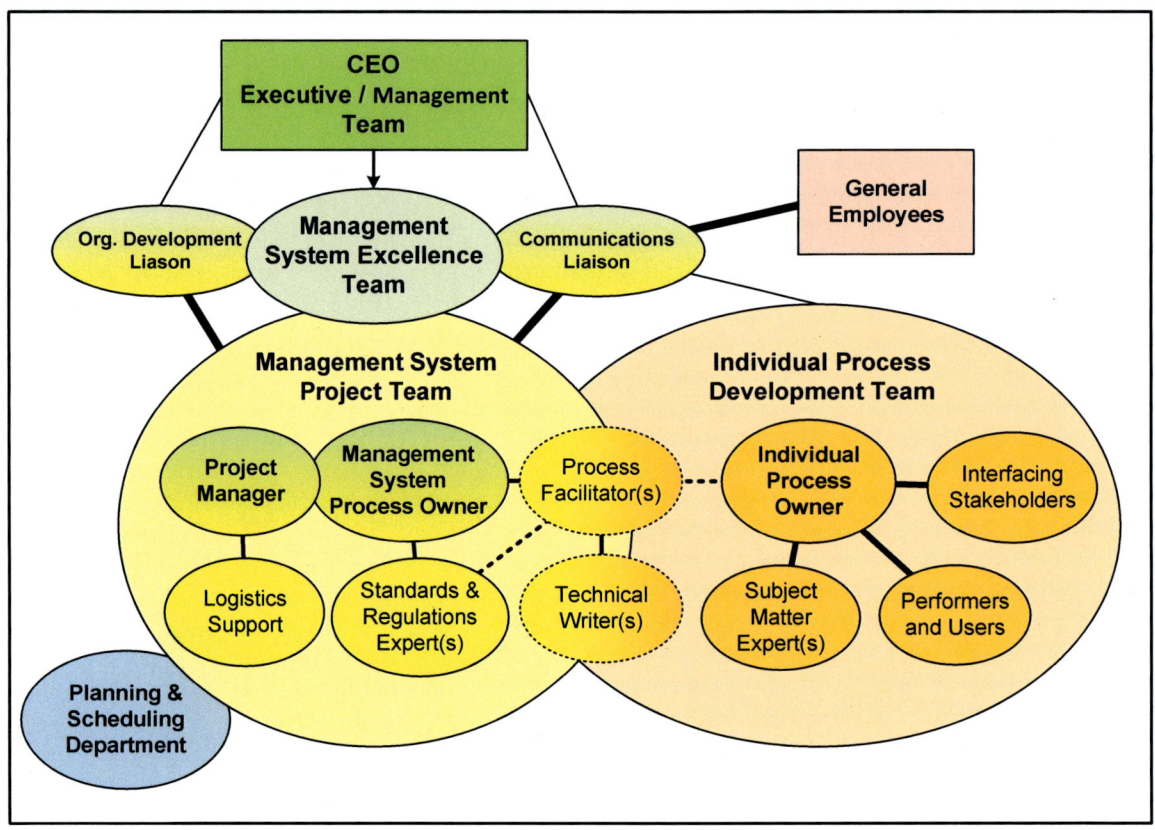

Figure 8-1: Sample Organization Chart for a Management System Development Project

EXECUTIVE / MANAGEMENT TEAM ROLE

The senior executive of the organization (e.g., CEO or President) is the primary owner of the overall management system and is therefore the person accountable for its effectiveness. In support of the senior executive owner, members of the senior management team have responsibilities for the effective functioning of the management system within their individual spheres of influence and responsibility. Together, the management team defines roles related to development, operation, monitoring, and improvement.

The senior team has several key initial tasks:

- Select a management system sponsor or champion
- Select members of the Excellence Team
- Select key members of the Project Team, specifically the Project Lead and the Management System Owner-Architect.

Typically, the senior executive assigns one member of the senior management team as the person responsible for the oversight of the management system and the go-to person on the senior team to resolve specific issues. For convenience we will call this individual the Management System Sponsor, although the term Champion is also used in some organizations. The sponsor role is distinct from that of Management System Process Owner or Owner-Architect discussed in Chapter 4, since the latter is more directly involved in the day-to-day functioning and improvement of the management system. In practice, the sponsor is the Owner-Architect's champion on the senior team.

Sometimes the role of sponsor is assigned to the Quality Assurance Manager; however, this approach has potential pitfalls if this is merely considered to be the logical default position on the organization chart and the individual does not have the requisite attributes. One also needs to consider potential conflicts of interest. For example, the Quality Assurance role includes audits and assessments, and it is problematic to audit a system that one also has responsibility for developing. In some organizations, a role of Performance Improvement Manager is identified as having a broader mandate than audits and assessments and may be assigned to the role of Management System Sponsor or Process Owner-Architect.

Of the many options available for a specific organization, the most important consideration is that the sponsor for the management system has attributes similar to those described for unitive leadership in Chapter 4. Key attributes for this individual include:

- A good understanding of the organization and its desired outcomes
- An interest in the human system dimensions of the organization and the way people work together to achieve the desired outcomes
- The capacity to think conceptually, strategically, systemically, and systematically in order to analyze complex systems, or a strong willingness to engage with people who do
- Good oral and written communication skills
- Good facilitation and negotiation skills
- Broad respect and credibility at all levels of the organization
- Willingness to engage multiple stakeholders in finding optimal solutions
- Willingness to tackle complex, cross-cutting organizational issues.

In simple terms, the sponsor should have credibility and influence within the organization beyond mere positional power. The sponsor will typically serve as chairperson of the Management System Excellence Team discussed in the next section.

Other members of the senior team will have specific responsibilities for aspects of the management system within their general sphere of responsibility and accountability. For example, a manager may have responsibility for a number of processes, and will typically appoint individual process owners to monitor day-to-day operation of each process. This has two practical advantages: (i) managers typically do not have enough time to pay day-to-day attention to the details of the process, and (ii) managers can better serve an oversight, interface management, and issue resolution role to ensure smooth functioning of inter-connected processes.

GAINING MANAGEMENT COMMITMENT

An IMS is a large-scale culture building exercise that involves a profound shift in meaning within the organization, including at the top. Senior managers need to understand how the IMS will change their role, enhance their effectiveness, and contribute to their success if they are to give it full support.

Proponents of integrated management typically build a case for an IMS by emphasizing requirements, control, and quality benefits. This 'factual' case was outlined in Chapter 1. Although this approach informs, it doesn't necessarily shape behaviour, and may leave some managers thinking that the IMS is merely another QA project. To counter this, one needs to consider motivation. At a personal level, people want to ***feel*** smart, emotionally safe, and in control. At a professional level, people want to ***be perceived*** as competent, in-the-know, and successful. Communication about an IMS needs to resonate at both the personal and professional levels in order to influence behaviour.

Primary responsibilities of any senior manager include:

- *Establishing and running an efficient and effective organization* that meets all relevant standards and expectations
- *Instilling and cultivating a conducive culture* that extends beyond the borders of the organization to include contractors, suppliers, and related organizations
- *Demonstrating commitment to systematic improvement* that keeps the organization learning and adapting.

Senior managers are typically fast-paced, decisive, forceful individuals who prefer to exercise initiative and wide degrees of freedom in order to have impact and get results. They typically view their job as controlling structures, people, and resources through active decision-making.

An IMS requires a shift in perspective and approach from directing and controlling people and resources, to controlling operations and outcomes through a defined system.

This may feel like a significant loss of autonomy and control. IMS proponents must help senior managers understand how an IMS better equips them to shape, direct, control and improve the organization.

It helps to shift the communication approach from ***informing*** to ***influencing***. To make this shift:

- Recognize and intentionally align messages with the personal and professional needs and agendas of senior managers
- Communicate with their goals and challenges in mind
- Position IMS as a system-wide performance enhancing and culture-building initiative

- Tie specific outputs and benefits to recognized organizational performance challenges and gaps, and how the IMS will help
- Reinforce that IMS may limit personal legal liability
- Speak to strengthening key levers that are fundamental to their role—how will the IMS:
    - Increase control at the level of aligning meaning and purpose across the system?
    - Improve synergy of the senior team, enabling them to focus more on strategy and exception handling rather than routine operation—in other words elevate their game?
    - Facilitate informed organizational changes, including staffing decisions?
    - Streamline resource planning, allocation, monitoring and control?
    - Enhance the rigor of operational decision-making through appropriate control points?
    - Enable performance monitoring, reporting and informed intervention?
- Evolve the system interactively
    - Position the IMS model as a systemic framework to assist in aligning the organizational structure, key processes, business model and plans, and other high-level strategies (holistic perspective)
    - Develop the IMS as a collaborative effort by the senior team to ensure it represents the specific activities and needs of the organization as they understand them (strategic alignment).

It is also essential for the Excellence Team and Project Team to sustain motivation by creating visibility for senior managers throughout the development process:

- Establish an ongoing role in the development process with specific engagement points for senior managers
- Engage them in mapping management processes
- Engage them in bringing line management and supervision on board
- Engage them in recognizing contributions and applauding success.

Senior management engagement and commitment will depend on their understanding of the impact of an IMS on their role, image, and autonomy. IMS development needs to anticipate and work towards enabling effective senior management control—personal, positional, and systemic. It is useful to develop a specific strategy for senior management engagement.

For those directly involved in implementation, sponsorship is a two-way street. Senior management sponsors the IMS project, and the project creates visibility and support for senior management.

SELECT A MANAGEMENT SYSTEM EXCELLENCE TEAM

As mentioned, another important task of the senior team is to select members for the Excellence Committee and Project Team. These are covered more fully in the following sections; however, the following two sidebars are relevant for both cases.

A note on departmental representation

In an effort to be fair and democratic some organizations feel a need to ensure that every department or interest is represented on cross-cutting teams or committees. This usually results in overly large teams that make weak decisions based on consensus and political considerations to avoid ruffling anyone's feathers.

A willingness to consult with all stakeholders is important, and team members should be selected for this propensity; however, teams should not be afraid to challenge the status quo. They should be willing to explain their decisions in relation to an overall strategy. They should also be able to explain how they used stakeholder input to make their decisions or recommendations.

> ### *A note on volunteers*
>
> In a similar effort to appear fair and democratic some organizations ask for volunteers or expressions of interest to find participants for projects or committees. This usually attracts 'perpetual' volunteers or those who simply want to enhance their résumés. Even worse, some departments may want to park problems on another doorstep temporarily. None of these options optimizes talent allocation.
>
> Managers should be expected to nominate their best people, the ones who they are "pained" to release for the project duration—the ones they believe have leadership potential and may therefore outgrow their departments. This sends a powerful signal to the organization regarding the importance of the management system project.

The Management System Excellence Team in Figure 8-1 monitors progress and provides guidance and oversight of the project as it unfolds. The term Excellence Team better represents its true functionality than the commonly used Excellence Team which is suggestive of control rather than creation. The team remains active for the duration of the project.

Typically, formal membership includes:

- Management System Sponsor or Champion named by the Executive Team
- Management 'owners' of key processes (added when appointed)
- Corporate representative(s) as appropriate
- Other key stakeholder(s) as appropriate (e.g., Senior union representative).

Regular attendees from the Project Team include:

- Management System Process Owner-Architect
- Management System Project Lead
- Organizational Development Liaison
- Communications Liaison.

Other specialists, stakeholders, or process owners may be invited to provide information depending on the project phase.

The role of the committee includes:

- Oversight of the management system project
- Approving the overall project strategy and plan
- Approving significant changes to the strategy or plan
- Approving appointments and changes to the Project Team
- Monitoring progress via periodic updates from the Project Team
- Making decisions related to corporate interfaces and alignment
- Making decisions related to information management technology and integration
- Ensuring the effectiveness of communications with all stakeholders
- Ensuring organizational alignment in terms of structure, groupings, and workforce development plans
- Allocating resources to support individual development teams
- Resolving issues and roadblocks.

The specialist liaison roles for communications and organizational development are described in the section on the Project Team.

Meetings are usually held weekly at the start of the project, and taper to bi-weekly or monthly as the project matures. It is useful to define the specific mandate and terms of reference for the Management System Excellence Team. There are many ways of doing this in a few pages. The sidebar lists typical contents.

Sample structure – Terms of Reference

A Terms of Reference document typically contains the following elements:
- Mandate (Purpose)
- Members
  - Identify standing members, chairperson, alternate, and recording secretary
- Roles and Responsibilities
  - For the committee overall, with specific roles as necessary
- Activities
  - Main activities of the committee
- Agenda
  - Standing items (e.g., status of open issues, routine progress reports)
  - New items (what can be brought before the Committee)
- Meeting Protocols
  - Frequency and duration
  - Material submission procedure
  - Decision-making authority (including dispute resolution if necessary)
  - Action tracking
  - Records

Organizations with well-developed project management processes and business processes often use a project charter to define project aspects such as objectives, deliverables, project risks, and risk mitigation strategies.

SELECT A MANAGEMENT SYSTEM PROJECT TEAM

The Management System Project Team has overall responsibility for the day-to-day management of the project. Project Team members are assigned on a full-time basis, and the team remains in place for the duration of project. Members then return to their original roles, although some may transition into support and improvement roles under the direction of the Management System Process Owner-Architect.

As indicated in Figure 8-1, membership includes:

- Management System Owner-Architect
- Management System Project Lead
- Communications Liaison
- Organizational Development Liaison
- Process facilitators
- Technical writers
- Logistics support (administration, coordination, scheduling, etc.)

The overall responsibilities of the Project Team are to:

- Develop and maintain a project strategy and plan
- Assist management in the development of a high-level Management System Manual
- Develop management system standards related to architectural controls, process mapping, and documentation
- Develop procedures, protocols, and training for facilitating the development of each process
- Develop orientation and training material on the overall management system and assist managers and supervisors in its delivery as needed
- Organize and facilitate development of each process in accordance with plans and standards
- Establish and maintain an issues tracking and resolution process
- Provide progress reports and refer key issues to the Management System Excellence Team
- Ensure management, staff, and key stakeholders are kept informed of the status of the initiative and related plans.

It is worthwhile to define the specific mandate and terms of reference for the Project Team (see previous sidebar). The project is not a typical project management involving schedules, milestones, cost controls, and checklists. It is a large organization-wide cultural change initiative with careful attention to the organization's "business" and context. The selection of staff should take this broader scope into consideration.

The specific roles of the Management System Owner-Architect and Project Lead were described in Chapter 4 and that information should be used to select these individuals. The other roles are as follows:

Communications Liaison – This individual is responsible for developing and implementing a communications strategy as part of the project plan. The liaison interacts on a continuing basis with the Excellence Team, Project Team, senior management, stakeholders and the workforce at large. At every step of the project, the liaison's role is to provide and receive information related to the status of the project, its impact on the organization, and emerging issues. The liaison may prepare and deliver some of the messages; however, a primary role is to organize face-to-face staff engagement sessions led by management, team leads, and team members to build shared understanding of the intent, benefits, and requirements of a successful management system. These may take various forms such as forums, focus groups, or informal discussions.

The purpose of a communication strategy is to ensure that everyone receives information in a timely manner. To avoid surprises and uncertainty, all stakeholders should be provided with ample opportunity to ask questions and provide advice or feedback. The individual serving this role may be seconded from the Information Department or Public/Employee Relations, and is clearly designated as a member of the Project Team.

The Communications Liaison also assists in optimizing methods for communicating management system information in the mature state. For example, this may involve input into document design, technology solutions, and communications media.

Organizational Development Liaison – This individual helps the team understand the human system implications of the readiness assessment and considers organizational impacts of new or changed processes. This includes determining what new knowledge, skills, training, and propensities are required to optimize performance of the process. It also includes determining whether broader aspects such as organizational culture, team performance, structure, interfaces and leadership require adjustment as a result of the planned changes. At a process level, the individual helps optimize the human system aspects to ensure the process aligns with human capability and conforms with best human factors practices.

The Organizational Development Liaison is also accountable for:

- Ensuring that the intended functionality aligns with the existing or proposed organizational structure
- Linking process functionality to position analyses and descriptions
- Linking process functionality to training program material.

Process Facilitators – These individuals facilitate the development of specific processes. This involves interacting with the process owner, helping select suitable team members, leading process mapping and documentation meetings, and producing process documentation. They provide just-in-time training to members of each process development team. Since it is difficult for an organization to progress more than two or three processes at a time based on the fact that individual team members are engaged in other routine work, 2-3 full-time internal facilitators are sufficient for most projects.

Technical Writers – These individuals perform the essential task of documenting the process during the evolution of the mapping meetings. They not only ensure that process and procedural documents are prepared to consistent formats, they actively participate in the mapping sessions to ensure clarity of presentation. Good technical writers are highly skilled at producing understandable, user-friendly documents, and are much more proficient and consistent than subject matter experts at this task. Technical writers are experts in written communication—they do not have to be experts in the technical-engineering-administrative process under consideration.

It is beneficial if they are skilled in designing documents for online use, including presentation on tablet devices.

Logistics Support – The project should be allotted full time administrative support to organize and schedule meetings, maintain documentation, prepare and distribute reports, respond to information requests, and maintain relevant databases such as issue tracking systems. Assistance will also be required from the organization's planning department to ensure the project schedule is integrated into other planned activities that the organization has committed to undertake. Integration is necessary to ensure resources are made available and that priorities are known to all parties.

PROJECT TEAM TRAINING

All members of the Project Team contribute to various tasks, including planning and organizing. The team has considerable preparatory work before initiating development of individual processes. Once formed, the team should receive initial training as a unit in the following areas:

- Process-based management systems
- Process mapping and optimization
- Implications of processes on organizational structure and development
- Human systems, human factors, and human performance
- Documenting processes and procedures
- Group facilitation methods
- Project management
- Communications and relationship management.

Some of this training will occur as protocols are developed by the team. Skills will develop on-the-job. The team itself will develop orientation and training material related to the overall management system to provide the workforce, including management and supervision, with information and understanding that will enable the workforce to implement the system in accordance with their responsibilities.

INDIVIDUAL PROCESS DEVELOPMENT TEAM ROLE

Once the processes are identified, a schedule established, and individual process owners named, each process is developed using a part-time team identified to develop that specific process. The team typically includes:

- Process owner for the specific process
- Process facilitator from the Project Team
- Technical writer from the Project Team
- Subject matter experts familiar with the requirements, purpose, and functioning of the existing process
- Representative performer(s) of the process
- Representative customer(s) of the process
- Major stakeholders such as representatives from key interfacing processes.

Selection of team members is by mutual agreement between the specific Process Owner and the Management System Owner-Architect. A team size of 7-9 people generally works best. Selection of team members is important in terms of their breadth of knowledge, willingness to gather essential information from specialists and stakeholders as necessary, and willingness to develop an optimized process that meets requirements and is human friendly in terms of implementation and maintenance. See the sidebar for notes on subject matter experts.

> ### *A note on Subject Matter Experts (SMEs)*
>
> When selecting members for individual process teams it is important to choose individuals who are knowledgeable and passionate about the process, but are nevertheless able to stay out of the weeds. Detail belongs at the procedural or work instruction level. The role of subject matter expert is to communicate to other team members the key activities and the rationale for including them in a particular order and level of detail.
>
> Subject matters experts should leave development of the documentation to the technical writer assigned to the team. There are two reasons for this: (i) consistency of documentation across the management system, and (ii) avoidance of the detail that subject matter experts tend to insert into documents. An astute technical writer knows when to create an appendix to satisfy a persistent subject matter expert, since such appendices can often be transferred at a later time to technical basis or training documents.

The mandate and terms of reference of individual process teams can be included as an addendum to the Project Team mandate.

The overall responsibilities of the team are to:
- Identify all requirements for the process
- Identify current state performance issues as required

- Develop and optimize the specific process such that it meets requirements
- Present the draft process to key stakeholders as part of the initial validation
- Perform pilots or table-top exercises to confirm the efficacy of the process
- Assist in developing orientation and training material for the process (if within scope)
- Review and finalize process and procedural documents required to implement the process
- Support the process owner during initial orientation and implementation of the process.

Preparation of orientation and training material may or may not be included in the project scope for the process team, depending on the capacity of the process owner and training department to develop such material using existing resources. The Organizational Development Liaison should be engaged in establishing the scope and general content of orientation and training material, since such material plays a key role in re-orienting people.

Just-in-time training of team members is provided as an integral part of process development.

The team works on a part-time basis through the design, development, and implementation of the assigned process and its related procedures until formal turnover from the primary Project Team to the process owner. A typical approach is to spend an initial 4-5 days mapping the process, followed by a number of 1-2 day sessions/week to finalize the process depending on its complexity.

QUALITY ASSURANCE AND IMPROVEMENT STAFF ROLE

Quality Assurance and Performance Improvement or related staff will need to support the project at various phases, and some may become team members. Although such groups provide essential information and support, it is important not to load teams with such specialists since they may inadvertently become the default decision-makers and shapers of the process. The primary developers should always be the process owner and performers. Specialists from other departments such as licensing, quality assurance, inspections, improvement, etc., provide input, information or reviews as requested by the team. A key reason for this approach is to ensure that ownership of the process does not drift from the specific process owner and performers who are ultimately responsible for successful implementation of the process.

A similar comment applies to external consultants, who are often needed to help with the methodology, strategy and team training, but should transfer process facilitation responsibilities to the Project Team following satisfactory development of the first 3-4 processes.

SUMMARY OF OUTPUTS

The following box summarizes the tasks that should be accomplished within this phase of the project.

Key Tasks and Outputs from this Chapter on Establishing an Excellence Team and Project Team

1. Select members of the Management System Excellence Team.
2. Select members of the Management System Project Team.
3. Establish an organizational map using the guidance in Figure 8-1.
4. Establish terms of reference for the Excellence Team, and Project Team. Include in the latter the terms of reference for a typical process development team.
5. Develop a strategy for senior management engagement.
6. Provide initial training to the Project Team in the following areas:
   - Process-based management systems
   - Process mapping and optimization
   - Implications of processes on organizational structure and development
   - Human systems, human factors, and human performance
   - Documenting processes and procedures
   - Group facilitation methods
   - Project management
   - Communications and relationship management.

Chapter 9

Establish a Top Level Model and Organizational Design

IN THIS CHAPTER

In accordance with Steps 3 and 4 of the flowchart in Figure 7-1, this chapter describes the approach to developing a top level model and an aligned organizational design. The topics include:

- defining the outcomes
- defining the organizational meaning system
- developing a top level management system model
- designing the organization including mobilizing constellations
- aligning the model and organizational design
- testing the initial concepts
- developing an organizational design basis document
- developing a management system overview manual.

All the activities in this chapter involve a collaborative effort by the senior management team, facilitated by members of the Management System Excellence Team and Management System Project Team as appropriate. Although the steps in this chapter are presented sequentially, the actual process is iterative. The outputs from the initial activities in this chapter are used by the Project Team to draft an Organizational Design Basis and Management Manual that serve as guidance for lower-tier development.

DEFINE THE CONTEXT AND OUTCOMES

Everything the organization does should be related in some way to what the organization wishes to accomplish. No matter whether this is expressed in business plans, mission statements, or goals, the role of the senior team is to define as clearly as possible the organizational outcomes that constitute success. Only they can do this, even though input from key stakeholders is essential.

Organizations typically develop vision and mission statements, and may also have a specific mandate defined by a governing body. It is also useful to describe the context in which the organization operates.

A vision statement describes the future. A mission statement describes what the organization intends to focus on now. There is much online guidance related to developing vision and mission statements. Such statements add value only when they are given enough thought to be useful as communication tools that help shape organizational culture. Spare your employees clichés such as "become a world leader in…".

Regardless of how good the vision and mission statements are they need to be translated into tangible outcomes. One of the interesting things about vision, mission, and values expressed in organizational communications is that the element that is often omitted is the vivid description or articulated view of what the organization (and society) will look like when the vision and mission are fulfilled. The vivid description is often the part that best resonates with people within the organization, but may seem 'idealistic' or 'less professional', as if management feels shy or embarrassed about stating its deeper wishes. Nevertheless, the vivid description often provides deeper insight into the organization's underlying meaning system, the cultural preferences of its membership, and the true desired outcomes.

As mentioned in Part A, outcomes fall into several categories:

- Human – what the organization desires for its employees and the people who use its products or are otherwise affected by the organization's activities
- Organizational – what the organization provides, produces or contributes, including attributes of its culture
- Societal – what role the organization plays in enhancing the quality of life beyond its immediate boundaries
- Economic – what the organization contributes to the local, national or international economy
- Ecological – the organization contributes to a healthy, sustainable environment.

In most organizations, many of these outcomes have been discussed and documented over time. However, the initial task for the management team is to revisit these desired outcomes to:

- add to or modify them
- express them as concisely and clearly as possible

- determine how well the organization is achieving them
- consider their relevance in the current context and projected future.

This task should be performed by the senior team with the assistance of a facilitator.

The output of this task is management's concise expression of the organization's context and desired outcomes. These provide requisite guidance to the Management System Project Team for the evolution of the management system. This information will also appear in the management manual discussed later.

Organizational Meaning System

Now that we have defined outcomes, we can turn to the question of what will make the organization function effectively and have people truly enjoy their contribution. This is often expressed as organizational culture and values.

As indicated in Figure 4-1 from Chapter 4, espoused values, guiding principles, and norms are at the second level of the cultural pyramid. Rather than devoting a lot of effort to defining espoused values, it is more useful, although more difficult, to explore the third level of the cultural pyramid, i.e., the underlying shared meaning system that reflects the beliefs, perceptions, and reasoning/relating patterns of the people in the organization. Articulating the shared meaning system provides a basis for maintaining the integrity of the fabric of the organization and expressing the culture of the organization.

Some of the elements to explore in order to articulate the meaning system are identified in Figure 9-1.

In some respects, the task is to construct a vivid description of the organization's shared meaning system. Every organization is unique. Where a sales organization may value people with flair and charisma, a high reliability organization might value exceptional levels of integrity and expertise.

There are a number of questions and ideas that the team can explore related to Figure 9-1. It is preferable for them to derive their own ideas about what each means; however, the following questions might help stimulate thought if the team becomes stuck.

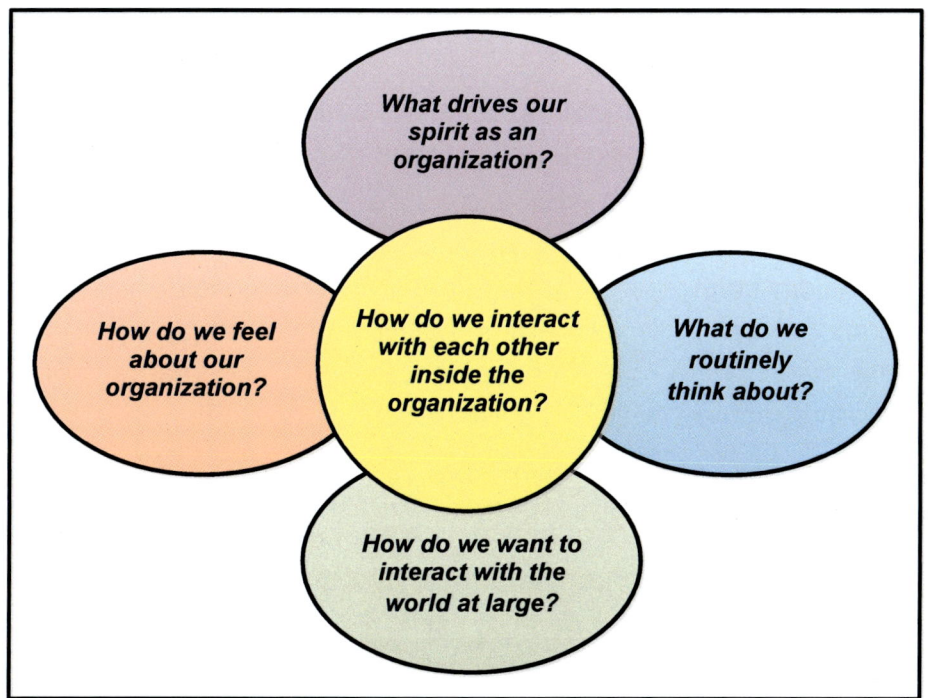

Figure 9-1: Organizational Meaning System Elements

Our Organizational Spirit:

- What maintains our esprit de corps and vitality?
- What do we believe about our value to the world?
- What beliefs do we hold about how the system learns?
- What beliefs do we hold about a successful future?
- What is bigger and more important than us?
- What do we want our legacy to be?
- Consider: greater purpose, learning, growth, contribution, ethics, innovation, creativity, entrepreneurship, agency, sustainability, conscience, philanthropy.

Our Feelings About Our Organization:

- What do we feel about what we do as an organization?
- What makes people valuable?
- What binds us?

- What makes us unique?
- What motivates us?
- What do we believe about ourselves and our contribution?
- What do we want people to be proud about?
- What are we to each other?
- What do we feel about work-life balance?
- Consider such things as: popularity, fraternity, visibility, empathy, humour, tact, guilt, concern, sensitivity, constraint, perfectionism, pressure, stress-tolerance, self-expression, acceptance, confidence, self-respect, respect for others, recognition.

Our Thoughts about the Organization

- What is the centre of gravity of our attention?
- What would we like people to hold 'top of mind'?
- What drives our perception of risk?
- What drives our decision-making?
- How do we approach problem-solving?
- Consider such things as: common sense, analysis, intuition, street sense, experiential learning, reflectiveness, profit awareness.

Our Interactions with the World at Large

- What behaviours are appropriate in our interactions outside the organization?
- What differentiates us outside the organization?
- What outcomes do we want to achieve together?
- What do we want our societal and ecological contribution to be?
- What do we want our societal and ecological footprint to be?
- Consider such things as: wealth, visibility, recognition, power, influence, leadership, trend-setting, responsiveness, service, adventuring, stability, longevity, security, status.

Our Interactions Inside the Organization:

- What behaviours are appropriate inside the organization?
- What characteristics describe our relationships with each other?
- What are the true expressions of our organizational culture and values?

- How much autonomy do we have to consult with each other?
- How much autonomy do we have to consult with people outside the organization?
- How much autonomy do we have to express creativity?
- What are the power dynamics within our organization?
- Consider such things as: cooperation, assertion, initiative, drive, competitiveness, discipline, determination, goal-setting, risk-taking, efficiency, conscientiousness, responsibility, flexibility, adaptability, versatility, self-expression, career, health, pace.

The output of this task is a thumbnail sketch of the shared meaning system that underlies the actions of the organization. It may provide insight into what may have to change in the current culture in order to achieve the goals of the organization.

DEVELOP A TOP LEVEL MODEL

Once outcomes and the organization's shared meaning system are defined, it is time to define the top level management system model that will form the bones of the organization. Chapter 6 and Appendix E provided examples of management system models and emphasized a few key points:

- The model(s) must be developed as a collaborative effort by the senior team to ensure it represents the specific activities and needs of the organization
- The model(s) must serve as a systemic framework to assist in aligning the organizational structure, key processes, business model and plans, and other high-level strategies.

Whether the organization prefers to use several models (e.g., business model, process model, accountability framework) the relationship between models must be clear. Generally, a top-level unifying model can be developed to show the relationship.

Hence, an early step is for the senior team to develop a relevant model to serve as a framework on which other process and human system elements can be built. It is important that the senior people who manage various aspects of the organization participate in this task, including the top executive. It is generally easiest to do this in a concentrated 2-3 day workshop with the senior team, and build directly from the key activities of the organization. For this task, it is desirable to use an internal or external facilitator familiar with management systems so that team members can focus their attention on each step. The specific focus is on the process dimensions of the organization.

Typical steps in such a workshop with the senior team include:

1. Provide a basic orientation on top-level integrated models, process-based management systems, the purpose of core, executive, governance, and support processes, and process naming conventions.
2. Identify all key activities necessary for the organization to accomplish its desired outcomes.
3. Group the identified activities in order to define top-level processes such that the process model contains a manageable number of processes (typically fewer than 30).
4. Confirm that each process is likely to have a sufficient number of sub-processes to warrant its position as a top-level process.
5. Bucket the processes into core, executive, governance, and support processes.
6. Develop with the team a top-level straw model that integrates all dimensions of the organization's activities.
7. Identify other elements that the team believes should be visible elements of the top-level model.
8. Elaborate the model(s) in a way that has visual appeal and resonates within the organization's operating context.
9. Confirm that the work of every department is reflected in the model.

Since this is a process-based approach it is important that the team not bog down by thinking in terms of departments or programs rather than pure processes. There is often a tendency to ensure a particular department or program is represented by a named process, rather than ensuring that each department can recognize the processes it uses to accomplish its work. Taking a departmental or program approach will make subsequent development steps far more difficult in terms of integration. Departmental or program boundaries are inherently more complex than process boundaries.

Since the purpose of this task is for the senior team to develop a model it truly believes reflects the work and context of the organization, the team should resist the temptation to simply import parts of other models. Nor should the Management System Project Team propose a model for 'management approval'. The absence of original thinking, discussion, and problem solving by the senior team will result in a model that they don't feel genuine ownership for, and will therefore have difficulty communicating and implementing.

The output of this task is a model the senior team believes is representative of all the higher level activities of the organization.

Once the senior team has developed the initial model(s), it is desirable to allow time for the Management System Excellence Team and Project Team to review the model(s) and provide joint feedback. At this stage it is not necessary to perfect the model but it is worth confirming there are no significant gaps in terms of key processes or elements. At this stage it is also useful to review comparable models available from similar organizations.

A systematic way of doing this review is to develop for each key process a high-level description. A sample template is given in Appendix G. This has the advantage of identifying the sub-processes that support each key process.

The senior team determines whether adjustments to the model(s) should be made.

DEVELOP AN ORGANIZATIONAL DESIGN

The senior team then convenes to map the organizational and human system dimensions related to the model(s). The general steps include:

1. What processes should we cluster into organizational units or functions?
2. What outcome focused process groupings, mobilizing constellations, meeting venues, or standing committees should we establish so that the right managers, Process Owners, and stakeholders convene to integrate activities and monitor key outcomes?

Mobilizing Constellations

As discussed in Chapter 3 on organizational design, outcome focused process groupings, or 'mobilizing constellations', are cross-cutting groupings of Process Owners and management focused around a key outcome. Some of these are common to many organizations (e.g., business/organizational excellence, continual improvement, organizational development), and some will be organization specific (e.g., equipment health, design and operational configuration management).

The task here is to look for inter-dependencies and synergies that contribute to achieving the desired outcomes defined by senior management. Such groupings should also include sufficient diversity of reasoning and relating to ensure risks are identified and all stakeholders are considered in decision-making.

Aspects to consider when forming mobilizing constellations include:

- What key processes contribute to the outcome?
- What talent sets and styles of reasoning and relating need to be present?
- What decision-making authority needs to be present?
- Are the right organizational levels and functional units represented?
- What input is required from support processes?
- What is the shared meaning that coalesces the group, and how does this relate to the organization's meaning system?

Having the right organizational levels present does not necessarily mean ensuring that the right senior positions are represented, since essential expertise may in fact come from field positions or the 'shop floor'.

The mobilizing constellation serves as the community of practice for all aspects related to process development, implementation and improvement. They should strive to monitor advances in their area of expertise, enhance professionalism and performance related to their activities.

Functional Groupings

This task involves grouping top level processes that have similar attributes or intents such that one can make use of natural synergies. Such groupings can be surfaced by asking such questions as:

- Which processes are a natural fit such that organizational levels, boundaries, and silos are minimized?
- Which processes require direct, day-to-day interactions?
- Which processes share common inputs and outputs?

- Which processes have a similar functionality?
- Which processes require similar infrastructure for effective implementation?
- Which processes would benefit from co-location based on efficient exchange of material or information, or specific demands of the technology?
- Which processes would benefit from similar styles of leadership?

The objective of this task is to identify clusters that make sense both for management and the people who work within each unit. As discussed in Chapter 3, one is not simply trying to develop a traditional hierarchical organization chart since different functionalities may require different structures that are better elaborated when the processes are analyzed. Nor is it necessary to make a perfect match whereby every top-level process has a separate unit, since organizations that have tried this approach have not found it to be practical. For the moment, we are not trying to define a specific structure. That comes later.

Design the Optimum Organization

Now that we have an idea of the functional groupings, cross-cutting outcome focused process groupings, and shared meaning system, we can design an organizational structure that integrates and optimizes these three dimensions. In this step it is worth reviewing the material in Chapter 3 and Appendix D.

Each organizational unit will have management responsibility for a cluster of specific top-level processes. The structure will likely reflect that it is built on processes, particularly for the core processes. The intent is to design an organization that is more organic in form than the traditional hierarchical organization chart, and that embodies the meaning system and functionalities wanted within the organization.

TEST THE INITIAL CONCEPTS

The purpose of the previous activities is for the senior team to develop the initial information that will be used for lower tier development. Sufficient attention at this stage will reduce the need for multiple revisions of the high level model(s). For this reason, the Management System Project Team should analyze the initial output to determine how well it fits an integrated, coherent structure. For example, it is useful to identify the sub-processes for each top level process, since this will typically result in suggestions for changes to the process model. As mentioned earlier, these sub-processes typically derive from some of the key activities identified using the worksheet in Appendix G.

It is also beneficial for the Excellence Team and Project Team to facilitate sessions on the proposed models and organizational structure with key stakeholders to gain insight into whether the approach is sufficiently robust and transparent. This can be a sensitive topic within organizations and must be done in a way that is inviting and mindful of stakeholder concerns. It is a necessary step to begin socializing the thinking related to an integrated view of the management system.

PREPARE A DRAFT ORGANIZATIONAL DESIGN BASIS

At this point, there should be enough information for the Management System Project Team to draft an organizational design basis document introduced in Chapter 3. There will be some gaps in the document; however, it is important to have a working draft that can be modified as development proceeds. The general purpose of the basis document is to describe how the senior team defines the human system elements related to the organizational structure. It is also a necessary element for organizational development, and for managing organizational and process changes.

As the project proceeds, the Project Team uses the design basis to ensure a consistent approach to the human system elements. The document is typically owned by the senior person responsible for organizational development and staffing.

A suggested Table of Contents for an Organizational Design Basis Document is provided in Appendix H.

PREPARE A DRAFT MANAGEMENT SYSTEM MANUAL

The Management (System) Manual provides a high level description of how all aspects of the organization integrate to accomplish the required outcomes. A typical manual is only about 25-35 pages since its purpose is to provide a concise picture of the important attributes of the organization. The target audiences are members of the organization and key external stakeholders.

The manual is not a promotional (public relations) document since it is factually descriptive. Nor is it a traditional quality assurance manual since it does not contain the level of detail typical of such manuals. The management manual often replaces the need for a quality assurance manual. It is the top level document in the document hierarchy that will be described in Chapter 10.

The Management Manual often has a distinctive design, and is useful in orientation sessions with new employees along with the strategic/business plan and annual report. For that reason, readers of the manual should not require prior knowledge of technical terms.

A suggested Table of Contents for a Management Manual is given in Appendix I.

SUMMARY OF OUTPUTS

The box below summarizes the outputs that should be achieved within this phase of the project.

Key Tasks from this Chapter on Models and Organizational Design

The outputs related to the tasks from this step of the process are:

- Desired organizational outcomes
- Organizational meaning system
- Top level integrating model
- Top level process model
- Draft Organization and Organizational Design Basis document
- Draft Management System Manual.

Chapter 10

Establish Architectural Controls

IN THIS CHAPTER

In accordance with Step 5 of the flowchart in Figure 7-1, this chapter describes the approach to establishing architectural controls for the management system. Steps 5, 6, and 7 provide a control structure for process development and an interactive approach is necessary as described in the related chapters 10, 11 and 12. The topics in this chapter include:

- The role of the management system architect or process owner
- Establishing the process development and change control processes
- Establishing an information technology system.

THE ROLE OF THE MANAGEMENT SYSTEM ARCHITECT

The Process Owner for the management system is the individual assigned responsibility for the process related to 'Manage processes', 'Manage system integration', 'Manage process integration', or similar title. We will use the term 'Manage system integration' as reflective of the intent. This individual is considered the go-to owner-architect of the management system since this is a hands-on role responsible for ensuring coherence and integration across the management system.

The role of the Process Owner is specified in Table 5-2. One of the first tasks is to establish controls for the overall system as described in this chapter and the two following related to process mapping (Chapter 11) and document control (Chapter 12). These chapters require an iterative approach to establish adequate controls, and are primary responsibilities of the Management System Project Team.

DEFINE THE PROCESS FOR CONTROLLING THE MANAGEMENT SYSTEM

The most straightforward way to look at the job of the 'Manage system integration' Process Owner is in terms of the related top level process map. This process will be developed and implemented in accordance with later steps in this handbook; however, for ease of discussion it is introduced here as Figure 10-1.

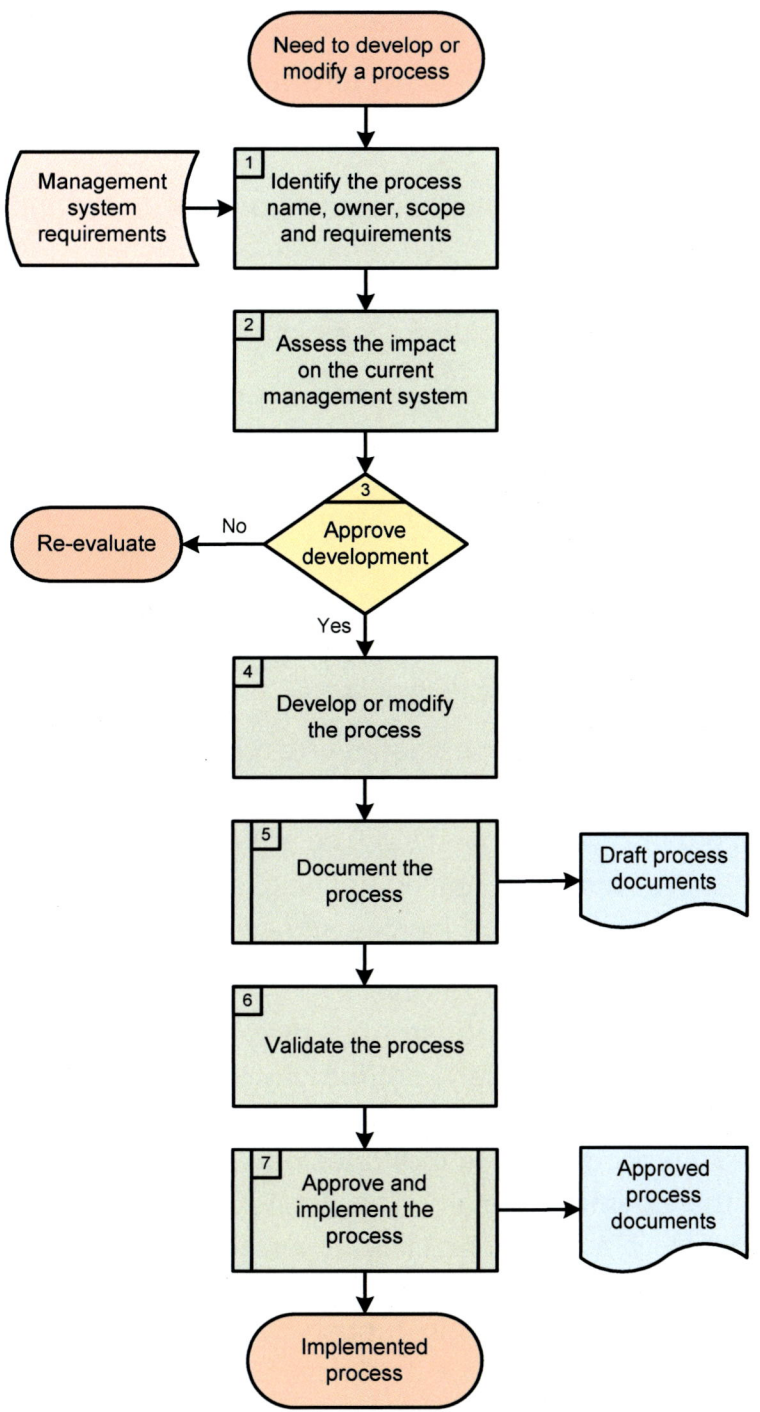

Figure 10-1: Example process map for 'Manage system integration'

The purpose of this process is threefold:

1. To control the overall architecture of the management system, including its interfaces between processes and organizational structure
2. To establish a consistent approach for developing and modifying processes
3. To ensure requirements are identified and allocated to the process(es) accountable for their implementation.

The document supporting this process establishes a number of elements that become standard practices for the management system. When a problem occurs in organizations, a common response is 'we need to change the process' or 'we need a new process'. Without adequate controls, processes emerge to satisfy local needs, with little regard to how the process fits within or impacts the overall system. Activity 2 of Figure 10-1 is intended to establish a systematic checklist to identify possible impacts on the management system of a new or modified process. Typical questions include:

- Can the work be accommodated within existing systems?
- What processes will be affected?
- What organizational aspects will be affected?
- What is the impact on staffing, training, and qualification?
- What is the impact on resources and infrastructure?
- Are there potential risks or unintended consequences?

The above are in addition to the business case questions (e.g., will the proposed work add sufficient safety, productivity, economic, and societal value?) although some organizations choose to integrate the questions into the business case development procedure. This illustrates one of the complex system aspects of designing a management system. The detailed information should appear in the most appropriate place (point of use), even if the requirement for it derives from a different process. In this case, an assessment of the impact on the management system may appear in a business process, with a pointer to the integration process for specific input or review since that process determines the criteria. The opposite would also work depending on how the owner-architect and respective process owners choose to optimize the work. Either way, the detailed criteria should appear only once in the management system. Often the decision on where to allocate a specific activity is aided by considering how many other processes require access to the information. Decisions as to which process should 'own' an activity are frequent, and cannot easily be made unless the top level model described in Chapter 9 has been developed since the model serves as the master reference.

Once management approves process development (Step 3 of Figure 10-1), work proceeds in accordance with the detailed sub-processes of 'Manage system integration' (Step 4).

Both Step 5 and 7 are call-outs to other processes that establish specific requirements and follow their own sequence of activities. For example, the details of developing, reviewing, approving, and issuing a process document are in the generic process for document production rather than embedded in the process 'Manage process integration'. Step 6 is the validation process prior to implementation. The criteria and acceptable approaches for verification and validation (table top, simulation, field test, etc.) are established within 'Manage system integration'.

The process associated with Figure 10-1 is developed in the context of the organizational structure in Chapter 8, Figure 8-1 and the responsibilities of the owner-architect in Chapter 5, Table 5-2. The primary sub-process is the specific procedure for developing and modifying a process. Although this process is engaged in change management for the management system, many other processes have a role in change management within their areas of activity.

It is worth pointing out that a comprehensive change management approach such as ProSci (www.prosci.com/adkar/adkar-model), that combines traditional change management and results-focused project management concepts into one user-friendly methodology, can be very helpful to achieving streamlined process implementation and improvement.

DEFINE THE APPLICATION OF GRADING

'Manage process integration' includes a number of standardized elements which will be discussed in later chapters where they are applied. As an example, it should define a standardized approach to grading to ensure that the development of each process builds in grading elements applicable to it. A definition of grading is provided in the following box.

> **DEFINITION: Grading**
>
> ***Grading*** is an approach to designing and applying requirements to an activity, item, or service based on its relative importance, complexity, variability, and potential impact on safety, production, and cost.

Appropriate grading improves efficiency and resource allocation by ensuring the controls applied are appropriate to the risk involved, and are reduced in situations of lower risk. In other words, scarce resources are allocated to matters of significance. Expecting employees to exert high levels of control in situations they believe have low potential risk is a recipe for introducing work-arounds and complacency into the organization.

Grading should not be confused with classification of components or systems, e.g., nuclear grade versus commercial grade. Although classification is a form of grading, it is a product of the design specification process, hence drives procurement and maintenance activities. Grading in the context of this handbook is broader in that it is applied during the development of every process, and embedded in the process as appropriate. Hence 'Manage process integration' is an appropriate spot in the management system to establish grading criteria.

Many variations of grading systems exist [IAEA 2014]. The task of the Management System Project Team and Excellence Team is to define an appropriate approach and criteria for general application, and embed this within the documented procedures supporting 'Manage process integration'. A simple example of a graded approach is given in Appendix J.

DEFINE THE APPLICATION OF VERIFICATION

For similar reasons of consistency, the approach to and general criteria for verification and validation are useful additions to 'Manage process integration'. Verification is a common quality assurance term defined in the box.

> **DEFINITION: Verification**
>
> **Verification** is the act of reviewing, inspecting, testing, checking, or otherwise confirming whether items, processes, documents, or services conform to specified requirements.

The method, extent, and timing of verification should be graded depending on the complexity of the work, the potential impact on safety, and on the ability to detect a nonconformity through verification.

Verification requirements, strategies, and activities should be identified as an integral part of developing a process, since the required activities should be built into each process as appropriate. This includes identifying:

- what is to be verified
- when to perform the verification
- who is to conduct the verification
- the method(s), and
- the acceptance criteria.

A number of generic criteria can be specified in 'Manage process integration'. For example, individuals who perform verification shall:

- be appropriately qualified and objective
- not inspect their own work
- record their name at the time of verification, and
- report all nonconformities.

Since the requirements for verification differ in definition and rigour with jurisdiction and safety significance of a system, the generic process needs to take such requirements into consideration.

DEFINE THE APPLICATION OF VALIDATION

In high reliability organizations, there is often a need to validate processes and changes before full implementation. Acceptable strategies and criteria for doing this should be included in 'Manage process integration' for consideration during the development of each process. In some cases criteria may be expanded and embedded in specific processes.

A definition of validation is provided in the box.

> **DEFINITION: Validation**
>
> **Validation** is the act of confirming that an item, process, document or service conforms to specified requirements and achieves the desired results under real or simulated conditions.

A validation is not simply a review by individuals who have not participated in development. It is intended to simulate actual conditions as closely as possible to confirm functionality. The validation should be graded depending on the significance of the item, process, document, service, and the consequences of failures.

Types of validation may include:

- table-top exercises
- walk-throughs
- field-tests, using either partial or full-scale scenarios
- tests using simulators.

In cases where full validation is not possible except in real circumstances, specific contingency and back-out plans should be in place until the process can be fully released for service.

CHOOSE AN INFORMATION PLATFORM FOR THE MANAGEMENT SYSTEM

One aspect requiring initial review and decision is the information system or technology platform that will be used to retain and disseminate information on the management system. This system serves as the repository of policy, process, and procedural documents, as well as all related information such as correspondence, technical information, drawings, maintenance manuals, records, and history of changes. Multiple systems such as separate databases for design, maintenance, documents, drawings, etc. are inefficient and problematic in the long run.

Modern systems enhance integration of information and facilitate retrieval of historical and real-time data. The project team should consider whether the current systems are adequate to support development and ongoing operation and propose a strategy to the Excellence Team.

Consideration should be given to the widespread availability of tablet devices, since their benefits include portability and paperless environments in which documents are extracted from an active database rather than a file cabinet. Their use has human factors implications for how information is presented. For example, a one-screen view of a flowchart or process step is preferable to scrolling through multiple pages. Such devices also enable real-time access to data, including equipment performance, and status of changing situations such as work progress and hazard conditions. Early clarification of this area is important to optimize the design and integration of management system processes and procedures with the technology selected. As with all modern technology, obsolescence issues should be considered.

SUMMARY OF OUTPUTS

The box below summarizes the tasks that should be accomplished within this phase of the project.

Key Outputs from this Chapter on Architectural Controls

The outputs from the tasks in this phase of the project are:

- A high-level process document for 'Manage process integration' that includes a process map and standard approaches for grading, verification, and validation for application across the management system.
- Supporting procedures for developing and modifying processes.
- Confirmation that management information systems are or will be in place to facilitate preparation, distribution, and retrieval of the variety of current and historical information users require on an on-going and real-time basis.

Chapter 11

Establish a Mapping Methodology

IN THIS CHAPTER

In accordance with Step 6 of the flowchart in Figure 7-1, this chapter provides guidance on selecting a mapping methodology to serve as the backbone for each process. The topics include:

- The purpose of maps
- Selecting a consistent approach
- The basic elements
- Types of maps, including advantages and disadvantages
- Mapping a process
- Documenting the approach.

PURPOSE OF MAPS

A process map provides a framework to guide users to the detailed information necessary to execute the process. A map looks like a flowchart, however, it should neither be construed nor constructed in the way one would build an engineering, manufacturing, scientific or software flowchart. It is intended to communicate the flow of a business or administrative process, hence the level of detail and attention to such elements as feedback loops present in standard flowcharts can be an impediment to understanding and performance. The process is a human system process, hence, the number of activity blocks in a management system flowchart should be kept to a minimum to facilitate comprehension of the overall picture.

The power of mapping lies not only in its ability to communicate the essential content of a process. It also ensures there are no loose ends, missing activities, or weak interfaces.

ESTABLISH A CONSISTENT APPROACH TO PROCESS MAPPING

The choice of mapping style is important since the project will involve creating hundreds of maps. Standardizing on an approach has a number of advantages:

- A consistent format makes it easier for individuals to interpret maps built by any individual or department within the organization
- Participants on mapping teams will learn a standardized approach that can be used in a variety of problem-solving situations both within their groups and within cross-functional settings, and
- A single software tool applied across the organization simplifies deployment and training.

Expect some resistance to standardization. Technical staff may hold particular views about flowcharts. Their familiarity with flowcharting standards such as IDEF0 may lead them to insist that such a standard should be adopted, despite the fact that it is unwieldy for the intended application. Individual departments may be attached to their current approach. Some people may want the maps to "look pretty".

Guess what? The design of process maps is so straightforward that organizations can, and should, establish their own standard as part of the management system architecture. With this in mind, the Project Team should solicit input on a number of design options from people in the organization who will have to develop and use the maps. This will help socialize the concept and aid in choosing an approach that users will accept. Be sure to include groups that are heavily invested in current flowcharting approaches, but do not be overly influenced by them. At this stage it is worthwhile to gather examples from similar industries.

THE BASIC ELEMENTS

A simple approach to mapping makes it easier to provide 'just-in-time' training for process mapping teams. Effective maps can be built using fewer than ten basic elements found in any software application for flowcharting:

1. Initiator
2. Terminator
3. Activity box
4. Callout box
5. Decision box
6. Connectors
7. Arrows
8. Input / Output symbols (optional).

1. Initiator or 'Start' Symbol

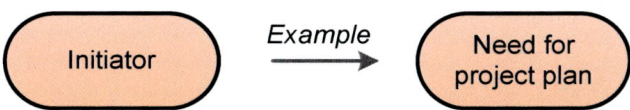

Figure 11-1: Initiator symbol

An initiator symbol:

- is not numbered
- is used as an entry, starting point, or 'trigger' to begin the process
- contains text indicating the reason for entering the process (e.g., need for a project plan, new licence application)

An initiator may also be a call-in from another process (see item 4).

2. Terminator or 'End' Symbol

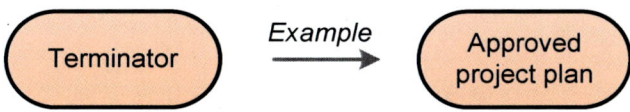

Figure 11-2: Terminator symbol

A terminator symbol:

- is not numbered
- is used to exit or terminate a process
- contains text describing the need that has been satisfied or the reason the process has been terminated.

A terminator may also be a call-out to another process (see item 4).

Initiators and terminators help define the process boundaries. Choose the wording carefully.

3. Activity Box

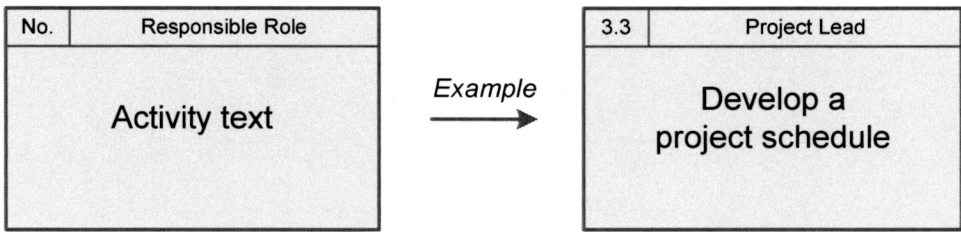

Figure 11-3: Activity box

A process activity symbol or box:

- is numbered to align with the corresponding section of the document that describes the required tasks
- identifies the primary role responsible for ensuring the activity is performed, even though action by others may also be needed to complete the activity
- contains text beginning with an active verb describing the required action.

An activity box is the primary symbol used in flowcharts.

4. Call-out Box

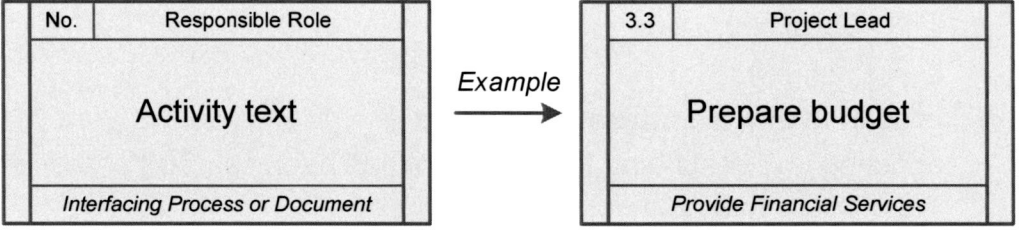

Figure 11-4: Call-out box

A call-out box:

- identifies a connection to another process
- may be left un-numbered when used to indicate a call-out to another process with no return link into the flowchart

- may be used to show a link to another document in the same or a different process by using the document title or number in place of the interfacing process name
- may be used as an initiator or a terminator.

Call-outs provide systemic links that indicate how one process integrates with another. Ensure such links are consistent with the process being referenced.

5. Decision Box

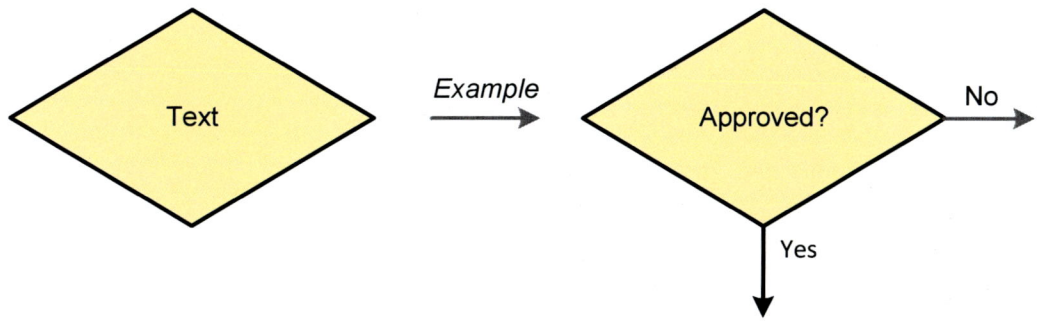

Figure 11-5A: Simple decision box

Decision boxes may be simple or complex. Use an unnumbered decision symbol as shown in Figure 11-5A when:

- the decision is simple and does not require explanation in the text (e.g., yes/no decisions)
- a simple switching or routing function is needed (e.g., Action status requiring three exit branches labelled 'new', 'open', and 'closed').

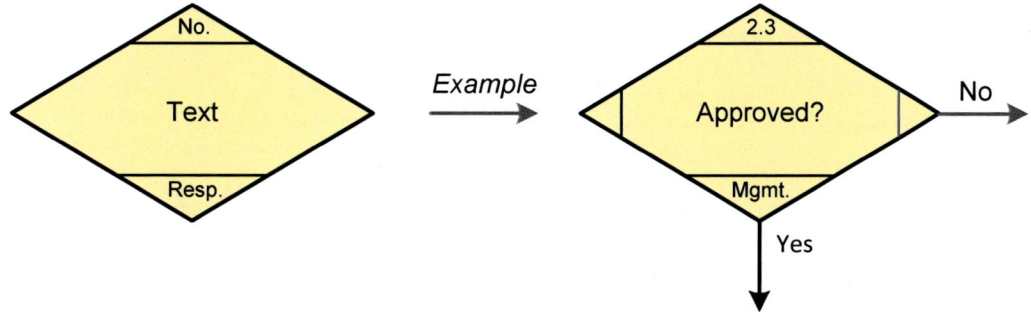

Figure 11-5B: Complex decision box

Use a numbered decision symbol when decisions are complex or need to be evaluated against criteria that require explanation in the text related to the numbered section.

If the decision is made in a different process, indicate this by adding sidebars as shown on the right side of Figure 11-5B.

6. *Connector Symbols*

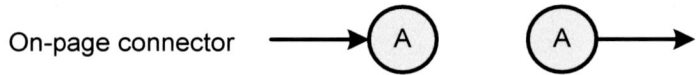

Figure 11-6: Connector symbol

A connector symbol with an enclosed letter is used to indicate transfer to, or entry from, another part of the same flowchart. These are rarely needed if one uses the one-page flowchart rule.

7. *Connecting Arrows*

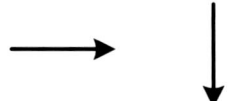

Figure 11-7: Connecting arrows

Connecting arrows link symbols and indicate process flow. Apply the following guidelines:

- avoid double arrows since they mask the flow
- avoid feedback arrows unless the feedback loop is important and expected to be frequent
- avoid crossing lines over each other
- label the arrow with text if clarity is improved, particularly when routing several arrows from one activity symbol.

Input / Output Symbols

Although they are rarely essential and can clutter a map, some developers favour the use of input and output symbols. They should be used sparingly, if at all, and then only for an input or output of major significance. Some common examples are given below.

Document   Data   Database   External Data

Figure 11-8: Example input-output symbols

The decision to establish a standard colour scheme for symbols is cost-neutral in an online environment, but can become costly in an organization where users prefer printed copies. Some organizations tend to 'prettify' or 'humanize' flowcharts by using realistic symbols. This is especially easy with modern software tools. While we do not oppose a degree of elegance in presentation where appropriate, too much glitz in user documentation can become tedious and detract from the basic intent of process mapping, which is to put a consistent tool in the hands of nearly everyone in the organization so that it can be used in everyday problem solving.

A few additional tips are given in the following box.

> ### *Tips for better process maps*
>
> The following tips may help make process mapping easier:
>
> - Use a consistent (standardized) approach to facilitate organizational use and understanding. Flowcharting should be a routine part of the organizational toolkit.
> - Simple is better – avoid complexity wherever possible.
> - Use a one-page rule for process maps (fewer than 10 activity boxes).
> - Select software responsibly – a fancy flowchart doesn't mean an effective process. Choose software that will be easy to use across the organization rather than software that requires extensive training or experience.
> - Don't over-analyze – not every feedback loop needs to be shown, particularly if they are 'common sense' such as returning to an earlier step if a problem occurs.

TYPES OF MAPS

Now that we have covered the basic symbols, let's look at several common types of maps and their advantages and disadvantages. Once again the objective is to decide on a consistent representation that makes the most sense for the organization.

We will look at three types:

- Simple maps
- Swim lane maps
- Explanatory maps.

For simplicity of illustration we will use a high-level procurement process.

Simple Maps

Figure 11-9 shows a simple process map. Note the absence of feedback loops that might occur for example if the material received was defective or inconsistent with the purchase order. Although the map could include other supplementary symbols such as an output document from activity box 3 to indicate the purchase order, such embellishments should be avoided if they are obvious outcomes of the step. Put only important reminders on the map. For example, the inputs to boxes 1 and 2 could be removed without significant loss. Assume the individual using the map has a reasonable understanding of the process.

Table 11-1 lists pros and cons for this type of map.

Table 11-1: Advantages and Disadvantages of simple process maps

Simple Process Maps	
Advantages	**Disadvantages**
<ul><li>Primary focus is on the process flow</li><li>Activity boxes can be balanced in terms of the number of tasks despite having several performers</li><li>Overall responsibility for activities in a box can be assigned even when different organizational units are involved</li></ul>	<ul><li>Organizational (department or group) aspects are not as evident</li></ul>

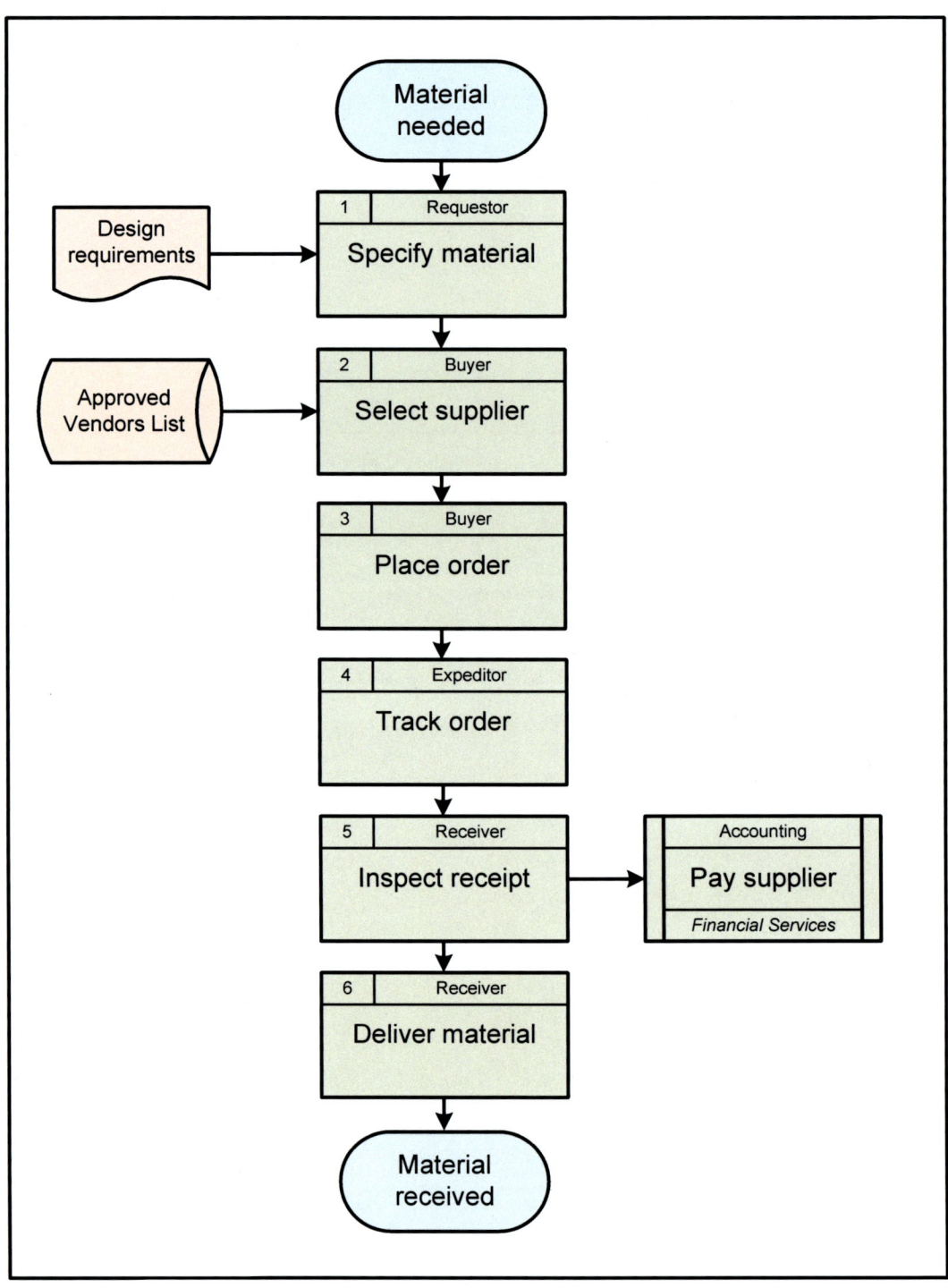

Figure 11-9: Simple process map

Swim Lane Maps

Swim lane or cross-functional maps are often favoured in organizations with a strong functional or departmental orientation. They provide a clear indication of the role of each department so it knows exactly which activities in the process are its responsibility. Figure 11-10 gives an example of a swim lane map based on the procurement process in the simple map. For simplicity, the inputs to the first two boxes are not shown.

Table 11-2 gives some of the advantages and disadvantages associated with swim lane maps. One advantage of swim lanes is that the horizontal axis can be used as a timeline to show various phases of an operation. The main risk is that the organizational focus of swim lanes can shift attention away from activities that the department doesn't perform, leading to the potential for sub-optimization as a department focuses on its activities. This can make the job of the process owner more challenging. Effective integration means that all departments involved in a process have a clear picture of how others contribute to process effectiveness.

Table 11-2: Advantages and Disadvantages of swim lane process maps

Swim lane Process Maps	
Advantages	**Disadvantages**
• Shows organizational functions that perform activities involved • Amenable to showing phases along the horizontal axis	• Emphasizes organizational silos rather than the process • Sensitive to organizational changes • Minor roles need separate swim lanes • Difficult to keep to one portrait page • Requires effective process owners to overcome departmental bias

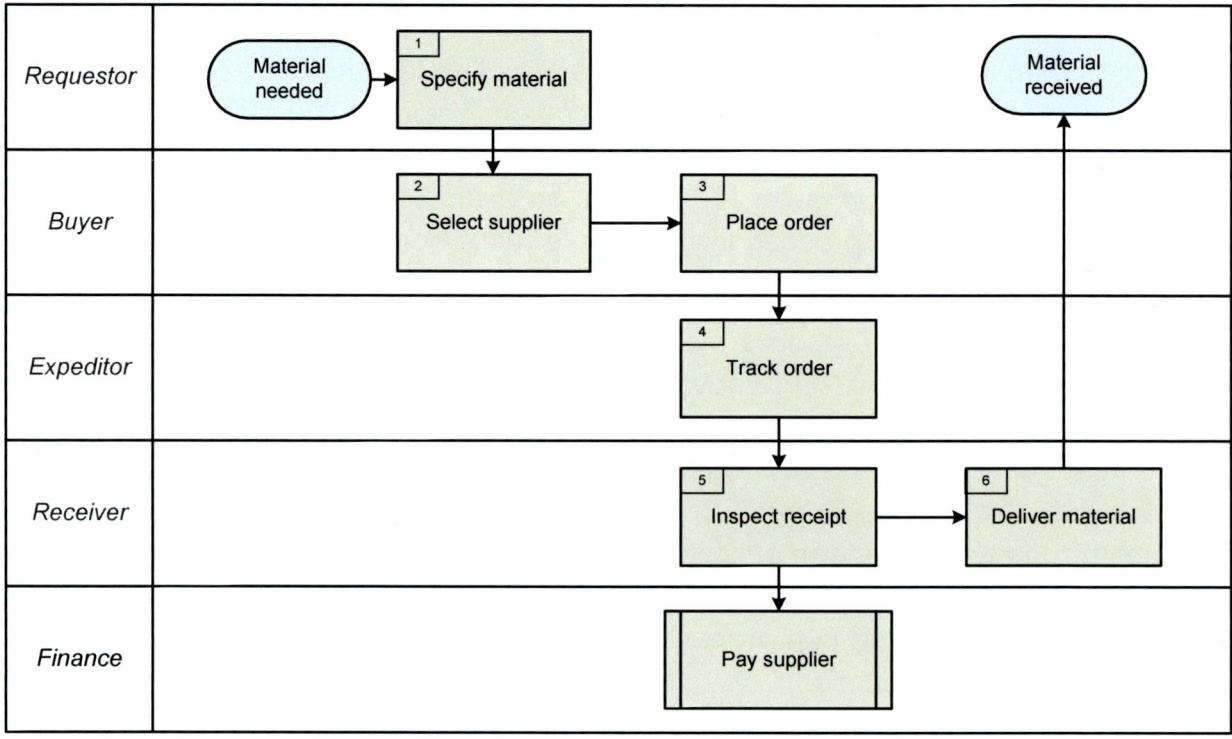

Figure 11-10: Swim lane process map

Explanatory Maps

Figure 11-11 provides an example of an explanatory map, followed by a list of advantages and disadvantages in Table 11-3. As their name implies, such maps allow for more explanatory information at the expense of using more space. They are useful for the highest level maps. For simplicity and space considerations, the inputs for the first activity boxes (see Figure 11-9) have been omitted.

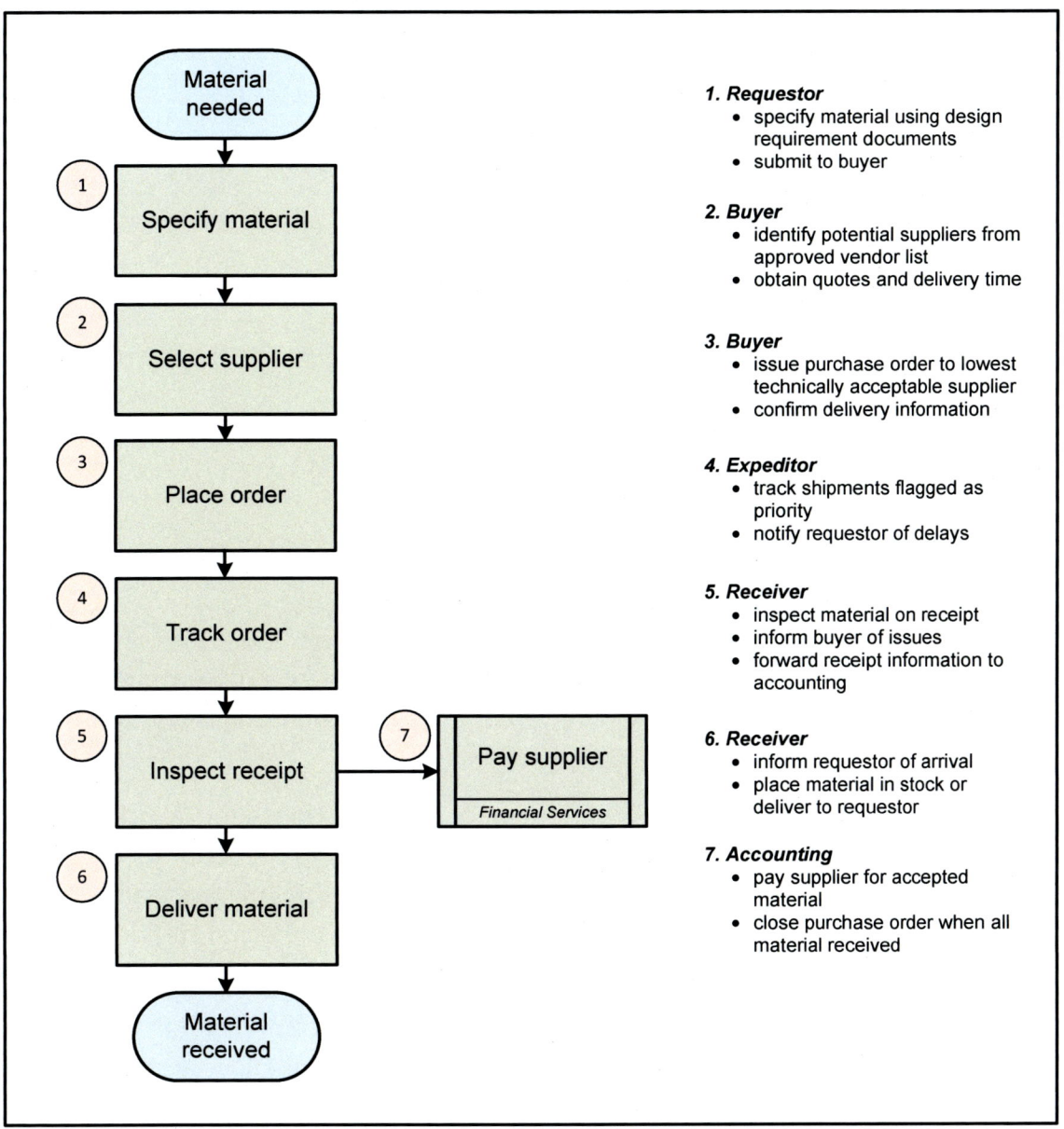

Figure 11-11: Explanatory process map

Table 11-3: Advantages and Disadvantages of explanatory process maps

Explanatory Process Maps	
Advantages	**Disadvantages**
• Similar to the simple map in structure • Provides additional explanatory information • Good for top level maps	• Difficult to fit on one standard sized page for maps with several branches • Text does not replace the need for details

Representational Styles

The examples in Figures 11-9, 11-10, and 11-11 are a few of many possibilities.

Project teams will often encounter individuals or groups who express a desire to have more flair and variety in flowcharts. Alternate representational styles may have merit for some applications, e.g., for high-level presentations or training. The project team should not prevent the use of styles that meet the needs of a specific audience; however, variety for the sake of variety can lead to visual fatigue or confusion.

A cautionary note is warranted. An essential consideration for developing "working level", user-friendly maps that tie directly to documentation is to apply a consistent standard that provides the discipline to avoid missing activities or interfaces, and can be applied in most situations across the organization.

An example of an alternate visual representation is the map for a safety culture self-assessment process (Figure 11-12) that the authors helped develop for an IAEA publication [IAEA 2016]. Such representations allow embellishments to provide context and intent. Many possible variations exist.

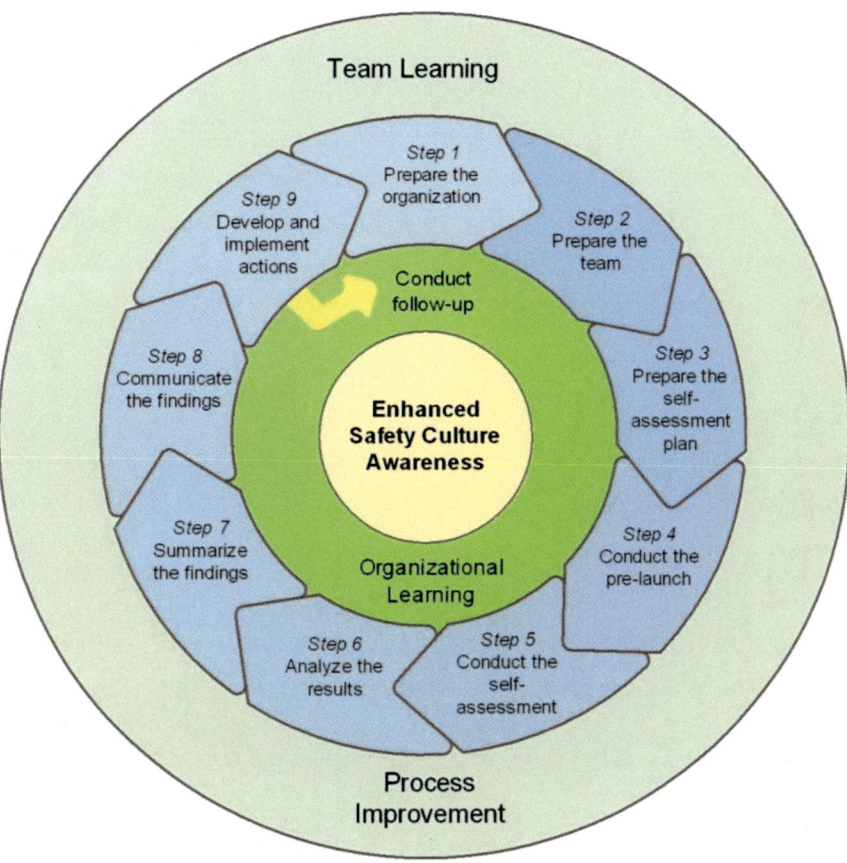

Figure 11-12 Process for safety culture self-assessment [IAEA 2016]

Process maps form the structure for documents. They are not a visual add-on to be parked in an appendix.

The primary objective of the Project Team is to examine various approaches and define one that will best suit their organization for 90% of the situations likely to be encountered. Being too loose with guidance will not be helpful, and will result in rework. A standard format used across the organization is beneficial. Success requires that process maps are human friendly, and this can only be achieved through engaging users and stakeholders during development.

MAPPING A PROCESS

We will address the detailed approach to mapping in a later chapter, but it is worth outlining the basic elements of how to apply the approach with a mapping team. It isn't necessary for the facilitator to have in-depth knowledge of the process. In fact, this can be a disadvantage since such individuals tend to become too invested in the decisions that lead to the outcome. Nevertheless, the facilitator has to do some homework, namely:

- Review existing documents related to the process
- Meet with knowledgeable sources to get a sense of what the process is intended to accomplish (the template in Appendix G is a useful guide for such discussions)
- Determine whether there are known issues with process effectiveness or efficiency
- Gain initial familiarity with the applicable governing requirements and standards.

To map the process with a team, the following steps generally achieve the intended results:

1. Gain consensus on the purpose, scope, boundaries, and major outputs of the process (Appendix G).
2. Identify the major activities. These do not have to be in order, nor will all of the ones identified survive as major. A brainstorming approach works well.
3. Determine whether some activities can be combined or whether some are sub-tasks within an identified activity. The objective is to reduce the number to no more than 10 activities.
4. Identify an approximate order for the major activities.
5. Confirm, through general consensus, that each activity contains enough tasks to warrant its status as a major activity.
6. Begin developing the map from initiator to terminator, working out sequence, branching, decision points, etc.
7. Obtain consensus that the initial process will meet key requirements once developed more fully.

8. Identify the role or position with overall responsible for ensuring each activity is accomplished, even though others may have sub-roles within the activity.

At this stage the map will be sufficient to use for the documentation stage described in the next chapter. It does not need to be refined since it will evolve during detailed development.

Note that the final step in the sequence is to assign responsibilities. This is deliberate. It helps mediate the tendency of individuals to force or defend a positional role too early in the process. The objective is to design the cleanest, most efficient process first, then decide who most logically should perform each activity.

TIP – The Ben Graham Method

There will be times when developers may wish to map an existing process. One of the most effective tools for doing this is the process mapping methodology developed by the Ben Graham Corporation (*www.worksimp.com*). Using only eight symbols, one can quickly map complex processes by following the work activities as they flow through the organization. This allows easy identification of redundancies, delays and non-value-added steps such as unnecessary signatures.

Although the tool is excellent for rapid mapping of an entire process, it is not designed to chunk information into user-friendly processes as described in this handbook. Nevertheless, it is an effective tool for process developers and should be considered as an element of their training program.

DOCUMENTING THE APPROACH

The approach to documentation is covered in the next chapter; however, one point is worth addressing here.

The mapping methodology adopted needs to be documented within a particular process. Although it is tempting to place this within the process for *Manage process integration* it more appropriately belongs in the process associated with document development. The reason is that the latter process applies to all documentation produced within the organization, hence it has a broader mandate. This is a good example of where the Project Team develops an element of the management system that it may feel the urge to retain under its primary process (*Manage process integration*), when doing so isn't actually beneficial to the overall system. As indicated previously, assigning activities and documents to the right process requires a good overall process model.

As mentioned earlier, this chapter on mapping works in parallel with the next chapter on documenting processes since the two methodologies must be integrated.

SUMMARY OF OUTPUTS

The following box summarizes the tasks that should be accomplished in this phase of the project.

Key Outputs from this Chapter on Process Maps

The output related to the tasks from this phase of the project consists of a single item essential for management system development:

- A documented, standardized approach applicable across the organization for the development of process maps.

Chapter 12

Establish Document Standards and Controls

IN THIS CHAPTER

In accordance with Step 7 of the flowchart in Figure 7-1, this chapter describes the elements required to ensure documentation related to the management system is well-structured, user friendly, and easy to maintain. Topics include:

- Developing document standards
- Developing a document hierarchy or framework
- Types of documents
- Document identification systems
- Establishing a technical writing strategy
- Writing effective documents.

DEVELOP DOCUMENT STANDARDS

Systematic control of the management system requires consistent writing guidelines, document formats and templates across the organization.

Document quality, control, and usability are diminished when an organization distributes responsibilities for document production, allowing departments or subject matter experts can use whatever style they prefer. If 'document control' is viewed solely as numbering, registering, distribution, and retention for records, the result will be the production of inconsistent documents with gaps in content and weaknesses in knowledge transfer.

Two early decisions are required:

1. Establish single point control

Establish single point control for the production and revision of process documents and related procedures. This control typically resides with the process owner for the overall management system, even though the formal documented process normally resides in the support process related to document production and distribution. The key is to ensure that the structure and requirements are defined and controlled. The sooner this is established, the better.

2. Develop writers' guides

Develop writers' guides to ensure a consistent style and format for documents (including forms and templates) across the organization. Although a number of useful guides exist from which to develop in-house guides, adopting them in their entirety is rarely sufficient because they do not include the specific needs of your organization with respect to such aspects as document types and terminology. Nevertheless, review industry specific writer's guides where available and adopt relevant material, particularly related to best practices in human performance and error reduction. Focus on the specific needs of your management system. Adopt accepted reference material such as 'approved for use' dictionaries and grammar guides.

The benefit of consistent document format, style, terminology, and 'feel' may not seem immediately evident. The advantages lie not only in easier production and revision, but also in training and use in cross-functional environments. For example, situations may require an engineer, mechanic, operator, electrician, safety person, and quality assurance inspector to perform steps of a common procedure such as a work plan.

Some of the material discussed later in this chapter would be included in the writers' guide. Preparing internal guides is useful professional development for in-house technical writers. Nevertheless, even well-prepared writer's guides are not a substitute for technical writer training.

DEVELOP A ROBUST DOCUMENT HIERARCHY

Spend enough time to develop a document hierarchy or framework. Since the hierarchy is intended to include every type of document used within the organization, this requires the Project Team to identify every type of document needed by the organization. This task is easily accomplished by obtaining actual examples from each department or unit.

Figure 12-1 gives an example hierarchy for a Canadian regulatory agency [CNSC 2013] showing both the regulatory framework documents and the hierarchy for documents controlling the internal work of the organization. Most organizations only require a hierarchy similar to the right side of the figure, however, the example illustrates that the number of document tiers depends on the needs of the organization and what best communicates the differences in the various levels.

The pyramids encompass all active user-level working documents. The rectangle below designates records of items that are generally not subject to revision. In reality, everything is a 'record' in the view of specialists in information management, but the distinction between working documents and records is of practical value within operating environments.

Once the team has identified all types of documents used within the organization, a suitable hierarchy can be built. Resist the temptation to make it highly detailed or contain more than 5 tiers or levels. The hierarchy is typically included in the management manual.

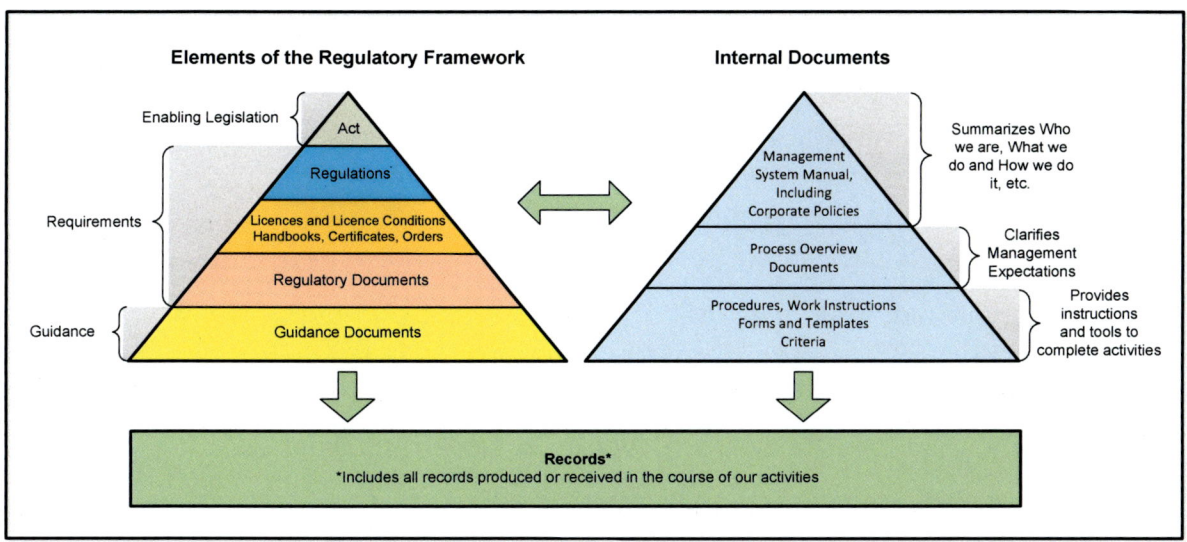

Figure 12-1: Example document hierarchy for a regulator [CNSC 2013]

DEFINE DOCUMENT TYPES

One reason the hierarchy doesn't require detail is that it needs to be supported by a table of all document types. Table 12-1 gives an example of internal working documents (right pyramid) developed for use by a regulator.

Similar types of documents may be assembled as manuals (e.g., operating procedure manuals, safety manuals) but the type of document within the manual should still fit within one of the defined categories.

In each case, the document type will have a standard format. Appropriate levels of production guidance should be provided in writers' guides or standards.

A common question is how to distinguish a process from a procedure. Here are a few features:

- A process:
    - is administrative in nature
    - is always supported by a process map
    - often has cross-organizational interfaces or broad application
    - may allow flexibility in the way tasks are accomplished.
- A procedure:
    - provides step by step work instruction on how to perform a specific task
    - doesn't usually require a flowchart because the actions are performed in sequence and have fewer interfaces
    - is often highly prescriptive
    - is generally performed by one or a few people together.

A significant feature is that a procedure or work instruction always derives from and supports a process, not vice-versa. A process is a higher tier document.

Table 12-1: Examples of Document Types

Tier	Type	Description
1	Management Manual	• Tier 1 description of management approach • Management system description and model(s) • Policies • Requirements • Senior management responsibilities and structure

Tier	Type	Description
2	Process Description or Overview	• High-level descriptions of top level (Tier 2) processes • Governing requirements, responsibilities, process map, key activities, inputs and outputs, suppliers and customers • Management 'contract' with the Process Owner • Shows links to or list of Tier 3 documents
3	Process	• Working level information to support Tier 2 processes • Process map linked to activities • Shows interfaces with other key processes
4	Procedure	• Detailed instructions at the task performance level • Flowchart optional
4	Non-procedural controlled documents	• Version-controlled documents that are outputs from processes or procedures (e.g., organization charts, work plans, training documents, technical basis documents, design drawings, program description documents, information reports, contracts) • Technical references from external organizations (e.g., manufacturer maintenance manuals, design manuals, drawings)
4	Internal standards	Organizational standards and guidance applicable across the system (e.g., writers' guide, lexicon of terms)
4	Forms	Standardized format for recording repetitive information. A checklist is one type of form.
4	Templates	Standardized format for a specific document type, including section titles, fonts, layout, and style.
	Records	• Provide institutional memory and include completed output information (e.g., audit reports, inspection reports, research, annual reports, completed forms, completed contracts) • Documents received from other organizations Note: Records include non-document items such as photographs, x-rays, physical specimens, etc.

ESTABLISH A DOCUMENT IDENTIFICATION SYSTEM

A standard quality assurance requirement is for all documents to have a unique identifier. Some organizations simply resort to a bar code type approach in which every document is assigned a unique numerical code. Some organizations devise letter-number schemes where the letters have significance such as type of document (OM – Operating Manual, DM – Design Manual, FS – Flow Sheet, etc.) or related process (MA – Maintenance Process, FP – Fire Protection, etc.) Sometimes a number series is related to a particular file system or physical system such as primary coolant system. Such numbering schemes present several issues:

- Whatever the system, it will eventually become obsolete or irrelevant
- If the system is defined by the designer, supplier, corporate office, or historical usage, changes may introduce other human system issues.

The more complex the system, the more likely problems will arise; however, the issue has to be addressed and deserves thought to avoid future problems. Some considerations include:

- Consider aligning identifiers to the process that 'owns' the document, since this facilitates searches to identify all documents related to a specific process. This aids knowledge management, retention, and transfer when a new process owner is assigned.
- Consider the search capabilities of the technology being considered, since not all search engines are adequate. Ease of retrieval is important for any document, including external correspondence and internal memos. Relying on key words for retrieval is problematic since people are rarely consistent or sufficiently diligent to select adequate key words.

Whatever the system, identifiers are no substitute for effective titles.

ESTABLISH A TECHNICAL WRITING STRATEGY

The ability or propensity to write clearly and concisely is relatively rare. Document quality is enhanced significantly if an organization pools writing talent as a primary resource to help develop processes and procedures for technical staff. Doing so means that a smaller number of people require training on how to write documents to consistent standards. Without such controls, documents will be of widely varying quality, notwithstanding technical review mechanisms.

Technical subject matter experts (SMEs) are likely to resist this approach in the beginning, since they believe their engineering or science competence includes writing ability. Nearly everyone thinks they can write well, simply because what they write makes sense to them. The best technical writers we have encountered have language training rather than engineering or technical backgrounds.

Engineers, operators, and other technical subject matter experts (SMEs) tend to:

- write what they would like to have happen rather than what can or does happen
- focus on one document at a time without adequate consideration of interactions with other documents, especially outside their process
- ignore process boundaries because they want their document to include everything they believe is important.

A much better use of technical SME time is to have experienced technical writers 'translate' SME needs into a concise, user-focused document that maintains integrity across the management system. A small group of technical writers will substantially reduce overall work and more readily incorporate best practices. Documents based on best practices are easier to:

- develop
- review
- use for training
- use in the field
- revise (keep up to date), and
- translate into other languages where applicable.

The decision to use technical writers who incorporate best practices requires organizational commitment, but return on investment is significant.

Research on how people best absorb information indicates that information is more readily absorbed if writers apply criteria such as the following:

- use concise, active language

- 'chunk' or group 5-9 items at a time
- use white space liberally
- eliminate extraneous or obvious information.

Information mapping is one of our favourite best practices for technical writers. It significantly changes how a typical organization writes technical documents. A real-life example of its effectiveness is shown in the box. The box does not show the 'white space' associated with the method, a factor which improves readability for both on-screen and printed material. As mentioned in an earlier chapter, readability on portable devices such as tablets is virtually a requirement in modern organizations.

The essential skills for information mapping can be obtained in a short training course (Google *'Information Mapping International'* for information on courses suited to your organization). We have no business connections with the product. It is simply one of the best research-based documentation tools we have encountered. Although it provides efficient documentation techniques, it does not include process mapping skills.

Example of the Power of Information Mapping

The following is the actual text of a published procedure. It contains **233 words**.

4.3.3 Identification and Incorporation of Verification Requirements in OMs

Operating Manual procedures involve activities such as positioning of components (e.g. switches, breakers, dampers or valves) or confirming that stated conditions exist. These activities could cause an upset or impair the safety and reliability of the facility if they are not performed correctly. Verification provides a means to prevent, or detect and correct, any errors by using a second qualified individual to "double-check" the operation.

Authors of OM procedures must consider the risk of error when the procedure is performed. If successful performance of the task is important to safety, OM authors must propose appropriate verification criteria and methodology that will provide the required rigor to meet Quality Assurance requirements and be in line with constraints such as schedule and resource requirements. Procedure *'Event Free tools – Verification'* [3] provides guidelines to consider when identifying verification requirements. In addition, OM authors shall ensure that OM procedures satisfy mandatory requirements for verification as identified in the Facility Licence or other safety documents. Note that, in order to satisfy the requirements in CAN/CSA N286.0 – Appendix A *"Guidelines for the Application of Safety-Related Systems"* [4], verification activities must be performed by an independent qualified individual (i.e. not involved in the performance of the activity being verified).

The format to be used for steps in an OM procedure that requires verification is specified in Appendix B of this procedure.

The following is the info-mapped version of the above text. It contains **95 words**.

4.3.3 Identifying and Incorporating Verification Requirements in OMs

Authors shall:

- incorporate verification steps where improperly performed activities could impair safety or reliability; and
- ensure procedures satisfy mandatory verification requirements identified in the Facility Lisence or other safety documents.

Procedure 'Event Free tools – Verification' [3] gives additional information on identifying verification requirements.

Verification must be performed by an independent qualified individual who was not involved in the performance of the activity being verified. [Requirement of CAN/CSA CAN/CSA N286.0 – Appendix A *"Guidelines for the Application of Safety-Related Systems"*] [4].

Appendix B provides the format for verification activities.

The info-mapped version contains 41% of the words in the original with no loss of content.

After reviewing the examples in the box, which one would you prefer reading, reviewing or revising? The example is typical of the 50-70% reduction in word count for documents that are information mapped rather than written in prose style. This translates into equivalent gains in preparation or revision time, reading time, and human performance benefits for the end user.

WRITING EFFECTIVE DOCUMENTS

Appendix K contains tips on writing effective process and procedural documents. The following are a few important elements typically included in writers' guides.

Titles

Use a consistent format for titles beginning with an active verb:

- Initiating a project
- Developing mobilizing metrics
- Inspecting stainless steel welds.

Choose titles that clearly reflect the purpose so users can retrieve the right document.

- Preparing budgets NOT Budgets
- Performing internal audits NOT Audits.

Purpose and Scope Statements

The purpose explains what the document is used for or what it accomplishes.

The scope (or application) explains when, where, how, and to whom it applies (as needed). Avoid describing cases for which it doesn't apply unless there is a potential for significant mis-application.

The purpose and scope should be short and precise.

Reference Categories

Careful consideration of the definition and bucketing of references helps in:

- specifying standards and requirements that the document must comply with

- identifying linked documents that must be considered when changing the document, and
- listing useful supplementary documents

Good references aid knowledge retention and transfer. Table 12-2 provides an example of classification of references. Such a table would be embedded within each document, listing references relevant to that particular document.

The table should contain only essential references. It is not advisable to include every related document when other lists adequately cover the information (e.g., internal training manuals related to the topic). Nor is it necessary to list the current revision date or number of internal documents since such lists soon become superseded. The expectation is that one always refers to the most recent published version of an internal document. This requires that document owners ensure their documents are up to date and consistent with interfacing documents. This places an onus on the owner of the document being revised to consult owners of interfacing documents if a change may affect other documents.

Table 12-2: Examples of Reference Types

Reference Type	Description
Governing	Contain requirements the process must meet such as: • Acts, regulations, and government policies or directives • Standards, codes, and licenses • *Memoranda of Understanding* with other organizations • Management policies or directives.
Interfacing	Management System documents called up within the document to accomplish tasks. Changes to interfacing documents may impact the current document, and vice-versa, hence this list is a valuable cross-reference when revising documents. **Note:** Documents produced by external organizations should be referenced as supplementary or governing as appropriate, not as interfacing references.

Reference Type	Description
Supplementary	Documents not essential for understanding the process but which contain useful information. • Guides, standards, or best practices not formally adopted as governing references, but which contain useful information • External reports, papers, websites, or texts • Documents of value for knowledge transfer and retention.
Forms and Templates	Forms or templates referenced within the document.

There are many other decisions required when establishing a document control system, including document design, standardized tables of contents, review and approval structures, human factors considerations such as procedure use category (e.g., in-hand, at work location, or reference), and on-screen presentation. Many of these items are worked out during the preparation of internal writers' guides. The number of writers' guides should be kept to a minimum, otherwise consistency becomes a problem. Some organizations develop separate guides for process documents and field procedures. If these are developed by a single group, inconsistencies are much less likely.

Don't include forms as appendices in documents that use them. This allows the two to be updated independently.

Standardized Templates

Each document type should be supported by a standardized template to make production easier. Such templates include a cover page, table of contents, mandatory sections, style elements, and embedded guidance to help each writer achieve consistency.

SUMMARY OF OUTPUTS

The following box summarizes the tasks that should be accomplished in this phase of the project.

> ### Key Outputs from this Chapter on Document Standards and Control
>
> The outputs related to the tasks from this phase of the project are:
>
> - A document hierarchy that encompasses all types of documents used within the organization
> - Standard writers' guide(s) to provide consistency across the organization
> - Standard templates to support development of documents and forms
> - Decisions related to the organizational structure to support document preparation during the project phase and long-term (e.g., pool of technical writers versus distributed writers).

Chapter 13

Assign Process Owners and Develop a Roadmap

IN THIS CHAPTER

In accordance with Step 8 of the flowchart in Figure 7-1, this chapter describes how to select process owners for each top level process and how to develop a roadmap for implementation. The topics include:

- Process owner mandate and key responsibilities
- Process owner propensities
- Additional considerations for selection
- Prioritizing process development
- Developing a roadmap.

PROCESS OWNER MANDATE AND KEY RESPONSIBILITES

A definition for process owner is given in the box below. A process owner is accountable for the life cycle of a process from its inception through its continual improvement.

DEFINITION: Process Owner

A ***process owner*** is the individual accountable for the design, development, implementation, maintenance, effectiveness, and continual improvement of an assigned process.

Process owners have a mandate to develop, document, implement and continually improve their assigned processes within the standards and practices specified for the management system. They coordinate work with other process owners to monitor effectiveness and manage integration and interfaces.

Selecting effective process owners is an important task of senior management. It is unlikely that effective assignments can be made through a simple allocation based on position or level in the existing organization chart. The choice of process owner provides an early opportunity to serve notice of a cultural change within the organization. Process owners are both cultural ambassadors and change agents. Table 13-1 provides information of value for selecting process owners. The specific process under consideration will add other elements.

Table 13-1: Process Owner mandate and key activities

Process Owner Mandate: <ul><li>To develop, document, implement and continually improve the assigned process(es) within standards and practices specified for the management system.</li><li>To coordinate work with other process owners to monitor effectiveness and manage interfaces.</li></ul>
Functionalities
<ul><li>Process effectiveness and efficiency</li><li>Communication and engagement</li><li>Systemic and systematic integration</li><li>Alignment with standards</li><li>Continual improvement</li></ul>
Key generic activities
<ul><li>Develop and document the process consistent with management system internal standards and practices</li><li>Ensure the process meets applicable regulations, standards, codes, and stakeholder requirements</li><li>Effectively implement the process</li><li>Monitor effectiveness using defined performance metrics</li><li>Maintain the process and its documentation up to date</li><li>Establish and maintain effective interfaces and integration with other processes and owners</li><li>Resolve emerging issues and problems</li><li>Continually improve the process</li><li>Consult affected parties prior to changing the process</li><li>Provide orientation and training on the process</li><li>Periodically review internal controls</li><li>Assess and mitigate risks to the process arising from context changes</li><li>Address findings from assessments and reviews of the process</li></ul>
Specific activities
<ul><li>Dependent on the process under consideration</li></ul>

Experience of value
• Organizational experience—knowledge of organizational functionalities and required performance • Experience in process methodology • Experience managing processes • Experience in engaging and facilitating groups • Familiarity with the process under consideration or related process(es)

PROCESS OWNER PROPENSITIES

Although Table 13-1 contains elements of value in creating a 'position description' for a process owner, it is far from sufficient in terms of selecting the right candidate. As discussed in Chapter 5 on team selection, one needs to consider the desired propensities for an effective process owner. Attributes for successful performance are similar across processes. Figure 13-1 shows the profile for a process owner. It is based on the individual performance model first introduced in Chapter 2.

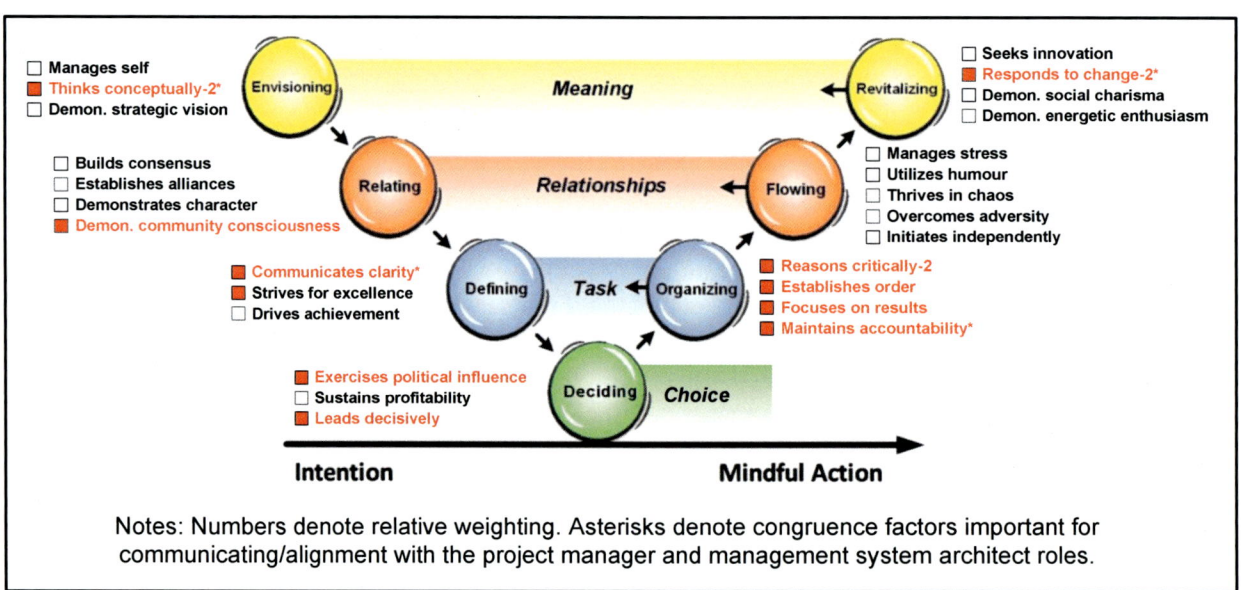

Figure 13-1: Process owner propensities

Aspects related to organizing dominate—namely the propensities to reason critically, establish order, focus on results, and maintain accountability. These propensities enable the process owner to systematically orchestrate assessment and improvement activities across multiple workgroups. Conceptual thinking enables the process owner to hold the activities, connectivities and interdependencies of the process in their mind's eye and to see how best practices can enhance process performance. Responsiveness to change helps prevent the rigidity associated with overly bureaucratic process management and increases openness to continual improvement. Demonstrating community consciousness enables the process owner to think beyond their specific wants and needs to ensure outcomes benefit others within the organization. Communicating clarity, exercising political influence, and decisiveness are key to resolving issues related to implementation and continual improvement.

Similar to the profile for the owner-architect of the overall system (Chapter 5), the preferred leadership style is transformational-utilitarian. This opens the individual to continually improving the process while not losing sight of the importance of ensuring that it meets organizational and stakeholder needs effectively and efficiently. The nature of the specific process and the overall dynamics of the team engaged in performance will also have an influence on the preferred leadership style. It may be useful to review the discussion on leadership in Chapter 5 prior to selecting candidates.

ORGANIZATIONAL CONSIDERSATIONS IN SELECTING PROCESS OWNERS

Management and Organizational Charts

Process owners are accountable for the day-to-day functioning and continual improvement of their process. With the possible exception of a few executive processes, managers should not feel they need to take on the role of process owner for all processes. Management efforts are better directed at coordination across organizational boundaries and oversight of management system integration and effectiveness. They use information from the process owners and associated measures to better direct and manage the organization. In many cases they may have several process owners reporting to them directly or indirectly.

Select individuals who are ideally suited to the role, and push responsibility for process ownership to the lowest practical level within the organization. As mentioned earlier, this usually makes selection based on the existing organization chart somewhat problematic.

Organizations have successfully implemented process ownership systems without tying ownership to additional compensation. Ownership may be assigned as part of normal duties to positions at supervisory level and above. This increases flexibility for staff rotation and removes the perceived 'status' often associated with increased pay.

A process owner is required for each key process. Ownership should be limited to one, or at most two, key processes to ensure each gets enough attention. We do not recommend assigning process owners to sub-processes since this increases complexity. It is appropriate to designate alternates to support professional development, transition, and decision-making when the process owner is unavailable.

Control of Resources and Authority

Process owners should control the major resources required to implement the process. This provides the authority to make changes to the process and re-allocate resources as required. This helps ensure that the process owner has the greatest stake in ensuring the process works well, and will 'feel the pain' when it does not.

Mobilizing Constellations

Process owners will participate in, and in many cases lead outcome focused process groupings or 'mobilizing constellations'. This is one reason why it is important to select process owners for their leadership capacity or potential. Their experience with their process and its integration into the larger system will make them more adept at developing strategies that benefit the organization. Similarly, this broader experience better positions them to contribute to the work of corporate offices or external organizations that set standards or focus on enhancing industry-wide performance.

Risk Management

One of the key activities listed in Table 13-1 relates to the ability to identify and mitigate risks related to context changes. In its simplest form, when proposing a change to the assigned process, the owner must be able to assess the organizational impact of the change. Conversely, changes to the organization, its strategy, or governing regulations are but a few of the elements that may impact a process. The process owner must be able to foresee and mitigate potential risks such as personnel changes, equipment issues, technology changes, common mode failure scenarios, and peak effort requirements. This is one reason why conceptual thinking is included as an element of the propensity profile in Figure 13-1.

In a similar vein, a contingency response during adverse conditions requires the process owner to exhibit decisive leadership, responsiveness to change, and the ability to communicate clarity as identified in Figure 13-1.

Position Description

A generic position description consisting of the mandate, roles, responsibilities, accountabilities, and authorities of a process owner should be developed. As indicated above, the position description should include key activities and propensities. For some key processes there is value in including information specific to that process.

Ensure that the position description is consistent with the Organization Design Basis document discussed in Chapter 9, or adjust either document as necessary. At this stage, the team should also be able to identify where the position description fits within the management system process structure.

Timing of Selection

Although process owners will not be fully engaged until the development of their process begins, it is worthwhile selecting all process owners near the start of the project. This allows them to participate in the planning, orientation, training, validation sessions, and special meetings to review strategy and make key decisions.

The list of designated process owners and their alternates should be formally maintained within a process. This can be within the 'Manage process integration' process since this process often initiates actions for process owners, or it may be contained within a process related to human resources. Once again, a well-defined top level model will make the decision on placement easier. The list of owners should be kept up to date and be readily available online.

Training Process Owners

The Project Team will have to develop orientation and training for process owners related to their roles and process management. This is often best done in a series of short (2-3 hour) modules that can be delivered at appropriate times during the project.

DEVELOPING A ROADMAP

Once management has identified the process owners, the Project Team can refine its project plan by working with the process owners and the Excellence Team to identify which processes should be mapped first. This involves four basic steps:

1. Identifying the first processes on which to pilot and refine the methodology
2. Prioritizing the remaining processes
3. Estimating realistic timelines
4. Developing a logic structure.

Identifying Pilot Processes

The objective of a pilot project is to work out bugs in the methodology or its implementation. Although the team might be tempted to tackle a 'broken' process to demonstrate what is sometimes called a 'quick win', the team should weigh the considerable risk of getting bogged down in a complex or problematic process. So-called 'low hanging fruit' may also be tempting, but is only useful if it helps the team improve processes it will itself need to use. Nor is it strategically wise to pick a process that is already working well, since the gains to the organization are not as evident, and the owners of the process may not engage or change enthusiastically.

A valuable place to start is with processes needed to support the overall project. These are typically related to the team's primary process '*Managing system integration*' and processes involving the document hierarchy or framework, namely development of various document types, and their review, approval, publication, and revision. If these processes are not efficient, the project will quickly stumble.

Identify other candidates that will help the team perform their role in a manner consistent with the integrated management system they have been tasked to develop. One area to consider is project management. Since the Project Team is, after all, managing a project, it should follow the methodology used within the organization for improvement projects. If that process is weak, fixing it early has direct benefits to the team and the organization.

The pilot(s) should involve testing and refining the entire methodology, including implementation at the procedural level. Although some value is gained in developing internal processes for the project team itself, an early start on a "real" organizational process is important. Insufficient attention to running a successful pilot will impede future process development and potentially damage credibility and support.

Prioritizing the Remaining Processes

A relatively simple way of prioritizing the remaining processes is for the Project Team to develop a simple rating worksheet so that all managers, supervisors, and process owners can individually prioritize all key processes based on their experience and understanding of the process. For example, 1 would indicate the highest priority for improvement and 10 the lowest priority. This will force scoring over a broader range than high, medium, and low. A category for 'no opinion' may be included, with instructions to use it only if the individual has no direct or indirect interaction or knowledge of the process.

The Project Team tabulates the results, analysing any differences in scores between levels of the organization, and presents the information for discussion to the entire group if possible, or at minimum to an expanded session of the Excellence Team. The team should consider whether there is a preponderance of core, support, or executive processes listed as high priority. If an important executive process such as *"Direct and manage the organization"* is listed late in the development, the rationale for this decision should be discussed.

After any adjustments agreed in the meeting, this prioritization list is used as the initial basis of the roadmap.

Estimating Realistic Timelines

Realism means not underestimating the work involved. A project covering the entire management system may take 2-4 years to complete depending on the resources applied. Mapping a key process at tier 2 (i.e., excluding supporting procedures) may take 3-4 weeks based on part-time participation of a team of subject matter experts from the line organization. Each new document or major revision may take 4-person weeks of technical writer time, and will involve interaction time with subject matter experts.

To estimate the work, the Project Team members should meet with process owners and department managers to identify and review the status of every document that should be owned by that process. Such detailed work may seem tedious but is essential for determining the scale of the project. It will not seem tedious to those assembling the information if they are selected for their propensity for detail and interest in establishing order.

For ease of updating, information can be maintained in a tabular spreadsheet form similar to Table 13-1, or captured in a visual form such as listing the documents on a document hierarchy diagram for each process. Many variations of this table are possible. Other fields may be included as desired, such as estimated person-weeks for technical writers and specialist subject matter experts, facilitator name, technical writer name, etc. One should not include information (e.g., schedule dates) that will be kept in another form. In many organizations, planning support and software can be used to good advantage.

Completing the table requires the process owner and facilitator to make a number of initial judgments, but even such tasks as choosing titles and combining documents will help socialize process-based thinking. Process owners need to understand that these initial efforts will be refined with time.

In Table 13-1 the work required may involve a minor or major revision of an existing document, creating a new document, combining one document with another, making a document obsolete, splitting content with another process, or transferring the document to another process for dispositioning. The transfers in Table 13-1 are shown for illustration but would not be maintained on this process owner's table. In some cases such as manuals which contain many procedures that are frequently applied, the manual may be recorded, but only those procedures requiring individual effort should be listed. For large initiatives such as revision of multiple maintenance or operating procedures, a sub-project should be established and resourced.

Table 13-1: Sample document table for a single process

Process Name: Manage Process Integration					
Process Owner: Jane Doe					
Existing Identifier	Existing Title	New Identifier	New Title	Work required	Current Status
Tier 2					
-	-	PI-2	Manage process integration	New	In progress
Tier 3					
3780-1	Documenting processes	PI-3-1	Developing and modifying processes	Major revision	Scheduled
3780-3	Revising processes			Combine with above	Scheduled
3780-4	Managing regulatory requirements			Transfer to regulatory process	Done
3780-6	Process assessment			Transfer to assessment process	Done
Tier 4					
37801-1	Tracking regulatory requirements	PI-4-1	Assigning and tracking mandatory process requirements	Minor revision	Scheduled
37801-2	Process measures		Developing, monitoring and reporting on mobilizing metrics	Transfer to direct and manage process	Done

Assembling the Roadmap

When all processes have been assessed, an initial roadmap and schedule may be prepared based on the agreed priorities. Adjustments are usually required due to resource loading considerations (e.g., not scheduling parallel mapping that will require a group to provide multiple resources). This initial roadmap is not a rigorous schedule to be driven by project management, but an attempt to identify and order the sequence of events. It is a dynamic vehicle that is important to keep as realistic as possible as new knowledge becomes available.

A number of elements should be included in the plan for each process:

- Development time for Tier 2, 3, and 4 documents (i.e., a timeline for each tier dependent on the number of documents and projected development team meetings)
- Validation events and duration
- Orientation and training events and duration
- 'Go-live' or implementation date when formal turn-over from the Project Team to the process owner occurs (this may be a staged turnover and implementation)
- A 'burn-in' or enculturation interval over which any discovery issues are worked out and the process builds maturity (typically 6 months)
- A scheduled assessment to evaluate the effectiveness and efficiency of the process (after the allotted 'burn-in' period).

Much of the above will involve parallel activities. It is wise to do the pilot process in the absence of competing work, and then to schedule two processes in parallel assuming two facilitators and two technical writers are available. The roadmap schedule can be presented as a simple Gantt chart or other tool used within the organization for project management; however, a schedule alone is not sufficient to explain the strategy, assumptions, and contingencies covered in the roadmap.

SUMMARY OF OUTPUTS

The following box summarizes the tasks that should be accomplished in this phase of the project.

> ***Key Outputs from this Chapter on Selecting Process Owners and Developing a Roadmap***
>
> The outputs related to the tasks from this phase of the project are:
>
> - Definition of the generic 'position description' for process owners, with information on specific processes where necessary
> - Identification of individual process owners for each of the key processes
> - Development of orientation and training modules for process owners
> - Identification of processes for pilot development
> - Proposed prioritization for developing all processes
> - Document disposition lists for all processes
> - Road-map for developing all processes in the management system.

Chapter 14

Develop Processes, Confirm Alignment, and Establish Mobilizing Metrics

IN THIS CHAPTER

In accordance with Steps 9, 10, and 11 of the flowchart in Figure 7-1, this chapter describes how to work with a team to develop an individual process. The topics include:

- Establishing a standardized approach
- Facilitator preparations
- Selecting the process-specific development team
- Developing the detailed process
- Sample contents for a Tier 2 document for a key process
- Developing mobilizing metrics.

ESTABLISHING A STANDARDIZED APPROACH

Steps in a standardized approach for mapping a specific process are shown in Figure 14-1 which represents the detailed tasks connected with activity box 4 "Develop or modify the process" in Figure 10-1. We will assume that the team will develop a key process and its associated document at Tier 2. The approach is similar at lower tiers, although some of the specifics may not be needed for simpler processes.

To illustrate the advantages of writing lean documents, we will use an information mapping approach for each step associated with the flowchart, and follow this with explanatory text. Steps are numbered A.B where A is the block on the process map in Figure 14-1 and B is the sub-step associated with that block. The actual process document would not contain the explanatory text, although such information could be included in training material.

There are many ways in which one can construct step-action tables and this chapter illustrates only one of those ways. Some organizations, for example, reproduce the activity block from the process map in the margin beside the details associated with the block.

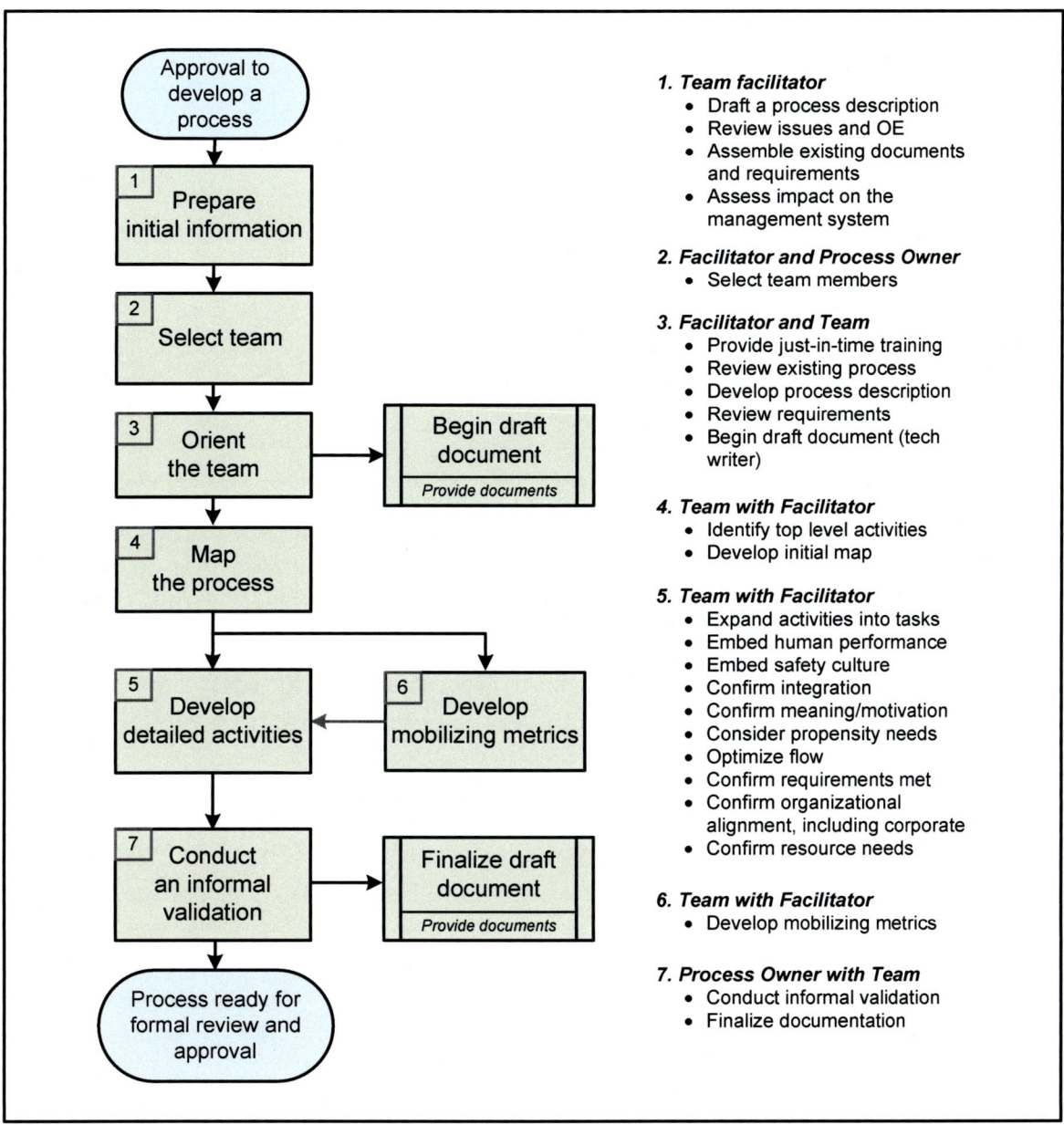

Figure 14-1: Approach for mapping and documenting a process

STEPS IN DEVLOPING AND DOCUMENTING A PROCESS

Step	Action
1. Prepare the initial information	
Team Facilitator	
1.1	Gather initial information on the process: • Draft the process description (Appendix G) • Assemble existing process documents • Assemble existing requirements • Review issues and operating experience • Assess impact on the management system.

In Step 1 it is not necessary for the facilitator to become an expert in the process. In fact, this is often a mistake since even a well-intentioned facilitator may inadvertently influence the outcome based on his or her understanding of how the process should work. The purpose of preparation is for the facilitator to gain enough familiarity with the process to help prevent the team from going too far off course, jumping process boundaries, or getting stuck on a particular issue or detail.

Assessing the impact on the management system should be done with input from the Process Owner of the management system. The issue is whether aspects of this process should be moved to another process, or conversely, that elements of another process be brought into this one.

Step	Action
2. Select the Team	
Team Facilitator and Process Owner	

2.1	Select team members:
	• From the Project Team
	   – Process facilitator
	   – Organizational development liaison
	   – Technical writer
	• From the process
	   – Process owner
	   – Subject matter experts familiar with the requirements, purpose, and

	functioning of the existing process
	- Representative performer(s) of the process
	• Others
	  • Representative customer(s) or user(s) of the process
	  • Major stakeholders such as representatives from key interfacing processes
	  • Requirements specialist(s) from regulatory affairs or quality assurance (part time)

Team members should be selected not simply for their expertise, but their demonstrated commitment to performance improvement, willingness to entertain new ideas, and willingness to solicit input from people outside the team. As mentioned elsewhere in this document, an optimum team size is from 7-9 people, excluding the Project Team representatives.

Step	Action
3. Orient the Team	
Team Facilitator with Team	
3.1	Schedule team meetings and facilities.
3.2	Introduce the team members, task and approach: • Identify role of project team, facilitator, and technical writer • Identify role of team members • Develop team conduct or 'ground rules' with the team to establish a climate of shared space and appreciative inquiry • Establish an issues list or "parking lot" maintained by the technical writer.
3.3	Explore the meaning system associated with this process from the perspective of: • What is the <u>intent</u> of this process? • What are the <u>essential outcomes</u> of this process? • How do performers and recipients of the process think and feel about the process now? • What do you want performers and recipients to think and feel about the process in future? • What are some of the essential attributes of this process that will ensure it works well? • How does this process contribute to our desired organizational culture? • What principles should govern this process? • What propensities are needed to run this process effectively?

		• What learned competencies are needed to run this process well?
	3.4	Explore team perspectives on the current state versus future state to identify gaps for potential resolution by the new or modified process. Identify aspects of the current process that function well.
	Technical Writer	
	3.5	Begin development of the document in accordance with the standardized template. This is an on-going activity throughout the team sessions.
	Team Facilitator with Team	
	3.6	Define the <u>purpose</u> and <u>scope</u> statements for the process. *Note:* This and subsequent steps are intended to validate any draft information gathered while developing the Process Description Worksheet in Appendix G.
	3.7	Develop a vivid description of the user-performer-organization's experience when the process is working well.
	3.8	Identify key: • inputs and suppliers • outputs and customers/receivers • performers • stakeholders • interfaces with other processes or organizations.
	3.9	Identify: • mandatory requirements specific to this process (regulations, licences, codes, standards, local and corporate policies) • other constraints or limitations imposed by stakeholders or organizational context, if any. *Note:* Use the team to extract this information. Invite quality or regulatory experts to supplement team understanding and knowledge as needed.

	3.10	Deliver just-in-time training on process mapping:
		
		• Identify basic terms, symbols, and conventions (Chapter 11)
		• Present examples relevant to the management system work
		• Have the team develop a sample process map that includes culture/meaning and propensity dimensions. Examples:
		    – choosing a place to live
		    – buying a house.

The objective of Step 3 is to get the team to agree on the basic dimensions of the process. It is counter-productive to "word-smith" at this early stage since the team will revisit each element as work progresses. Using a projection system to enable the team to see the words captured by the technical writer is helpful, although the technical writer or facilitator should only project the content when he or she feels the team needs to see whether their input has been captured sufficiently well. Keeping the screen visible all the time can turn the sessions into a group writing exercise, which is not desirable. At the beginning of each session the technical writer can review any sections that require clarification. The team will quickly gain confidence in the technical writer's ability to capture information, and can devote their attention to developing the process rather than writing and editing.

At this stage the current state versus future state and gap analysis discussion is intended to align team members on the issues, rather than go into detail on how to fix them. The issue of whether the proposed process will resolve issues (if any) associated with the current process may require the team to undertake some subsequent field investigation of the current process. People do things for a reason, and it is important for the team to understand what works well in the existing process as well as the causes of work-arounds and performance issues. Useful techniques for exploring what actually happens in an existing process will be discussed in a later chapter on continual improvement. The team should not hesitate to explore the reality of what is going on at the workface rather than rely only on their impressions and assumptions.

An important requisite for successful teams is to establish an atmosphere of appreciative inquiry where individuals do not feel a need to construct arguments, defend positions, or criticize others or their input.

Step	Action
4. Map the process	
Team Facilitator with Team	
4.1	Identify the initiator and terminator for the process to establish the process boundaries.

	4.2	Identify the top level activities associated with the process, independent of order.
	4.5	Consider at a broad level whether activities need to be added to cover: • Philosophy, culture, climate, or context • Organizational alignment • Risk management • Safety implications • Propensity implications.
	4.3	Combine similar activities until a maximum of 12 activities have been identified.
	4.4	Order or sequence the activities to develop an initial map. Consider: • interfaces with other processes that are important enough to show • alignment with other organizational structures and processes (e.g., corporate) • flow optimization.

The intent of Step 4 is to develop a map of the key activities showing the order of activities and essential interfaces with other processes. Since further work on the details of each activity will likely influence the flow, the team should avoid trying to get it perfect at this stage. The team will work over multiple days and it is inevitable that new ideas will surface. At the beginning of each session, the facilitator should review the work of the previous session and solicit any changes that the group would like to make before proceeding to the next activity.

Step		Action
5. Develop detailed activities		
Team Facilitator with Team		
	5.1	For each key activity, identify the tasks required to complete the activity. Consider: • Whether the activity is consistent with and promotes intended meaning, motivation, climate and culture • Whether each task adds value • Optimizing sequence of tasks • Optimizing personal flow [see Chapter 2] • Critical approvals – legal, local, and corporate authorities • Critical activities and consequences of improper performance • Safety implications (danger, caution, or warning notes) • Human performance and error reduction tools [Appendix L] • Control of risks and inadvertent consequences

		- Contingency actions - Quality requirements - Propensity and training qualification implications - Verification requirements - Validation requirements - Oversight requirements - Opportunities to standardize - Environmental impact controls - Opportunities for grading.
	5.2	Adjust the process map if required.
	5.3	Confirm the following elements: - Does the process meet all legal, management, corporate, and other stakeholder requirements? - Does the process align with organizational plans, goals, and objectives? - Are the resource requirements realistic? (e.g., infrastructure, human resources and structure, training, ongoing operational requirements) - Is it aligned with the organizational design basis? - Is it aligned with the management manual? - Are there quality program implications? - Does it resolve known issues with the current process?
	5.4	Identify the records that must be retained and their retention time.

	5.5	Identify responsibilities, accountabilities and authorities by position, workgroup, or process role:
		
		- Identify who should perform each activity (primary role)
		- Identify oversight roles
		- Define decision-making authorities
		  - Review and revise existing authority rosters as required
		- Review, revise or create position descriptions as needed
		  - Consider propensity implications
		  - Consider training and certification implications.

Step 5 describes the details of the specific tasks that need to be accomplished to achieve the objectives of the process. This helps determine whether the order in the process map needs to be adjusted. Although it is generally easy to identify the specific tasks, optimizing the sequence and ensuring compatibility with the preferences and limitations of the performers is an important consideration.

Responsibilities are identified as one of the last steps in the process evolution. This helps ensure that organizational biases are not built into the process at the outset.

Step	Action
6. Develop mobilizing metrics	
Team Facilitator with Team	
6.1	Review each activity to identify potential performance indicators or measures that mobilize collective effort through alignment with human motivators and the desired organizational culture. Consider types: • Input, in-process, and output measures • Proactive measures • Quantitative and non-quantitative measures Consider rationale and value: • Who needs and cares about the measure • Value-added benefit of tracking the measure • Whether the measure is related to the purpose of the process • Motivational aspects of the indicator, i.e., does it promote the desired behavior and measure success rather than failure • Effort required to track the measure.
6.2	Consider the relationship to measures already monitored by the organization to determine where the measure fits in the overall monitoring system.
6.3	Select a small number of essential measures to include as part of the organization's top level monitoring program.

Selecting the right performance measures or indicators is an art as much as a science. Appendix M provides information on selecting measures. Organizations can easily end up tracking an abundance of measures that provide marginal value. Spending time to identify the minimum set is worth the effort. One of the most important considerations is to select measures that motivate rather than punish those associated with the measure. It is preferable to think in terms of mobilizing or motivating measures rather than 'performance' measures. For this reason we use the term mobilizing metrics in this manual.

Organizations usually establish a central process for monitoring indicators somewhere within the 'Direct and manage' process, hence it is not generally wise to build indicators directly into individual process documents because of the frequency of change. This means that indicators for the entire organization can be rationalized and modified within a single process. This does not mean that Process Owners lose accountability for monitoring the indicators.

7. Conduct an informal validation	
Process Owner with Team	
7.1	Where warranted by the complexity or extent of the change, assemble a knowledgeable group of key stakeholders who have not participated in the development. This should include: • Relevant management and supervision • Customers, users, and performers • Representatives of interfacing processes • Other key stakeholders.
Process Owner	
7.2	Present the essentials of the process, including purpose of the process, map, and key elements. Solicit feedback from the participants. Team members should support the presentation as needed, and record issues.

IF the validation…	THEN…
• identifies significant errors or omissions • identifies a need for modifying the process to accommodate interfaces • presents questions that require further investigation	• reassemble the team to resolve outstanding issues
is successful	finalize the documentation and proceed to orientation and training

Technical Writer with Process Owner	
7.3	Finalize the document in accordance with the process for reviewing and publishing internal documents.

Facilitator and Team	
7.4	Conduct a debrief with the team to capture lessons learned.

The purpose of the informal validation meeting is to obtain general organizational agreement that the proposed process will accomplish its intended objectives and that no significant issues will impede its implementation as designed. The validation meeting is led by the Process Owner to ensure the Project Team is not perceived as the owner. It is obvious that the Process Owner has to be fully conversant with the new or revised process, and this can only occur if the owner has participated in critical decisions as the process development team proceeded with its work.

SUMMARY OF OUTPUTS

The following box summarizes the tasks that should be accomplished in this phase of the project. This step is repeated for every process under development.

Key Outputs from this Chapter on Develop Processes, Confirm Alignment and Establish Mobilizing Metrics

The outputs related to the tasks from this phase of the project are:

- Documented process, including map and detailed activities/tasks.
- Mobilizing metrics related to the process
- Validation to confirm organizational support for the intended process.

Chapter 15

Conduct Pilots, Train and Implement

IN THIS CHAPTER

In accordance with Step 12 of the flowchart in Figure 7-1, this chapter describes how to conduct pilots, training and implementation activities. The topics include:

- Determining the need for and scope of pilots
- What to look for during pilots
- Finalizing implementation planning
- Conducting training
- Implementing the process.

CRITERIA FOR PILOTS

A pilot is simply a test run to confirm that key elements of the intended change work in practice. Criteria for determining whether a pilot is necessary include:

- The degree of change in relation to existing practices, especially if the change is novel or complex
- Consistency with the intended culture and methods of operating
- Potential consequences if the change is incorrectly conceived or executed
- Familiarity of the target group with the existing process, their depth of knowledge and ability/receptivity to absorb the change.

TYPES OF PILOT

The pilot may be graded according to need, and various elements may be tested using combinations of the following methods. In each case the people selected for the pilot should not have been involved in the development of the process or procedure.

- Table top – individuals who represent different users, performers, or customers do a round-table full read through the procedure or process.

- Walk through – similar to the above except that the actual activities are performed with as much realism as practical.
- Limited pilot – this involves beta-testing specific portions of the change, typically those considered to represent the biggest challenge for participants.
- Full scope – a complete test in the actual operating situation. The test may involve a selected department or group prior to being rolled out to a larger audience.

Planning for a pilot requires careful selection of aspects that are important to confirm prior to full implementation. Pre-training required, duration of the test, and support requirements must also be considered. Determine the approach to observing, gathering data, and reporting findings from the pilot.

WHAT TO LOOK FOR

Some aspects to look for during the pilot include:

- Gaps, redundancies, and unintended consequences
- Effectiveness of exchanges and transfers at organizational interfaces
- Response of participants in terms of satisfaction and ease of use
- Human factors aspects of the process-performer interaction
- Confidence level that the desired outcomes are achieved related to the process and the desired human system dynamics (cultural, organizational, relational, and value to internal or external customers)
- Utility of proposed mobilizing metrics
- Likelihood of satisfactory performance in real-life situations with multiple activities and diversions
- Agreement of the process owner to accept accountability for their role.

Although one is looking for efficiency and effectiveness, one needs to observe the impact on participants and the 'cost' of performance. By their nature, pilots are simulations with the benefit of recent familiarity, few distractions, and progress at a measured pace. A key question is how well this will translate into the typical work environment with its distractions and competing priorities.

Debrief for any changes required prior to full implementation. Changes that affect safety or impede the ability to perform as intended must be made prior to full implementation. It is unlikely that a pilot will uncover all issues, hence it is not usually necessary to fix every minor issue identified since this can prove counterproductive. One can be certain that more issues will be found on full implementation.

IMPLEMENTATION PLANNING

In Chapter 13 we described the development of a roadmap for the entire project. Confirm that the project plan associated with the roadmap is still valid and that the process is ready for implementation. The project plan will include the intended go-live date and assessment milestones.

For each process, finalize the training plan and materials including type of training (e.g., orientation, formal training, detailed skill training). Identify the list of participants who should include managers, supervisors, task performers, users, customers and any other key inter-dependent participants. Confirm that the Excellence Team and process owner agree to proceed with implementation of each process. Deliver training and implement the process.

Monitoring During Implementation

During implementation, the following are good practices:

- The process owner should take the lead role. The Project Team should only monitor implementation and provide backup support when required.
- Fix safety issues and other serious problems promptly. Defer minor changes to the end of the implementation phase.
- Managers and supervisors should conduct direct observations to confirm that implementation is proceeding effectively and that any barriers or issues are resolved.
- Conduct periodic review meetings with participants including interfacing processes to resolve issues and identify improvements. Consider using engagement tools such as focus groups, Appreciative Inquiry, or Open Space Technology to maximize constructive participation.
- Provide progress reports to the Excellence Team who are responsible for monitoring success of the overall system.
- Allow sufficient burn in time to identify issues or problems including interfaces and human dynamics issues.
- As identified in the project plan, conduct self-assessments and a formal audit 4-6 months following implementation.

- Capture lessons learned to improve the implementation of upcoming processes.

Since only a few processes are implemented in parallel, the Excellence Team must ensure that as new processes are implemented, the entire system continues to function smoothly. Adjustments will normally be required as more processes are brought online. The process of continual improvement of the management system begins before the entire project is completed. This is discussed in Chapter 16.

PROJECT DEVOLUTION AND CLOSEOUT

Once the formal management system project is complete and all processes are implemented and under the direction of their process owners, the project may be formally closed. The following actions should be undertaken during close-out:

- The project team should prepare a close-out report for the Excellence Team with specific emphasis on lessons learned, items that require ongoing monitoring, areas that should be targeted for priority improvement with respect to integration of the system, and opportunities that should be explored to enhance the management system, including development needs for process owners.
- Management should formally declare the end of the project. Communication should include lessons learned during the journey, where we are now, and what everyone needs to do to maintain the integrity of the management system and help improve it.

Typically, the Project Team members will be reassigned to their originating work group. The Excellence Team may be dissolved with some members distributed among mobilizing constellations as appropriate. Some organizations may choose to keep the Excellence Team until there is confidence that the management system is functionally mature.

Summary of Outputs

This box summarizes the tasks that should be accomplished in this phase of the project.

Key Outputs from this Chapter on Conduct Pilots, Train and Implement

---

The outputs related to the tasks from this phase of the project are:

- Pilots for each significant process as required.
- Implementation plan for each process aligned with the overall implementation plan.
- Process implementation.
- Compilation of lessons learned.

Chapter 16

Monitor, Assess, and Improve/Innovate

IN THIS CHAPTER

In accordance with Step 13 of the flowchart in Figure 7-1, this chapter describes how to monitor, adjust and improve the management system once it has been implemented. This is a never-ending process of evolving the organization from where it is currently to where it wants to go. In order to be successful, the elements related to continual improvement should be designed as an integral part of the management system processes, particularly in the areas of processes related to direct and manage, manage the human system, performance assessment, performance improvement, and information management. The improvement process works most effectively in environments that foster shared space and healthy human dynamics.

The topics include:

- Types of monitoring
- Types of assessment
- Tracking systems
- Key recipients of data for decision-making
- Key insights into improvement
- Evolution of PDCA by stage of organizational evolution
- Strategies for improvement.

MONITORING, ASSESSING AND TRACKING ISSUES

The following sections discuss monitoring, assessing and tracking systems that may be used in high reliability organizations. Such methods are based on a defense-in-depth approach that monitors performance across all six systems in Figure 1-1 to proactively identify areas that may signal a need to improve or modify performance to ensure organizational effectiveness and sustainability.

Types of Monitoring

- Surveillance – from a quality assurance perspective, this involves such activities as inspections or direct observations of tasks undertaken for a specific purpose. These activities may be random or planned.
- Field observations – involve routine observations of work activities, work environment and housekeeping by managers, supervisors, process owners, peers or program specialists (e.g., safety inspections)
- Review and feedback – involves information gathering on the general conduct of work from performers, customers, and interfacing parties
- Operating experience – involves learning lessons from internal and external incidents, events and good practices
- Environmental scanning – proactively obtaining information about what is going on outside the organization technologically, economically, competitively, politically, etc.
- Mobilizing metrics and targets – these are pre-established indicators and measures used to determine whether performance is on track.

Types of Assessment

- Self-assessment – a structured, objective process whereby individuals and groups, including management, evaluate the effectiveness of their own performance against predetermined standards and expectations.
- Internal audits and assessments – involve systematic and independent examination to determine whether activities and related results comply with standards, planned arrangements and are effective at meeting objectives.
- External audits and assessments – involve systematic examination by third parties to determine whether activities and related results comply with stated internal and relevant industry expectations and requirements.
- Root cause investigations – involve a formal examination of a specific undesirable occurrence. The objective is to examine the chain of events to find the causes where an intervention could reasonably have occurred to prevent the undesirable occurrence. Modern methods include analysis of culture and management influences. Depending on the severity of the event, organizations may grade analysis from

apparent or proximate cause to formal investigations conducted by trained people.
- Program reviews – a senior-level examination of organizational performance in a broad area usually involving cross-boundary interactions. Such reviews are often periodic, for example, an annual review of the effectiveness of the management system. They involve a review of metrics, outcomes, assessment findings, and opportunities.
- Benchmarking – a systematic comparison of an organization's processes and outcomes with industry best practices or top performing organizations in the same or comparable field. Benchmarking often includes focused visits to high performing organizations. Findings are often adapted to improve performance in the initiating organization. Benchmarking should be considered a stimulus for innovation rather than merely a method of emulating best practices. For this reason benchmarking teams should include not only people familiar with the process being benchmarked, but also include some members with the propensity for innovation.
- Safety culture assessments – these focus on the underlying beliefs and assumptions within an organization that drive accepted practices and behaviours which may contribute to or negatively affect safety performance. They are normally conducted by teams which include specialists in behavioural, organizational and social sciences.
- Organizational assessments – these focus on the alignment between structure, functionality and task; the distribution and diversity of propensities to achieve the required functionalities; and the effectiveness of team and unitive leadership at optimizing organizational intelligence to achieve desired outcomes and advance strategically
- Regulatory inspections and audits – involve verification by a regulatory body that the organization's activities are conducted in accordance with regulatory requirements
- Oversight – involves several dimensions
    - Formal programs similar to those listed above that systematically monitor organizational performance across all six systems in Figure 1-1 and feed into management decision making

- Management's on-going attentiveness to what is happening real-time inside and outside the organization and how it might impact current and future performance. This can only be effectively performed if management establishes strong personal relationships and communications vertically and horizontally across the organization, and consciously promotes a culture whereby individuals willingly approach management on potential concerns or issues. It also requires effective communication with relevant external organizations including industry peers and regulators.
- Roles and responsibilities for oversight strategies may be established at several levels in the organization
    - *Senior management*
    - *Mobilizing constellation*
    - *Process owner*
    - *Management and supervision.*

Tracking systems

Monitoring and assessment processes typically result in vast amounts of information, much of which is related to the need for change or improvement. Many organizations establish 'corrective action programs' to track issues from identification to closure. Generally, prioritization systems are used to distinguish important safety or economic issues from less significant enhancements to organizational performance. High reliability organizations also often trend precursors or low level events such as human performance errors that may not individually be significant but can indicate systemic weaknesses. In many cases, anyone at any level in the organization can enter an issue into a formal tracking system.

Making sense of these large amounts of data can be problematic. Regardless of the criteria for reporting, the criteria for elevating issues, or the methods used to decide the resolution strategy, it is essential to have a single integrated information system for managing such issues. In many organizations, the role of managing this system falls to a performance improvement function. Their role is to filter and synthesize the large amounts of data from across the organization into meaningful information for key recipients who can take action on the related issue.

Since data is coming in constantly, both from internal and external sources e.g., external operating experience, many organizations establish an initial screening team to do an initial prioritization and assignment of the issue. There are some pitfalls related to this. Screening teams often struggle with understanding the true significance of a particular item which is why they want to tag it to a responsible individual as quickly as possible. There is a natural tendency for every issue that is raised to be seen as needing action. This leaves the receiving group with the task of prioritizing the issue with other work, and in many cases the associated action either displaces other work, is written off in the most expeditious manner, is deflected to another work group or remains in backlog.

It is the role of the performance improvement group to understand how the organization works so they can act as an intelligent filter to determine whether the issue requires prompt action or should be assigned to trending. They also ensure that the action is tagged to the person or group who can do something about it. Typically, the most effective method is to tag issues to the relevant process owner. When necessary, the process owner can take issues of broader significance/scope to the relevant mobilizing constellation or senior management.

Key Recipients of Data Required for Decision-making

We will discuss the key recipients in the order in which issues would normally be escalated from process owner, to mobilizing constellation to the management team.

The process owner is accountable for the effectiveness of the assigned process. The following lists information inputs for a process owner.

- Direct observation, informal review and feedback from line supervision, users, customers, and related processes regarding:
    - Process efficiency and effectiveness
    - Process requirements
    - Boundary issues
    - Human system impact
    - Performer satisfaction

- Client satisfaction
- Outcome accomplishment
* Process metrics
* Process and interface focused self-assessments
* Audit and assessment results
* Operating experience – internal and external.

Mobilizing constellations are focused on key outcome areas, are accountable for integration, performance monitoring and decisions related to improvement actions. They make decisions on resource allocations and priorities related to achievement of their collective outcomes. The following lists information inputs for a mobilizing constellation.

* Input from individual process owners on issues relevant to the mobilizing constellation
* Mobilizing metrics related to common outcomes (multi-process)
* Results of self-assessments of member processes
* Filtered audit and assessment issues including regulatory issues
* Key operating experience
* Environmental scanning.

The management team is responsible for overall organizational effectiveness and integration. The following lists information inputs for the senior management team. These issues are all at the organizational level.

* Direct observation, informal review and feedback from across the organization and externally with a particular focus on:
  - Systemic integration
  - Management system performance
  - Process and structure boundary issues
  - Human system health
  - Outcome accomplishment
* Escalated issues from the mobilizing constellations
* Input from oversight committees
* Benchmarking results
* Organizational metrics
* Key filtered audit and assessment issues including regulatory, peer reviews and organizational/management system assessments

- Environmental scanning to identify industry and regulatory trends.

KEY INSIGHTS INTO IMPROVEMENT

Introduction to Continual Improvement and Change

The term continual improvement is in common usage world-wide but is often understood in a limited context such as the cyclical application of plan-do-check-act.

Improvement is always about change. Change can be either reactive or proactive. There are many dimensions to improvement because there are so many different degrees of change [Snowden 2015]. Change involves adaptability; the capacity to react to emergent or disruptive circumstances, and a focus on ensuring long term sustainability. Improvement may require incremental change, transformative change, anticipatory change or resilience in the face of disruptive change.

- Incremental Change is often considered to be equivalent to continual improvement. It applies when you recognize a need to make improvements to or refine an existing situation but don't feel a need to reengineer the process or practices. This is typically in the hands of the line organization. To give an analogy, this would be like moving from a 3-speed to a 10-speed bicycle.
- Transitional Change happens when you recognize the need to implement a different course of action in an area where outcomes are not being realized. This generally involves only part of the management system rather than a wide-scale change. This would likely be handled at the process owner or mobilizing constellation owner. This change might be equivalent to moving from a bicycle to a motorcycle or car.
- Transformational Change is necessary when you recognize that the current way of operating is not sustainable because of significant changes in the internal or external environment. Hence a very different strategy is required. This would involve the mobilizing constellation and senior management. This is akin to moving from an automobile to an airplane.

- Disruptive Change occurs when something totally unexpected happens that has a major influence on the organization. This might be a disruptive technology, a disaster, a financial crisis, or any other thing such as political instability that makes the status quo untenable. This is solely the role of senior management to manage and resolve. Some disruptive changes can be foreseen and mitigated e.g., data disaster recovery plans, fire contingency plans, labour disruption plans.

Since continual improvement is only one form of change, we will use the more general term 'improvement' when discussing strategies for enhancing performance or responding to change.

Evolution of Plan-Do-Check-Act by Stage of Organizational Maturity

In the following we discuss improvement in terms of different stages of organizational evolution and the change strategy they generally adopt.

- Stage 1 - Operating: find and fix
- Stage 2 - Managing: standardized controls
- Stage 3 - Leading: generating ideas through engaging people
- Stage 4 - Uniting and integrating: seeking and creating new opportunities.

These approaches are illustrated in Table 16-1. The leading capital letters and bold text indicate the degree to which each element is emphasized within that stage.

Table 16-1: Approaches to improvement by stage

Operating	Managing	Leading	Uniting and Integrating
React to problems	Resolve problems	Anticipate opportunities	Create new opportunities
Expected to do it	Assign people	Engage people	Inspire people
plan	**Plan**	look ahead	**Envision**
Do	**Do**	create	**Create**
Check	**Check**	Design	**Design**
act	adjust	**Plan**	Plan
		Organize	organize
		Implement	implement
		Monitor	**Oversee**
		Adjust	**Redirect**

All the elements Table 16-1 are strategic in nature. As discussed in the theory section, the ability to initiate, implement or react to these different types of change requires different propensities, and flexibility within the organization to assemble the right talent mix on short notice.

Improvement Strategies by Stage of Organizational Maturity

The fundamental nature of the 'Plan-Do-Check-Act' cycle changes with stage. 'Find-and-fix' approaches common to the application cycle become less effective for complex issues such as management effectiveness.

Many organizations believe that continual improvement consists of 'finding and fixing' problems or implementing the 'Plan-Do-Check-Act' cycle continually to achieve higher performance. This view limits organizations to incremental improvements that are reactive in nature, thereby obscuring emerging issues that require transformative change or may in fact result in disruptive change.

Most organizations perform the 'Plan' and 'Do' parts of the cycle, but evidence suggests that many are less adept at performing the 'Check' and 'Act' steps. Both 'Check' and 'Act' are important parts of the cycle that ensure the quality of implementation and ongoing improvement.

As shown in Figure 16-2, improvement methodologies change across the stages. For example, audits and assessments typical of Stages 1 and 2 work with "knowns", i.e., gaps between current and desired states. They shift into benchmarking, sharing operating experience, and exploring best practices in Stages 3 and 4. The latter stages begin to work with non-linear, complex systems such as culture, or emerging external contextual changes that require more anticipatory and developmental approaches. Stages 3 and 4 make extensive use of engagement techniques such as networking, focus groups, appreciative inquiry, world cafes, meaning-mapping and open space technology to tap into the intelligence of the human system. Successful application of these techniques requires different relational and problem-solving propensities.

Additionally, whatever the choice of tools, the organization needs to be sure that talent exists to apply the tools and that the organization at large will be able to adapt to the changes arising from the analysis. Enculturation is often the most challenging part of the journey.

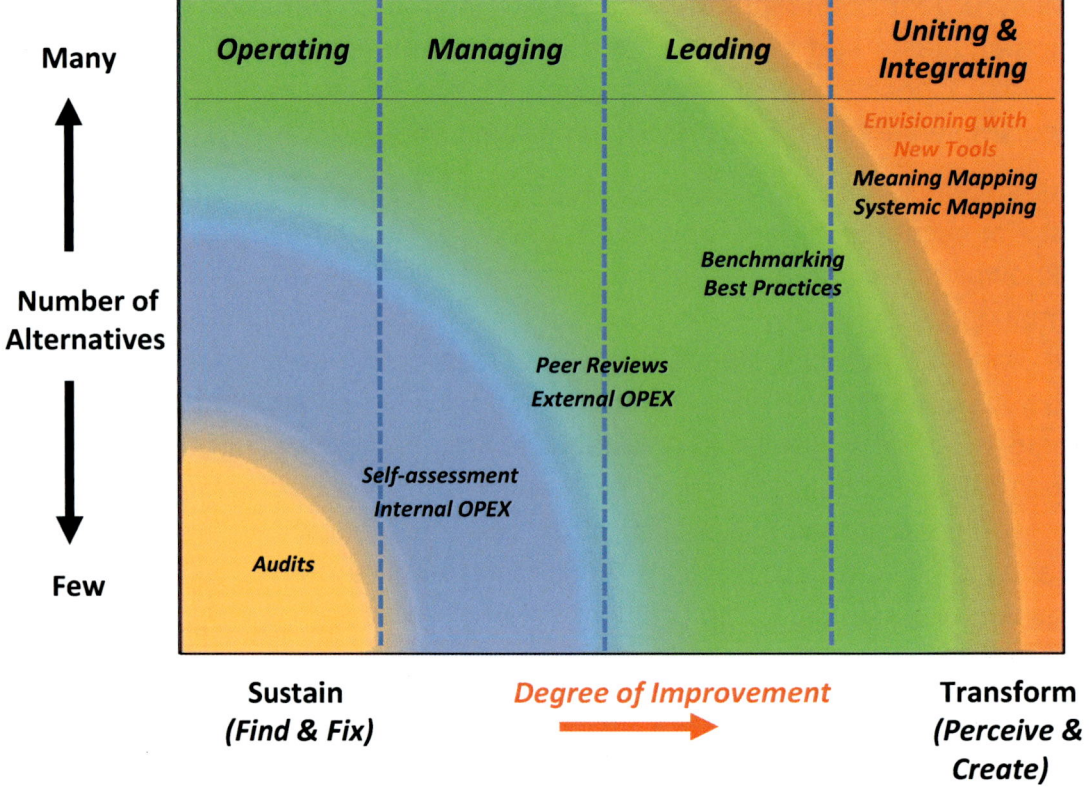

Figure 16-2: Approaches to continual improvement by stage

When determining the need for change and deciding on the appropriate strategy there are a number of questions to ask:

- What are we trying to change?
- Why are we trying to change it?
- Who owns the agenda?
- What is the root nature of the required change?
- What alternatives are available to us?
- Do we have the capacity for change – individual, team, culture?
- Do we have the tools and strategy to enact the change?
- What is the scope and breadth of the change?
- What is the timeline for the change?
- Who will lead the change management initiative?
- What are the cultural, system and human dynamics related to the change?

At this point it is worth remembering that change and improvement processes should already be imbedded in the management system for anticipated and contingency type situations. For example, a Design process requires a rigorous change process, Direct and Manage requires a disciplined lead and manage change process, Operations requires a robust configuration control process, etc. The objective for building in such change processes is to strengthen defense-in-depth and resilience. By the same token, when one of these processes requires changing, it should be done by the disciplined means described in this manual.

Ultimately the management system must be designed to support monitoring, assessment and improvement of all 6 simultaneous organizing systems set out in Figure 1-1. This encompassing approach will take the organization a long way towards adopting a systemic approach to safety and reliability. As we said in the beginning, everything your organization does is achieved through people. Smart organizations don't treat people as a means of production, but as the source of intelligence, conscience, resourcefulness, and connectivity. The formal management system, as well as the means by which it is improved over time must be engaging and supportive of their efforts. It should not restrict people from fixing simple things at the work group or team level. The management system in its broader dimensions is a reflection of how you want your organization to be perceived by people within the organization and the world at large.

SUMMARY OF OUTPUTS

The following box summarizes the tasks that should be accomplished in this phase of the project.

Key Outputs from this Chapter on Monitor, Assess, and Improve/Innovate

The outputs related to the tasks from this phase of the project are:

- Determining appropriate types of monitoring for your organization
- Determining appropriate types of assessment
- Establishing an integrated tracking system
- Identifying data required for key decision-makers (process owners, mobilizing constellations, senior executive teams)
- Expanding the traditional PDCA concept to encompass both reactive and proactive systemic thinking
- Selecting appropriate tools and strategies for improvement.

Chapter 17

Summary

IN THIS CHAPTER

This chapter recaps some of the considerations related to developing an integrated process-based management system. Successful implementation requires a significant shift in the meaning system and culture of an organization, starting at the top. Senior manager engagement and commitment will depend on their understanding of the impact of an IMS on their role, image, and autonomy. IMS development needs to anticipate and work towards enabling effective senior management control from a personal, positional, and systemic perspective, while remaining alert for dysfunctional power dynamics that inhibit performance.

Sponsorship is a two-way street – the senior management team sponsors the IMS project, and the project creates visibility and support for senior management.

In addition to the mechanics of doing the work, the following are some things to keep in mind along the journey.

1. Move beyond traditional QA systems.

    These focus on standards, policies, processes, audits, and corrective action programs, which, while important, are insufficient. Shift organizational thinking toward outcomes, system integration, diverse reasoning, and proactive change.

2. Consider all 6 complex interacting systems

    Each of these systems influence each other:

    - Technical basis or underlying hard or soft technology
    - Human system (meaning, propensities, competencies, behaviours, and power and relational dynamics)
    - Organizational structure, position descriptions, and boundaries
    - People-process interactions, and work execution accountabilities
    - Organizational, human, societal, and ecological outcomes, and
    - Evolving internal and external context.

3. Pick the right Management System Process Owner and Project Lead

   Balance organizational, process systems, and business knowledge with a strong understanding of human systems and relational dynamics.

4. Pick a diverse support team

   Include skills related to strategic thinking, promoting shared meaning, systemic and systematic understanding, sustainability, and willingness to create shared space.

5. Integrate beyond processes into the full interactive system

   Understand the relationships between outcomes, resilience, context, change, and communications.

6. Integrate leadership processes and propensities

   Define leader, manager, supervisor, and team leader propensities relative to each organizational function.

7. Pay attention to the order of development

   First ask what outcomes do we want? Then ask by what human system-process combination can we do this? Then ask what standards do we need to apply? The temptation to begin with the standards often builds unnecessarily complex systems less suited to human system capability.

8. Use tools of engagement

   Get as much input as you can from workers, users, and customers of the process. Use face-to-face encounters such as open space technology, shared space, appreciate inquiry, focus groups, world cafés, and social media.

9. Rethink Plan-Do-Check-Act, Corrective Action Programs, and Continual Improvement Programs

   PDCA can resolve known problems, but isn't sufficient to guarantee improvement. Similarly, Corrective Action programs, even when they include operating experience from other organizations, focus on known problems. True improvement is both preventive and anticipatory. It has to anticipate or create new opportunities. Improvement must be supported by effective change management processes that can accommodate both transformative and disruptive changes that are the true test of resilient organizations.

10. Build your Management System to:
    - Impart organizational meaning
    - Show how everything fits together
    - Be your knowledge management centre
    - Be your vehicle for continual improvement.

As we stated in the early part of this handbook, the journey is long and takes a lot of effort depending on where an organization is on the learning curve. Although perfection will never be achieved, the journey will build a stronger, more resilient organization with engaged, more satisfied participants.

Glossary of Terms

This glossary provides an alphabetical list of definitions of terms used in this publication.

Accountability

Accountability is the obligation to deliver agreed results within an agreed time frame in the assigned area of responsibility.

Activity

In the context of a process, an activity is a series of tasks undertaken by person or group.

Appreciative Inquiry

A facilitation technique that uses collective inquiry into the best of what is and works well, in order to imagine what could be, followed by collective design of an achievable desired future state. It overcomes excessive use of focusing on problems by emphasizing a positive approach that examines what works well and why.

Assessment

An evaluation conducted to determine whether activities and related outcomes are in accordance with defined expectations. An assessment generally focuses more on performance effectiveness rather than details of codes and standards.

Audits

Internal audits involve systematic and independent examination to determine whether activities and related results comply with standards, codes, planned arrangements and are effective at meeting objectives.

External audits involve systematic examination by third parties to determine whether activities and related results comply with standards, codes, and with stated internal and relevant industry expectations and requirements.

Regulatory audits and inspections involve verification by a regulatory body that the organization's activities are conducted in accordance with regulatory requirements

Authority

Authority is the right or power to make independent decisions or to direct resources to accomplish assigned work.

Benchmarking

Systematic comparison of an organization's processes and outcomes with industry best practices or the best companies in the same or comparable field. Benchmarking often includes focused visits to high performing organizations with the aim of adopting and sharing best practices. At its best, benchmarking fosters innovation rather than mere emulation.

Competency

A developed skill that may be enhanced through training or experience.

Environmental Scanning

A form of monitoring that involves proactively obtaining information about what is going on outside the organization technologically, economically, competitively, politically, etc.

Field Observations

A form of monitoring that includes routine observations of work activities, work environment and housekeeping by managers, supervisor, process owners, peers or program specialists (e.g., safety inspections).

Functionality

The capacity to perform a task or fulfill an intended purpose. (Functionality relies on the alignment of organizational structure, management system processes, and human propensities).

Grading

An approach to designing and applying requirements to an activity, item, or service based on its relative importance, complexity, variability, and potential impact on safety, production, and cost.

Human System

A multi-dimensional, self-regulating interplay of meaning-making, intentions, relationships, and capabilities at the team, organizational, and societal levels.

IMS – see Integrated Management System.

Integrated Management System (IMS)

The purposeful alignment and interaction of an organization's meaning system, human system, process system, and technology with its external context to achieve desired organizational and societal outcomes.

Interface

An established means of exchanging or transferring items or information between individuals, processes, or organizations.

Leadership

A willingness to take the initiative to build momentum for an idea, direction, or way of being or doing that has meaning and value to yourself and others.

Mandate

Formal written authority to carry out an agreed course of action.

Meaning System

An inner sense-making and response-formulating strategy evolved from assimilating perceived external cues over the course of one's life.

Mission Statement

A mission statement defines an organization's purpose, objectives, and approach to reaching those objectives.

Mobilizing Metric

A measurement that helps to mobilize the organization to achieve desired outcomes. It supports collaboration and builds on intrinsic motivation, rather than being reactive, punitive and based on short-term incentives.

Open Space Technology

A facilitation technique that can engage large numbers of people in self-organized, purpose-driven dialogue focused on topics of their own choosing without any formal agenda beyond the overall purpose or theme of the engagement.

Operating Experience

The practice of learning from and sharing lessons from internal and external incidents, events and good practices.

Organizational Design Basis

An organizational design basis is a framework of organizational requirements, principles, functions, and processes that is used to establish the structure, responsibilities, and authorities of the organization.

Oversight

Involves formal programs (e.g., audits, assessments, program reviews) that systematically monitor organizational performance and feed into management decision making. In addition, it involves management's on-going attentiveness to what is happening real-time inside and outside the organization and how it might impact current and future performance.

Performance indicator

A measure used to identify whether a process, system, or activity is performing as expected and achieving the desired results. A performance indicator may be used to trend performance over time and may be assigned specific targets.

Process

A group of interrelated activities that, when performed, utilize resources to transform defined inputs to outputs. Processes may be generally grouped into governance, executive / management, core, or support.

Process Owner

The individual accountable for the design, development, implementation, maintenance, effectiveness, and continual improvement of an assigned process.

Program Reviews

A senior-level examination of organizational performance in a broad area usually involving cross-boundary interactions. Such reviews are often periodic, for example, an annual review of the effectiveness of the management system. They involve a review of metrics, outcomes, assessment findings, and organizational and customer feedback to find opportunities for improvement.

Propensity

A natural, in-born preference to reason, relate, and act in a particular way or to be drawn to and succeed at particular activities.

Responsibility

Responsibility is a defined area (example: activity, process, or function) for which an individual accepts accountability.

Root Cause Analysis

A detailed examination of the chain of events related to a specific undesirable occurrence to find the causes where an intervention could reasonably have occurred to prevent the undesirable occurrence. Modern methods include analysis of culture and management influences. Depending on the severity of the event, organizations may grade analysis from apparent or proximate cause to formal investigations conducted by trained investigators.

Safety Culture Assessment

An examination of the underlying beliefs and assumptions within an organization that drive accepted practices and behaviours which may contribute to or negatively affect safety performance. They are normally conducted by teams which include specialists in behavioural, organizational, and social sciences.

Self-assessment

A structured, objective process whereby individuals and groups, including management, evaluate the effectiveness of their own performance against predetermined standards and expectations.

Shared space

A state of mutual, sincere receptiveness to diverse viewpoints, motivations, and desires with the aim of enhancing mutual growth, creativity, and understanding. Shared space embodies authentic engagement with others.

SME

Subject Matter Expert

System

A set of inter-related concepts or parts forming a complex whole.

Stakeholder

Any person or group with an interest or concern in the impact of an organization's activities or outcomes. Stakeholders may be internal or external, e.g., employees, unions, professional and scientific organizations, peer organizations, media, government agencies, and the public at large.

Surveillance

Direct monitoring involving such activities as inspections or direct observations of tasks undertaken for a specific purpose. Surveillance activities may be random or planned.

Systematic

Activities or tasks performed in a specific, logical, or planned method.

Systemic

A holistic view of systems that encompasses the interaction between a system, its internal and external environment, and its inter-connection with and influence on other systems.

Task

In the context of a process, a task is a specific piece of work to be undertaken in support of an activity (see *activity*).

Validation

The act of confirming that an item, process, document or service conforms to specified requirements and achieves the desired results under real or simulated conditions.

Verification

The act of reviewing, inspecting, testing, checking, or otherwise confirming whether items, processes, documents, or services conform to specified requirements.

Vision

A vision is a guiding philosophy that focuses the organization in a particular direction.

World Cafe

A facilitation process for leading large-group collaborative dialogue and knowledge-sharing. The process involves an iterative exploration of a question by successive groups to capture full knowledge and understanding within the collective.

References and Resources

REFERENCES

Antonsen, S. (2009) "Safety Culture and the Issue of Power", Safety Science 47:183-191.

Alvesson, M. (2012) "Understanding Organizational Culture", Sage Publications, London.

APQC (2014) Process Qualification Framework^{SM}, www.apqc.org.

Kelly, C., et al., (2005) Aspen Institute and Booz Allen Hamilton "Deriving Value from Corporate Values".

Briggs Myers, I., McCaulley, M.H., Quenk, N.L. and Hammer, A.L. (1998) "MBTI Manual: A Guide to the Development and Use of the Myers Briggs Type Indicator", Third Edition, Consulting Psychologists Press, Menlo Park, CA.

Cash L. (2011) Cash Lehman and Associates. Personal communication.

Cash L. (2013), "Pathfinder Career System," Cash Lehman and Associates, *www.cashlehman.com*. The Pathfinder Career System is owned by Optimum Talent *www.optimumtalent.com*.

CNSC (2009) Management System Manual, Canadian Nuclear Safety Commission, Ottawa.

CSA (2012) "Management System Requirements for Nuclear Power Plants", N286-12, Canadian Standards Association, Toronto.

CQI (2007) Certified Quality Institute, CQI IMSIG – IMS Definition and Structuring Guidance – Issue 1 – 12 June 2007.

Csikszentmihalyi, M. (1990) "Flow: The Psychology of Optimal Experience", New York: Harper Collins.

Csikszentmihalyi, M. (2004) "Good Business: Leadership, Flow and the Making of Meaning", Viking Penquin, New York.

Deal T. E. and Kennedy, A. A. (1982, 2000) *Corporate Cultures: The Rites and Rituals of Corporate Life*, Harmondsworth, Penguin Books, 1982

Drexler, A., Sibbet, D. and Forrester, R. (2011) Team Performance Model Abstract, San Francisco: The Grove Consultants International.

Grant, I. M., Travers, W., and Viktorsson, C. (2013) "Establishing the Independent, Effective Regulatory Authority in the United Arab Emirates", International Conference on Effective Nuclear Regulatory Systems: Transforming Experience into Regulatory Improvements, 8-12 April 2013, Ottawa, Canada.

EFQM (2010) "EFQM Excellence Model", www.efqm.org.

Harvard Business Review (2010), "Behold the Extreme Consumer…and Learn to Embrace Them", Harvard Business Review, April 2010, p. 30.

IAEA (2006a) "The Management System for Facilities and Activities", Safety Requirements No. GS-R-3, International Atomic Energy Agency, Vienna.

IAEA (2006b) Safety Guide No. GS-G-3.1: "Application of the Management System for Facilities and Activities", International Atomic Energy Agency, Vienna.

IAEA (2009) "The Management System for Nuclear Installations", Safety Guide No. GS-G-3.5, International Atomic Energy Agency, Vienna.

IAEA (2014) "Use of a Graded Approach in the Application of the Management System Requirements for Facilities and Activities", IAEA-TECDOC-1740, International Atomic Energy Agency, Vienna.

IAEA (2015) "Development and Implementation of a Process Based Management System", IAEA Nuclear Energy Series No. NG-T-1.3, Vienna.

IAEA (2016) "How to Perform Safety Culture Self Assessments", Safety Report No. 83, International Atomic Energy Agency, Vienna, in publication.

International Integral Leadership Collaborative (2014), http://www.integralleadershipcollaborative.com/sq/6617-ilc-free-content

ISO (2004) "Environmental management systems – Requirements with guidance for use", ISO 14001:2004, International Organization for Standardization.

ISO (2008) "Quality Management Systems – Requirements", ISO 9001:2008, International Organization for Standardization.

Kaplan, Robert S. and Norton, David P. (1996) *The Balanced Scorecard: Translating Strategy into Action*, Harvard Business School Press, Boston.

Marston, W. M. (2012) Emotions of Normal People, Perfect Paperback, Unabridged.

McGregor, D. (1960). *The Human Side of Enterprise*, New York, McGrawHill.

Mintzberg, Henry (1992) "Structure in Fives: Designing Effective Organizations", Prentice Hall, Englewood Cliffs, NJ.

NEI (2004) "The standard nuclear performance model - A process management approach", Revision 4, Nuclear Energy Institute.

OHSAS 18001 (2004) "Occupational health and safety management systems – Requirements", Occupational Health and Safety Group, Cheshire, UK.

PLGS (2014) Management Manual, Point Lepreau Generating Station, Lepreau Canada.

Roberts, K.H and Bea, R.G. (2001), *When Systems Fail*, Organizational Dynamics, Vol. 29, No. 3, pp. 179–191.

Schein, E.H. (2010), "Organizational Culture and Leadership", John Wiley and Sons, Hoboken, NJ.

Schein, E.H. (2013), "Humble Inquiry: The Gentle Art of Asking Instead of Telling", Berret-Koehler Publishers, San Francisco, CA

Senge, Peter (1990). *The Fifth Discipline*. Doubleday

Smircich, L. and Morgan, G. (1982) Leadership: The Management of Meaning. The Journal of Applied Behavioral Sciences 18(3): 257-273.

Snowden, D. (2015), Cynefin Framework, http://cognitive-edge.com.

Watts, G. and Paciga, J.J. (2011) *Conscious Adaptation: Building Resilient Organizations*, in Complex Adaptive Systems: Energy, Information and Intelligence: Papers from the 2011 Association for the Advancement of Artificial Intelligence Fall Symposium, Washington, D.C., 2011.

Watts, G., Paciga, J.J., and Whitcher, R. (2013) *Building Intelligent Organizations-Why Executives should Revisit their Management Systems*, Global Perspective on Engineering Management, February 2013, Vol. 2, Iss. 1, PP. 1-10.

RESOURCES

1. A substantial amount of information related to the design and use of processes is available at *www.APQC.org.*

2. Information on the EFQM Excellence model and its application is available at *www.efqm.org.*

3. Diverse explorations of management theory related to culture, lean principles, six-sigma, and leadership. Management Meditations by Larry Miller available at *www.lmmiller.com.*

4. British Standards Institution, BSI Group, *www.bsigroup.com.*

5. One of the most practical tools for real time mapping of processes in the field, and for rapidly building initial procedures. Ben Graham Corporation, *www.worksimp.com.*

6. Open Space Technology – a practical large group facilitation methodology. *http://openspaceworld.org.*

7. Appreciative Inquiry – a positive oriented facilitation technique focusing on what works and what can be rather than on conventional problem solving. *http://www.centerforappreciativeinquiry.net.*

8. World Café – a facilitation process for leading collaborative dialogue and knowledge-sharing. *http://www.theworldcafe.com.*

9. ProSci (ADKAR) – a five-part goal-oriented change management model that allows change management teams to focus their activities on specific business results. *www.prosci.com/adkar/adkar-model.*

Acknowledgements

Our early work on management systems began during an improvement project at Point Lepreau Generating Station in New Brunswick, Canada. We thank Jeanie F. McKibbon and Mike Haycox of Ernst and Young for their ability to visualize how complex systems connect, and Wayne Woodworth for project skills, meticulous attention to detail, and his wonderful sense of humour. Technical writers Cara Goodwin and Joyce Steinke blended their knowledge and Info-mapping to make every word count.

Thanks to our business partner Laurie Comeau for suggestions to improve clarity. Several others provided useful input, including Jeanie F. McKibbon, Yuzhakov Andrey from Russia, Lotko Paweł from Poland, and Haidi Tadros from the Canadian Nuclear Safety Commission.

We also appreciated the opportunity to participate in many discussions and working sessions with IAEA staff who work on safety culture and management systems, including Monica Haage, Jongile Majola, Jeannot Boogaard, and Abida Khatoon. We had the opportunity to participate in many consultancy meetings, technical meetings and workshops, in over twenty countries. We also thank the many participants of management system and safety culture workshops who provided insight into the questions and challenges faced by first-time and experienced developers.

Appendix A

Motivation

What really motivates you? What makes you feel energized and so totally absorbed that you skip meals? How can we bring others into that productive, creative space? Are there underlying principles and practices that we can mindfully apply, or is it all just happenstance?

This Appendix is intended to help you reflect on what motivation means to you. In the "value" column of Table A-1, rate yourself from 1-5 for each statement, where 5 means it is highly descriptive of you, and 1 means it is largely irrelevant to your usual behaviour. You'll gain more insight if you complete Table A-1 before reading further.

Table A-1: Motivational Statements

Key	Value	Statement
1		Wanting to succeed against challenging but reasonable goals
2		Experiencing acknowledgement of status, merits, achievements, service, etc.
3		Being in possession of required skills, behaviours, abilities, techniques
4		Seeking acceptance and harmonious relationships with others
5		Feeling connected through trust and empathy with others
6		Exchanging positive feelings of deference or esteem
7		Exercising the opportunity to participate fully socially, economically, and politically
8		Feeling empowered to make informed, un-coerced decisions
9		Seeking to direct others or to organize their efforts

As explained in Chapter 2, each of us is motivated by different things, and our underlying motivational pattern is decipherable.

Table A-2 (duplicated from Chapter 2) considers motivation in three categories shown by the columns. Those of us who pay close attention to our inner well-being and self-determination tend to be intrinsically motivated by feelings of personal competence, autonomy, and relatedness listed in column 1.

Those of us who pay attention to how we are perceived in the broader community, what impact we have, and how we can exercise influence to get what we want tend to be extrinsically motivated by achievement, social power, and affiliation in column 3. Inter-subjective motivators associated with column 2 involve our desire for 'shared space', our need to feel included, respected, and recognized as unique and valuable beings. In shared space we feel no need to prove our competence, we don't have to display evidence of our achievements because we feel recognized and appreciated, and we don't have to assert our power because opportunities and resources are equally shared.

Table A-2: Perspectives on Human Motivation

Intrinsic Motivation (Interior space) *Focus on inner well-being and self-determination*	**Inter-subjective Motivation** (Shared space) *Focus on engagement and appreciation*	**Extrinsic Motivation** (Visible/public space) *Focus on impact and outcome*
Competence	Recognition	Achievement
Autonomy	Respect	Social Power
Relatedness	Inclusion	Affiliation
I pay attention to my inner signals and rely on them to guide my behaviour.	I pay attention to the quality/safety of the "space" as a means of deciding my level of participation.	I pay attention to the signals around me and rely on them to guide my behaviour.

Return to the exercise you completed in Table A-1 and insert your answers from Table A-1 next to each descriptor in Table A-3.

Table A-3: Motivation Descriptors

Key	Value	Descriptor
1		Achievement
2		Recognition
3		Competence
4		Affiliation
5		Relatedness
6		Respect
7		Inclusion
8		Autonomy
9		Social Power

Now use the graph in Figure A-1, called a circumplex, to draw your motivational profile. Shade the radial pie segments in each descriptor corresponding with your values in Table A-3. For example, if you assigned a value of 3 to achievement, shade the first three rings of that segment, and so forth.

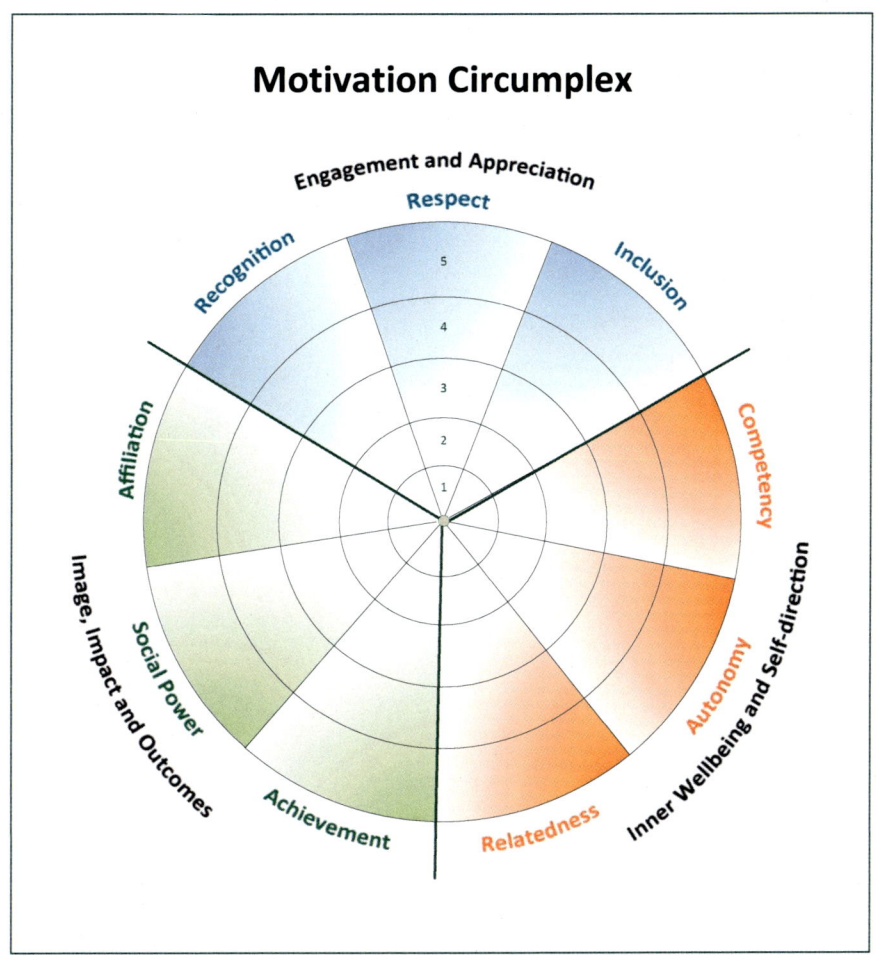

Figure A-1: Motivation circumplex by column of Table A-2

Each one-third wedge corresponds to a column of Table A-2. For example, the blue wedge (upper segment) corresponds to column 2 (inter-subjective motivation) of the table. Your completed circumplex provides insight into where you pay attention and what tends to motivate you. This profile provides a way of understanding why you prefer some arenas more than others. For example, if you prefer to focus on image, impact and outcomes, you likely feel energized through interaction with others, and invest considerable effort in this dimension. Notice that your preferences are not equal in each segment. They are also uniquely yours. You can prove this by sharing this exercise with someone you know well to see how their profile differs from yours.

We can take a slightly different view by plotting your data from Table A-3 into the circumplex shown in Figure A-2.

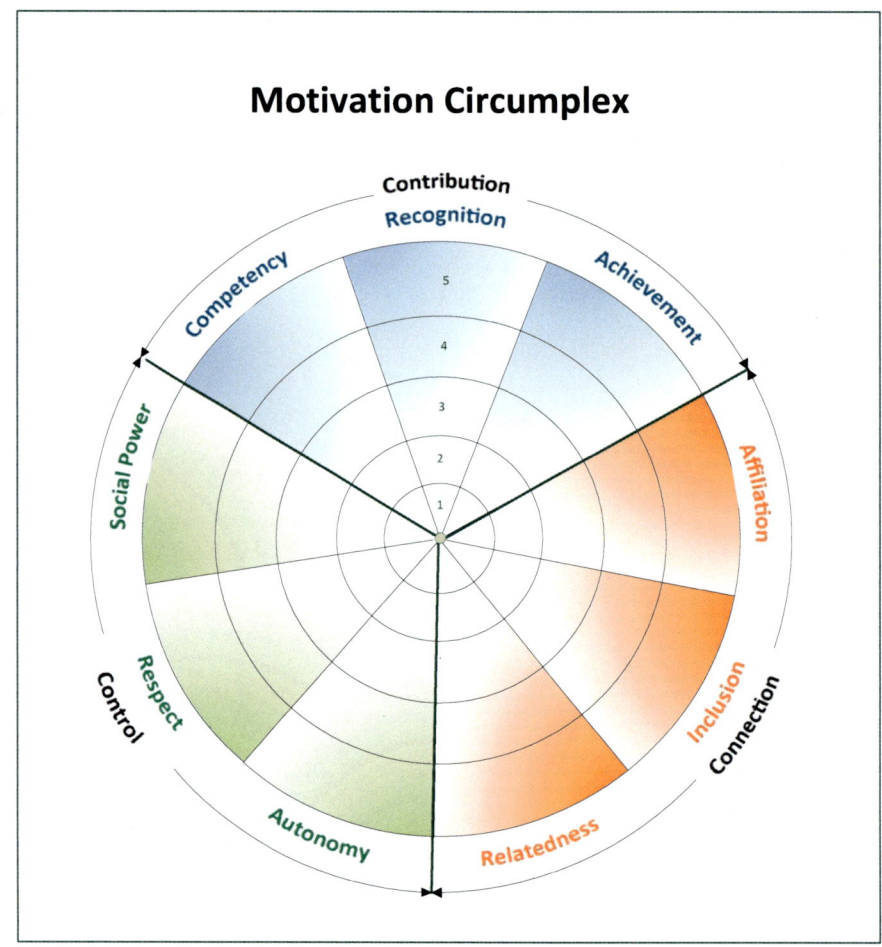

Figure A-2: *Motivation Circumplex by Row*

Looking at your motivation profile from the perspective of control, contribution, and connection gives insight into your root strategy for interacting with the world and expending energy. It also shows the balance you have struck with respect to each of these vectors and how strongly you value each one. This, in turn, provides deeper insight into fundamental dimensions of your natural preferences and aspirations. It can also help you appreciate that others may have very different profiles than yours.

Appendix B

Behavioural Factors, Career Themes, and Leadership Styles

This Appendix lists behavioural factors, career themes, and leadership styles based on the Pathfinder Career System developed by Cash Lehman and Associates [Cash 2013]. Information in this Appendix is used with the permission of Cash Lehman and Associates and is used to establish consistent terminology throughout this handbook.

Behavioural Preferences

Table B-1 lists 26 behavioural preferences or propensities used in the models for individual, team, and organizational performance.

Table B-1 Behavioural Preferences

Behavioural Preferences		
<ul><li>Builds consensus</li><li>Communicates clarity</li><li>Demonstrates character</li><li>Demonstrates community consciousness</li><li>Demonstrates energetic enthusiasm</li><li>Demonstrates social charisma</li><li>Demonstrates strategic vision</li><li>Drives achievement</li><li>Establishes order</li></ul>	<ul><li>Exercises political influence</li><li>Establishes alliances</li><li>Focuses on results</li><li>Initiates independently</li><li>Leads decisively</li><li>Maintains accountability</li><li>Manages self</li><li>Manages stress</li><li>Overcomes adversity</li></ul>	<ul><li>Reasons critically</li><li>Responsive to change</li><li>Seeks innovation</li><li>Strives for excellence</li><li>Sustains profitability</li><li>Thinks conceptually</li><li>Thrives on chaos</li><li>Utilizes humour</li></ul>

Behavioural Descriptors

The following are descriptions of each behavioural factor in Table B-1.

Builds Consensus: Enjoys working as part of a team. Emphasis is on appropriate compromise, demonstrating tact, maintaining emotional control and interpersonal tolerance rather than making demands.

Communicates Clarity: Demonstrates the capacity to deliver persuasive and articulate oral and written communications.

Demonstrates Character: Honours interpersonal commitments, maintains the courage of high-minded convictions, values living rightly and plays by honourable rules.

Demonstrates Community Consciousness: Demonstrates a commitment to making a worthwhile contribution to business solutions of public consequence and improving the quality of life in one's community, including respect for the environment.

Demonstrates Energetic Enthusiasm: Operates at a fast pace, possesses a high energy level and maintains a physically active, healthy lifestyle.

Demonstrates Social Charisma: Intentionally seeks to have a visible and forceful influence on others in order to convince, persuade and gain the support of one's agenda.

Demonstrates Strategic Vision: Takes a longer-term and purposeful approach to finding solutions, in order to actualize a more meaningful or worthwhile strategic goal.

Drives Achievement: Demonstrates an outstanding need to achieve exceptional challenges under competitive scenarios and is prepared to make lifestyle sacrifices for the sake of career advancement.

Establishes Alliances: Establishes friendly relationships, enjoys expressing one's views and participating socially with others in a manner that reflects genuineness and interpersonal intimacy.

Establishes Order: Establishes clear guidelines and expectations for others and implements departmental systems to effectively manage the orderly flow of work to ensure efficiency goal and disciplined effort.

Exercises Political Influence: Builds politically effective relationships and anticipates the hidden political agendas that could sidetrack or manipulate an appropriate outcome.

Focuses on Results: Prepared to make the personal sacrifices or expend extraordinary dedication to one's work when frequent overtime is required to complete assignments.

Initiates Independently: Demonstrates a preference for taking action, pursuing high risk and initiating projects independently of prior approval or requests.

Leads Decisively: Demonstrates assertive leadership by acting decisively and confidently.

Maintains Accountability: Demonstrates an attitude that is defined by taking responsibilities and loyalties very seriously, by assuming a sense of personal accountability for one's results, as well as co-workers' actions without seeking to blame or provide excuses for failures.

Manages Self: Seeks a deeper self-understanding of one's self and maintains a healthy self-acceptance without guilt and self-criticism.

Manages Stress: Demonstrates a capacity to function effectively under pressure without excessive worry or anticipating the worst.

Overcomes Adversity: Demonstrates an ability to persevere when pursuing difficult challenges and responds positively to adversity in the face of failure.

Reasons Critically: Demonstrates the ability to tackle difficult problems by using logical, quantitative reasoning to identify patterns relevant to problem solving.

Responds to Change: Demonstrates the ability and willingness to adapt, contribute, and support rapid change in response to different circumstances or objectives.

Seeks Innovation: Thinks expansively and combines novel ideas in unique ways to generate innovative solutions.

Strives for Excellence: Demonstrates a desire to produce the best quality products or serves and conscientiously tracks and double checks the accuracy of work.

Thinks Conceptually: Demonstrates the ability to comprehend theoretical concepts and be curious about the broader "why" or holistic perspective on problems.

Thrives in Chaos: Enthusiastically keeps on top of seemingly chaotic demands, rapid and overlapping priorities and displays intensity for getting everything done now.

Utilizes Humour: Exercises appropriate humour in the workplace and strives to maintain a relaxed, informal environment where people can have fun.

Career Themes

Table B-2 lists the 35 occupational themes in the Pathfinder Career System. Approximately half of the occupational themes are important contributors to management system effectiveness through process development or implementation.

Table B-2 Occupational Themes

Occupational Themes		
Administration Behavioural Sciences Construction Consulting Education Electronic/Computer Sciences Engineering Entertainment Farming & Ranching Finance Food Services Government Services	Home and Children Inspection Law and Politics Library Services/Languages Life/Environmental Sciences Management Manufacturing Marketing Mathematics/Statistics/Physics Mechanical Medical Services Medical Sciences	Personal Services Protective Services Religion/Philosophy/Ethics Retail Sales Self-Employment Social Sciences Sports Transportation Writing Visual Arts

Leadership Style Descriptors

The following are the descriptors for the seven behavioural-based leadership styles used in this handbook. The first six are from the Pathfinder Career System, the seventh (unitive) has been added by the authors to account for the unique characteristics of the associated leadership style.

Administrative – This is a traditional "manager" style best used where work environments involve risks and require significant rules and procedures. Leaders manage by the book and are there to enforce order and predictability.

Collegial – Best described as a participatory leadership style. Typically best used with employees who are highly trained, experienced and educated requiring minimal supervision. Leaders have a more 'hands off' style and prefer to provide little or no direction, giving employees as much freedom as possible.

Directive – Best described as the classical authoritarian or command and control leader. The focus is on maintaining control and power. Typically best used when employees require close supervision. Leaders expect employees to follow orders without question or challenge and seek little input from others when making decisions.

Entrepreneurial – The focus is on change and staying ahead of the curve and competition. Leaders are self-motivated, innovative and challenge the status quo. They encourage out-of-the-box thinking and empowerment. Typically best suited to environments where innovation and calculated, valued added risk taking is needed to shift organizational performance.

Utilitarian – The focus is on maximizing productivity and output. Leaders recognize the signs of lagging progress and overall effectiveness and seek to motivate employees to reach higher levels of efficiency, effectiveness, success and satisfaction. Typically best suited to environments where creating a sense of urgency and action is needed to achieve results and a higher level of performance.

Transformational – The focus is on engagement, building effective relationships and creating positive change linked to a common purpose. Typically best used with employees seeking challenge, autonomy and participatory decision making. Leaders seek to coach, mentor and influence to motivate employees to realize a different future.

Unitive – The focus is on understanding the interconnectivity of complex social, cultural, technical, political, economic, and ecological systems and how these systems create meaning and value in a universal context. Typically, best suited to environments where the issues are complex, solutions are not self-evident, and transformational attempts have had limited impact. Unitive leaders help create new meaning for a higher good.

Appendix C

Leadership Style by Stage of Evolution

This Appendix systematically examines the leadership characteristics typical of the four stages of evolution described in Chapter 3. Each stage represents a different way of perceiving reality and brings different strengths to the table. Leaders who have a predominant reasoning style associated with a specific stage need to understand the strength and contribution that other styles bring, otherwise organizational growth to the next stage is complicated because those that want to shape it differently may cause pain to others, especially when the current thinking appears to have served the organization to that point in time. Different styles of reasoning contribute different value to different situations. If the right reasoning isn't in the room, the outcome won't be achieved even when the goal might be clear to those present.

Leadership Styles by Stage

A useful tool for looking at leadership is to use spray diagrams that help explore the molecular structure of social chemistry and reasoning patterns. Spray diagrams allow people to compare respective viewpoints in a more systematic and visual way than arises through arguing individual perspectives. They reveal similarities, differences, irrelevancies, and missing viewpoints. They also provide insights on how different individuals view a specific topic, thus surfacing potential areas for bridging differences and applying the best set of talents to a particular issue. For example, it is fruitless to develop long-term strategies if the leaders involved favor short-term decision-making and action over long-term visioning. An effective leadership team recognizes its limitations and seeks talent to fill gaps within its own ranks.

In the following, we will follow a three-part structure to describe leadership propensities at each stage of evolution:

i.   A description of the perception of reality
ii. A spray diagram showing common reasoning patterns
iii. A V-diagram to explore related propensities.

Perceptions of reality shape leadership decisions and actions, including those who may not have formal titles within an organization yet may have considerable influence. Depending on personal perceptions, reality is something that one:

- reacts to
- observes and manages
- responds to and influences, or
- shapes and creates.

Perception is the root of culture. Perception of reality is grounded in various personal factors including:

- time perspective (past, present, future orientation)
- locus of control (internal or external)
- degree of internalization (introversion-extroversion), and
- innate preferences (propensities).

Individual propensities and ways of perceiving, plus shared experiences, create opportunities for insight, shared learning and shared meaning.

Stage 1: Technical Leadership

Stage 1 leadership (Figure C-1A) tends to perceive reality as "something I react to".

If reality is something I react to, then...

- Forces beyond my control shape my experience
- Satisfaction of needs, sense of self-worth, and motivation are dependent on things outside of me
- Change is a threat to my wellbeing and survival, and
- Who I am and how I should be is defined by others.

I lead by applying technical competence and lessons learned from the past to solve problems and avoid tangible risks.

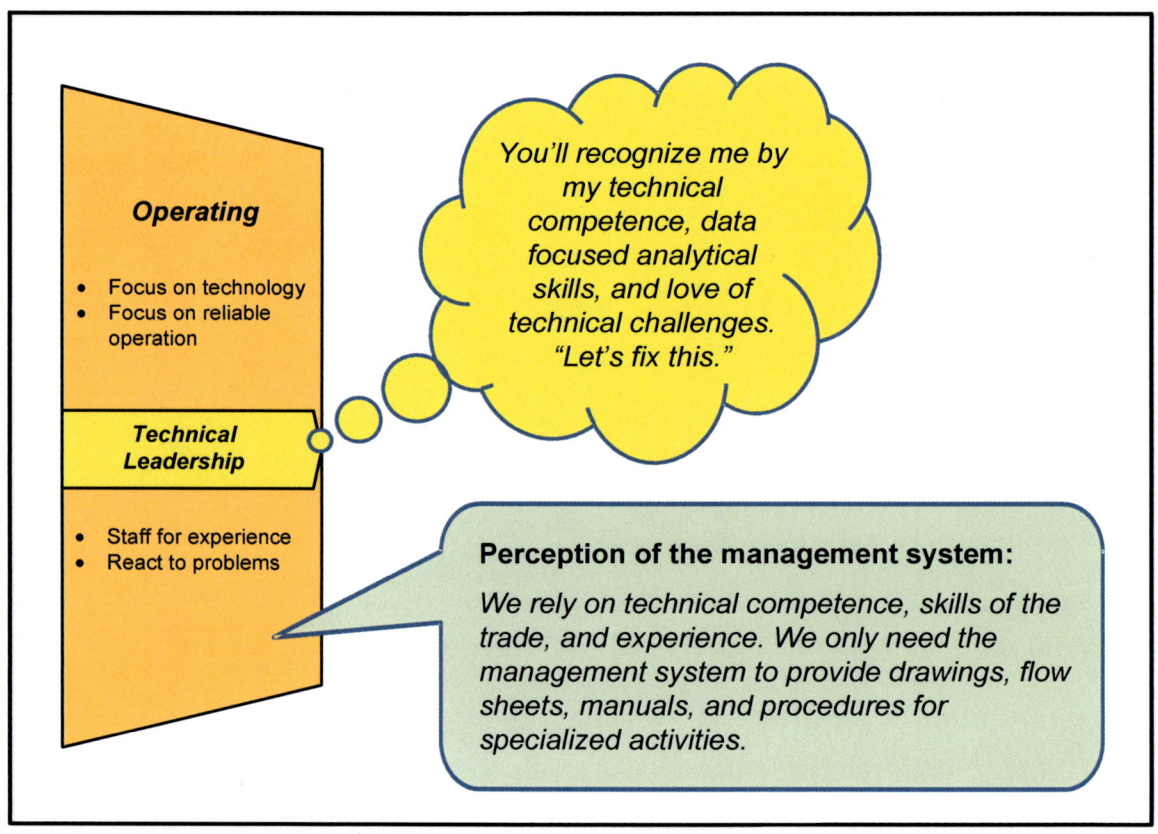

Figure C-1A: Stage 1 leadership and management system perceptions

To construct a spray diagram, one takes any concept or issue and circles it as the central theme on a sheet of paper. One then constructs related thoughts or aspects connected with the central theme. The thickness of the line joining each circle indicates the strength of its influence.

There are many similar concepts from mind maps to story-telling, however, spray diagrams are easy to construct and can be developed interactively in group settings. Figure C-1B uses a spray diagram to illustrate some of the focus areas and reasoning styles common to Stage 1 leadership.

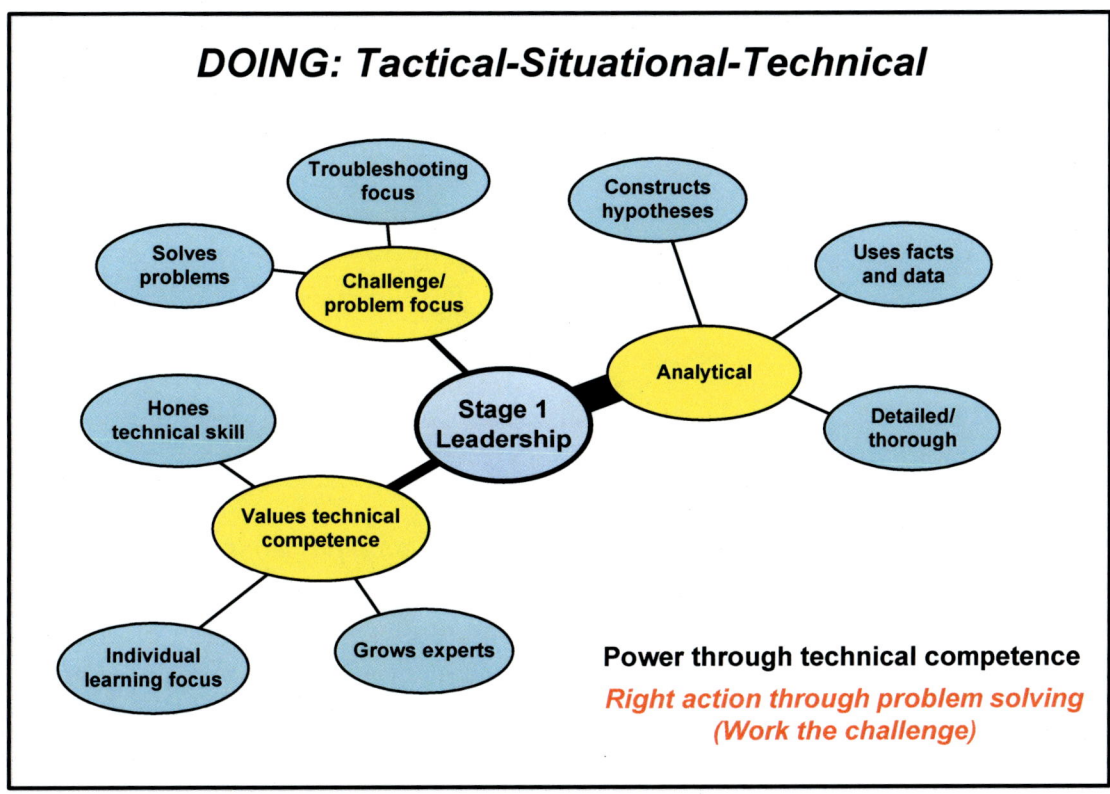

Figure C-1B: Stage 1 leadership spray diagram

Stage 1 leadership focuses on technical depth and individual learning. This style promotes continued competence and autonomy. The focus is on working the problem and seeking practical solutions.

Figure C-1C provides the underlying behavioural factors that drive reasoning and action for Stage 1 leadership. It is based on the individual performance model in Figures 2-8 and 2-9 of Chapter 2. The items in read are common propensity strengths associated with Stage 1 leadership.

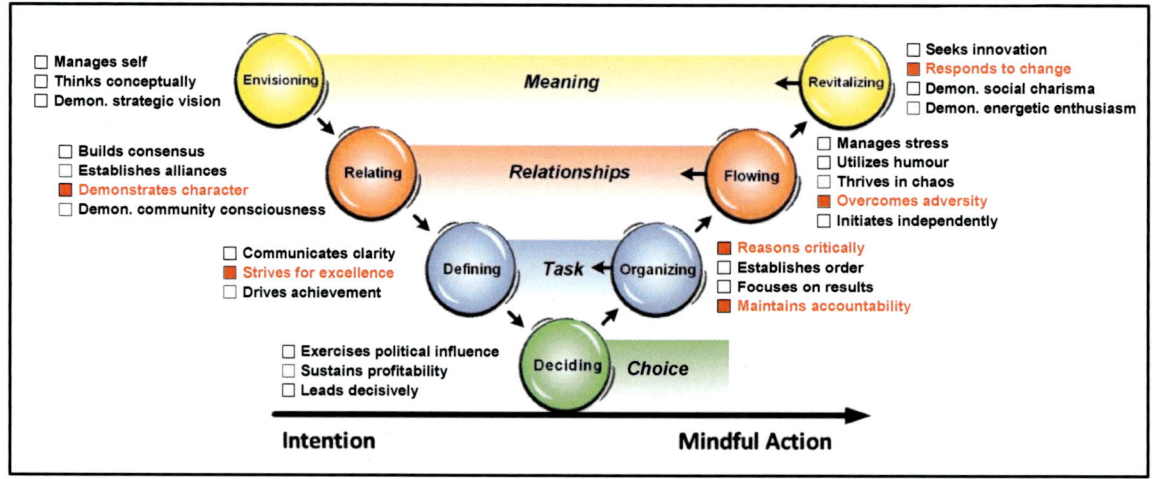

Figure C-1C: Stage 1 leadership behavioural propensities

Individuals possessing Stage 1 attributes function well in front-line leadership roles. They respond well to practical challenges and unanticipated change, and exhibit the discipline and critical reasoning skills that enable them to solve tangible, hands on problems.

Stage 2: Managing

Stage 2 leadership (Figure C-2A) tends to perceive reality as "something I can try to manage".

If reality is something I can manage, then…

- Astute observation, dedication, and perseverance will lead to 'the good life'
- Taking control and doing things perfectly will ensure success and reward
- Who I am and what I should be is defined by what I accomplish
- Change is supposed to reward me but can punish me too.

I lead by securing resources, making decisions, and managing logistics to control knowable risks.

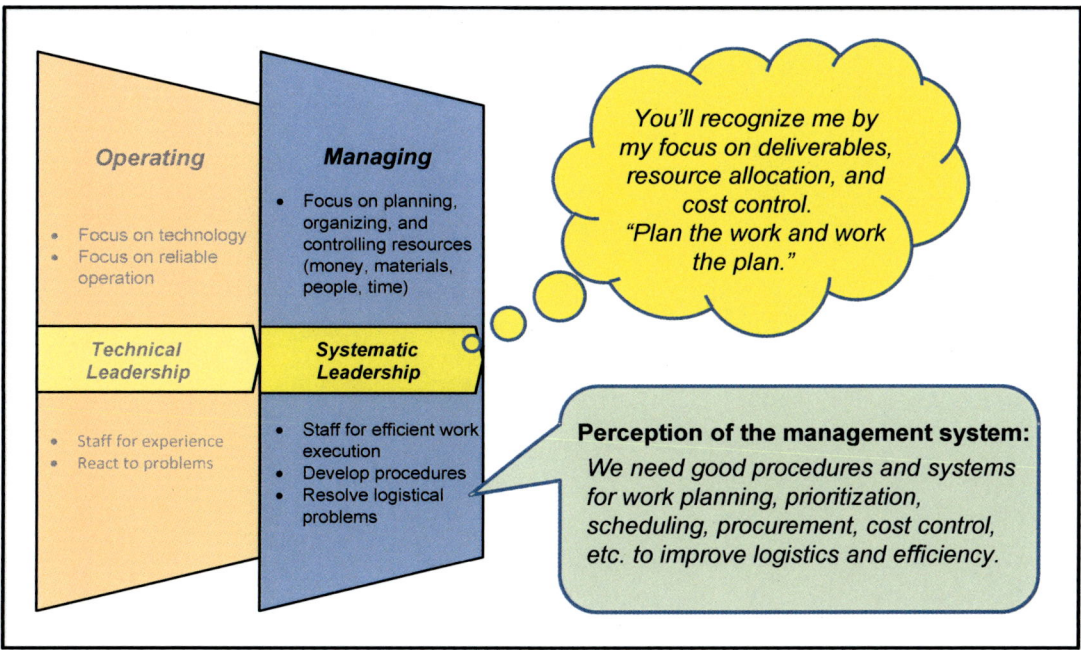

Figure C-2A: Stage 2 leadership and management system perceptions

The spray diagram in Figure C-2B illustrates some of the focus areas and reasoning styles common to Stage 2 leadership.

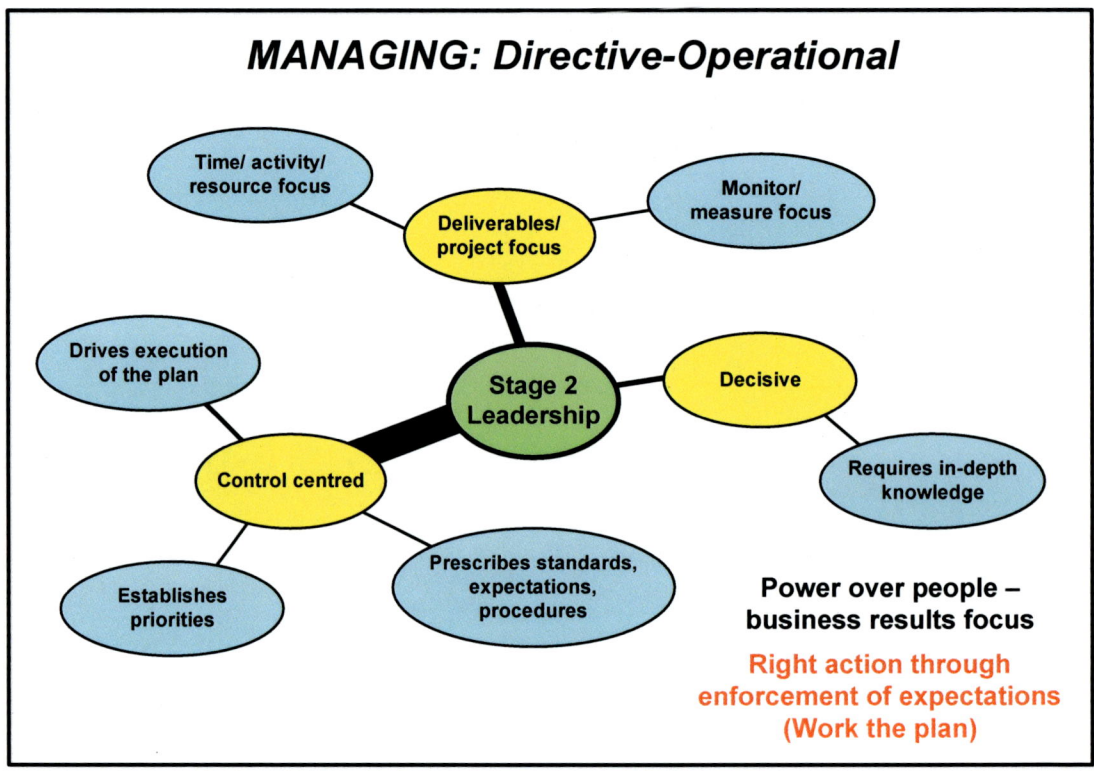

Figure C-2B: Stage 2 leadership spray diagram

Stage 2 leadership typically displays a utilitarian meaning system and a dominant sense of personal competence and autonomy. This results in low relatedness and low trust. The focus is on work-the-plan production, clean execution, and short-term results with little need for personal relatedness with the performers.

Figure C-2C provides (in red) the underlying behavioural factors that drive reasoning and action for Stage 2 leadership.

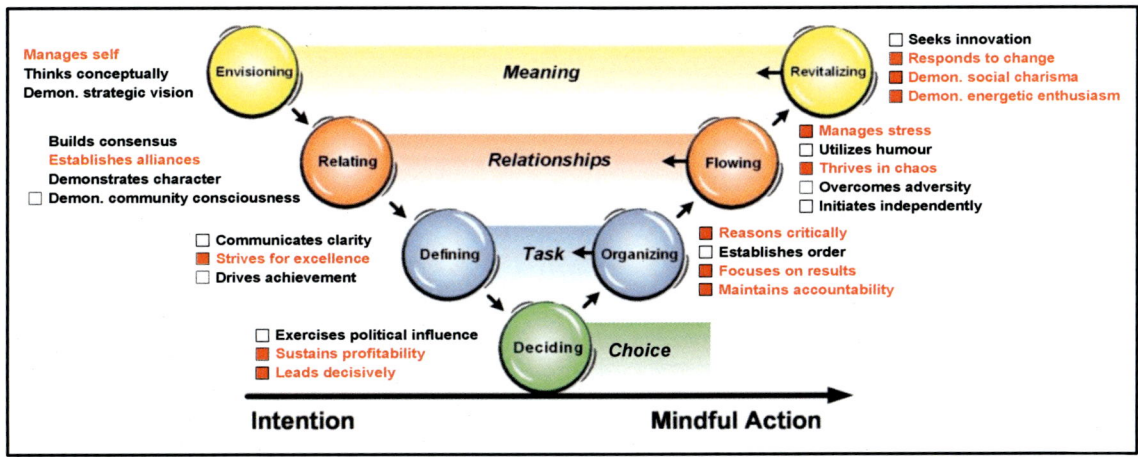

Figure C-2C: Stage 2 leadership behavioural propensities

Individuals possessing Stage 2 attributes tend to thrive in project environments where planning, organizing, and delivering results are essential for success. They often have an energetic, decisive, 'get-er-done' approach to organizational life.

Stage 3: Leading

Stage 3 leadership (Figure C-3A) tends to perceive reality as "something I can influence".

If reality is something I can influence, then…

- Recognizing opportunities and mitigating risks is my job
- Building alliances to get what I need and want makes sense
- Who I am and what I should be is my choice and I accept the consequences, and
- Change is an opportunity if I can seize it.

I lead by interacting, collaborating, and optimizing processes to achieve goals that minimize anticipated risks.

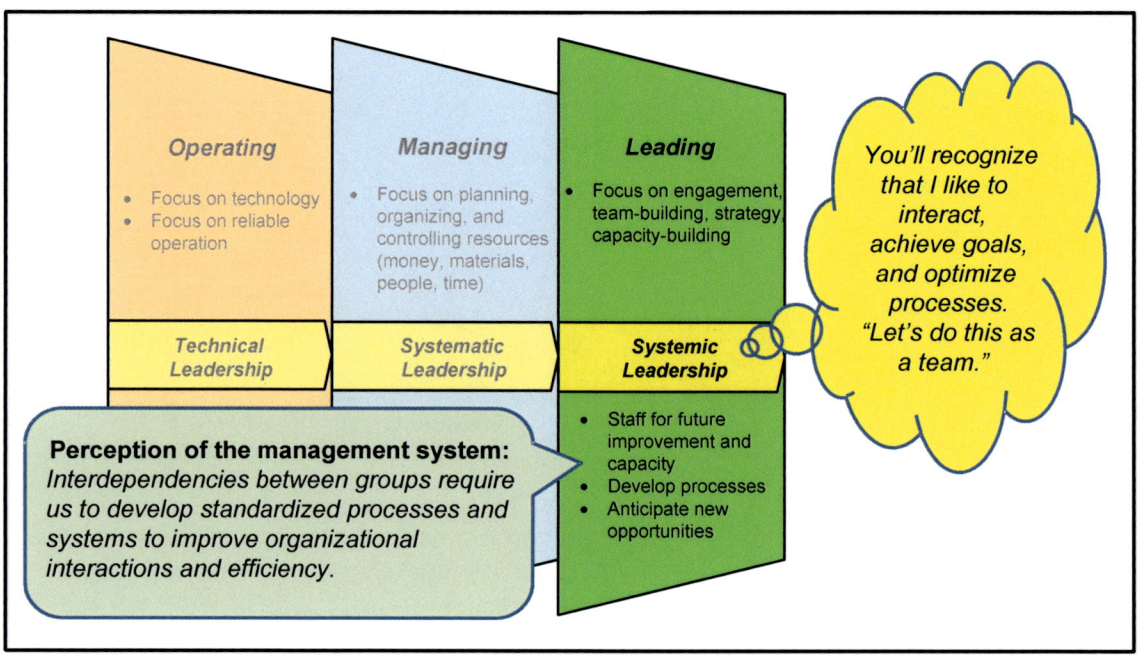

Figure C-3A: Stage 3 leadership and management system perceptions

The spray diagram in Figure C-3B illustrates some of the focus areas and reasoning styles common to Stage 3 leadership.

Figure C-3B: Stage 3 leadership spray diagram

Stage 3 leadership emphasizes relatedness, growth, and organizational learning. The approach is to work the strategy rather than the plan, thereby allowing more autonomy to achieve positive organizational outcomes. They interact well, promote trust, and tend to inject greater breadth when considering any issue.

Figure C-3C provides (in red) the underlying behavioural factors that drive reasoning and action for Stage 3 leadership.

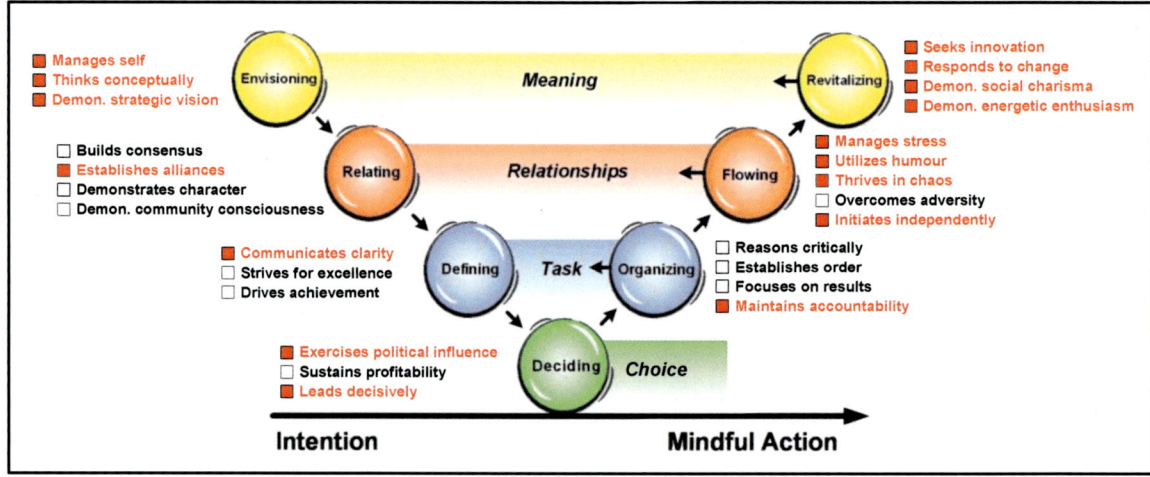

Figure C-3C: Stage 3 leadership behavioural propensities

Individuals who exhibit Stage 3 attributes tend to prefer organizing on a broader scale than individual projects. They favour team oriented goals, managing interfaces, and strengthening team relationships. Their strategic focus drives them to integrate organizational processes and activities.

Stage 4: Uniting and Integrating

Stage 4 leadership (Figure C-4A) tends to perceive reality as "something I create".

If reality is something I create, then…

- What is happening around me is a reflection of my inner state
- The criteria I use to evaluate my life determine the nature of my experience
- Who I am and what I should be depends on my values and intentions, and
- Change is a time for learning and growth.

I lead by defining purpose, designing systems, and striving for deeper meaning and innovation to avert potential risks. There is a strong unitive dimension to Stage 4 leadership.

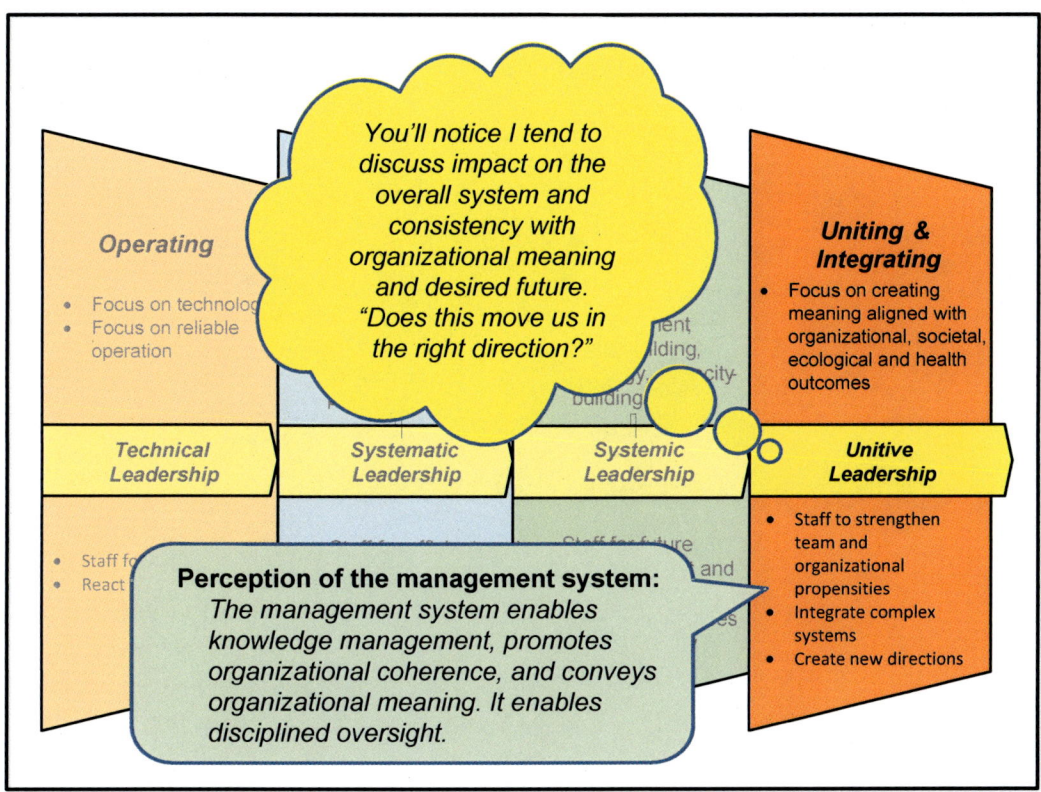

Figure C-4A: Stage 4 leadership and management system perceptions

The spray diagram in Figure C-4B illustrates some of the focus areas and reasoning styles common to Stage 4 leadership.

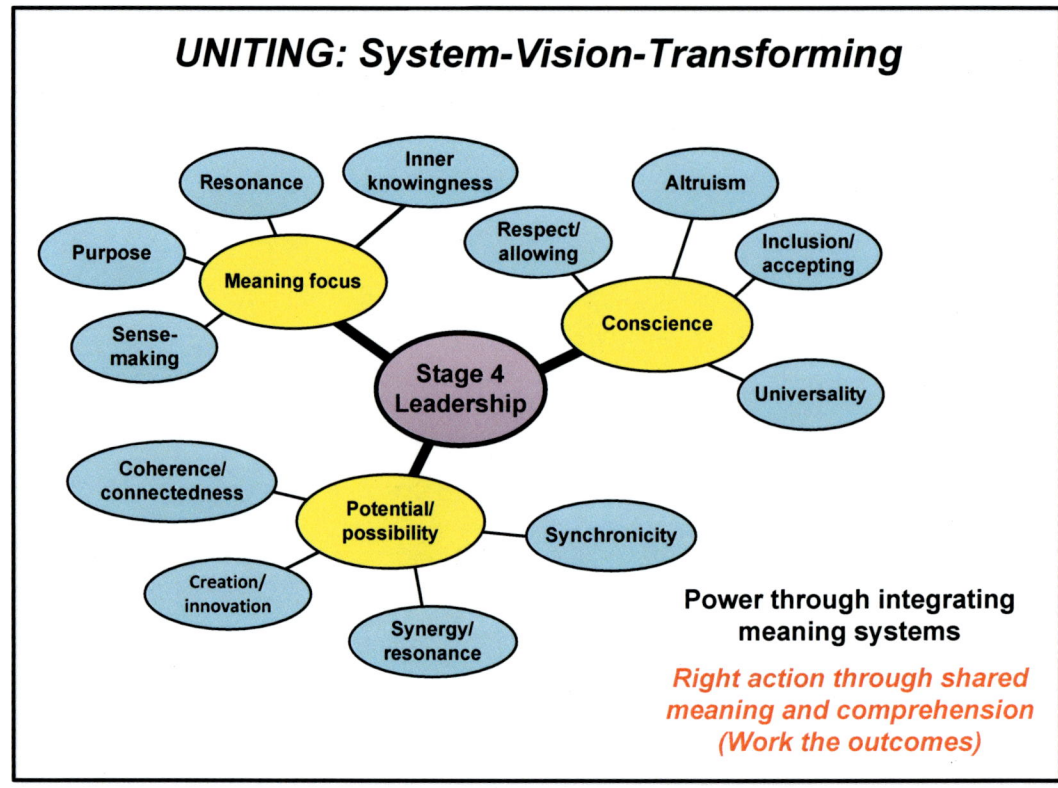

Figure C-4B: Stage 4 leadership spray diagram

Stage 4 leadership considers the connection between various elements of a system and how those connections and elements are perceived by the organization and its external stakeholders. Sense-making, purpose, inclusion, and overall impact, including the potential for unintended consequences, are considered in the course of making decisions. There is a strong unitive dimension to Stage 4 leadership.

Figure C-4C provides the underlying behavioural factors that drive reasoning and action for Stage 4 leadership.

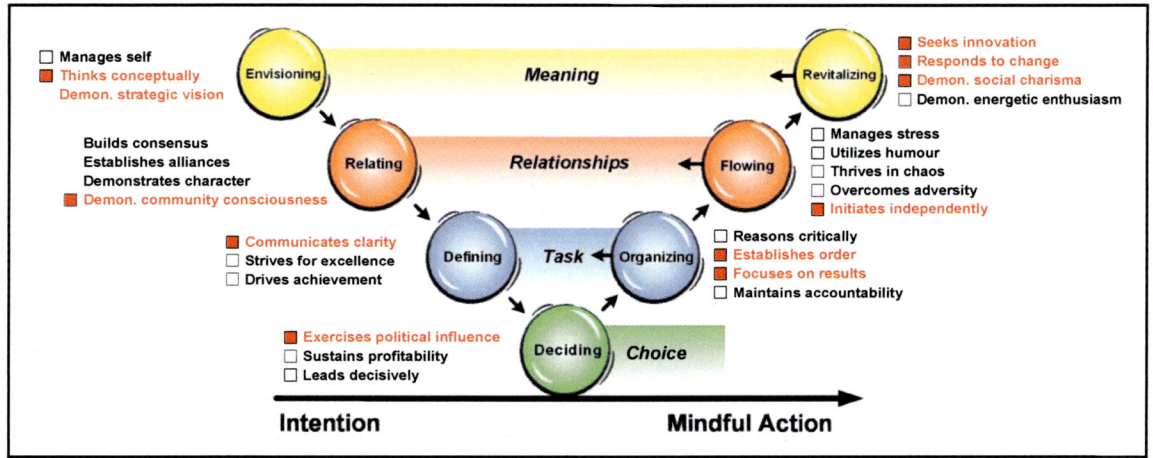

Figure C-4C: Stage 4 leadership behavioural propensities

Individuals with Stage 4 attributes tend to focus on the big picture, relationships between systems, and their 'meaning-making' impact in the context of the organization and society at large. This is one of the most challenging and vulnerable leadership styles since such individuals may be ignored or dismissed as dreamers. Aspects for success include political influence, focus on results, social charisma, and the drive to initiate independently.

Relevance to Organizations

Why is this rather analytical approach to leadership of benefit to organizations? Different leadership styles contribute different strengths. Organizations with leadership teams that include all strengths with generally be more effective if the leadership styles are applied in circumstances where a strength is appropriate for the intended outcome. A number of fruitful questions arise from such diagrams when a team considers their natural or default tendencies and their explanation of why these tendencies exist. For any situation, a team can explore what elements are relevant or irrelevant for that specific circumstance. A team can also explore what is limiting or missing from the perspectives that, if added, might benefit team performance.

For example, at an individual level, a Stage 2 leader's focus on control might limit patience with a Stage 3 leader's focus on organizational learning, compared with a Stage 1 leader who likes to develop experts. Stage 2 leader's focus on standards and expectations might not mesh well with Stage 4 leader's propensity for innovative approaches. On the other hand, Stage 2 leader's focus on deliverables aligns well with Stage 3's desire to achieve goals.

Thinking through the dynamics of leadership styles helps team members to understand their reactions and responses in a variety of situations.

As indicated elsewhere, the stages are not hierarchical, nor is any stage 'better' than another. What matters is whether the leadership style assignment is appropriate for the stage, whether the leadership team understands the value of different propensities that each style brings, and most importantly, whether gaps are hampering the organization's effectiveness and evolution.

Appendix D

Organizational Design Principles

This Appendix provides a synopsis of ten organizational design principles useful to consider when setting up or modifying an organizational unit.

Organizational structures result from the application of two generic principles:

- division of labour into distinct activities, and
- coordination among these activities.

To achieve the desired outputs, organizations assign activities, roles, responsibilities, accountabilities and authorities to various positions and groups. They also establish leadership and supervisory roles to sequence, prioritize and integrate the intellectual and physical activities of work performers. This process functions better if the following principles are considered.

1. Design for compatibility and integration

Compatibility and integration includes consideration of the:

- demands of the technology (particularly in high-reliability industries)
- individual work processes and interfaces with other processes
- organizational functionality and desired outcomes
- capacity of the people performing the activities.

2. Define minimum critical specifications

Specify only the essentials to avoid foreclosing options or being unnecessarily restrictive in the way the work is performed.

3. Optimize the human-technology interface

Keep people close to the technology. Control variance nearest the source to avoid reactive approaches such as inspections of the completed activity or product. This reduces re-work and reduces the likelihood of cumulative or latent errors.

4. Design for an appropriate level of adaptability

Some people need to perform specialized, fractionated tasks to a high degree of reliability, whereas others need to be able to respond quickly to internal and external changes.

Too much compartmentalization can limit:

- creativity
- adaptability to off-normal situations, and
- breadth of responsiveness.

Organizations have to make choices about the appropriate rate of adaptation for different units/functions/phases:

- Small 'container' operations involve free-flowing interactions with few significant differences. This increases the speed of adaptation to the environment through rapid achievement of shared meaning.
    - e.g., Emergency response team, or Fix-it-now team
- Large 'container' operations involve controlled interactions with multiple significant differences that can slow or even stop adaptation to the environment and are very slow to achieve shared meaning.
    - e.g., Top-heavy bureaucratic organizations, international codes and standards collaboration.

5. Minimize unnecessary boundaries

Organizations develop boundaries based on purpose, function, technology, location, and time. These boundaries often interfere with information transfer and knowledge/experience sharing. The greater the compartmentalization, the more leadership needs to manage interfaces through additional coordination and integration. This increases the likelihood of miscommunication across boundaries, increases potential for competing agendas, and ultimately increases cost and effort. Organizations often include bridging roles such as cross-functional planning units to facilitate coordination.

6. Streamline information flow

Provide timely information at the point where action is needed. Design information for the user, including representing information in formats readily interpreted by the receiver. Modern information systems are only valuable if information is integrated, easily extracted, and clear.

7. ***Design jobs to align with human needs***

   Some key factors to consider are:

   - Choose positive motivators related to competence, recognition, achievement, respect, power, etc.
   - Provide a balance between challenge and capability
   - Provide opportunities for on-the-job and continual learning that contribute to the individual and organization's future
   - Provide a sufficient degree of self-directedness and autonomous decision making – specify what, not how
   - Promote self-determination
   - Include mental and physical breaks
   - Avoid multi-tasking to reduce error rates
   - Promote relatedness, inclusion, and affiliation
   - Provide social support and recognition
   - Align what is done to individual/social meaning.

8. ***Design for programmatic congruence***

   Design organizational programs (e.g., reward structures, collective agreements) to reinforce the behaviours that align with the structure's intended functionality.

9. ***Design with meaning systems and propensities in mind.***

   Differences in individual meaning systems can create conflict and confusion, but also provide expanded capacities when actively integrated and supported.

   Team and organizational propensities represent the combination of member preferences that are allowed to manifest as a result of power relationships. For this reason, functionality and performance can be systematically enhanced by considering individual meaning systems and propensities when forming teams and staffing entire structures.

*10. **Consider impacts across the system when making changes***

An organizational change can have an impact on processes, technology, requisite leadership styles, roles, and interfaces. The converse is also true hence the organizational change process must consider impact from all dimensions.

An example of an organizational structure that doesn't align well with functionalities or processes is shown in the box below.

Example of a misaligned structure

One organization had distributed the following accountabilities across different departments, reporting to different levels:

- Quality assurance and regulatory accountabilities
- Permanent modifications
- Temporary modifications (in operations reporting to the Station Manager)
- Purchasing and contract development
- Verification against national purchasing policies (in the legal department reporting to the President)

Disjointed configurations such as these often indicate situations where organizational changes are made without adequate consideration of functionality and process alignment. They also indicate a weak organizational change process.

Appendix E

Samples of Management System Models

This Appendix provides examples of top-level models of management systems. Some of the examples are pure process models, others combine organizational or business model elements. They are presented here to illustrate the many ways that such models emerge within organizations.

As you look at each model, notice the following aspects:

- The overarching structure of the model
- The grouping of various elements within the model
- The location and proximity of elements in terms of what this might indicate about the perceived importance of and relationships between various elements
- Whether the name of the element clearly communicates its intent
- What the name of each element suggests about what one might expect to find as sub-processes or lower-tier elements (i.e., how easy would it be to drill down to find a desired element?)
- How much the model attempts to communicate broad aspects of the organization – processes only, business model, philosophy such as values, etc.
- What the model might communicate to employees, stakeholders, and the public.

Nuclear Model – British Energy/ Électricité de France

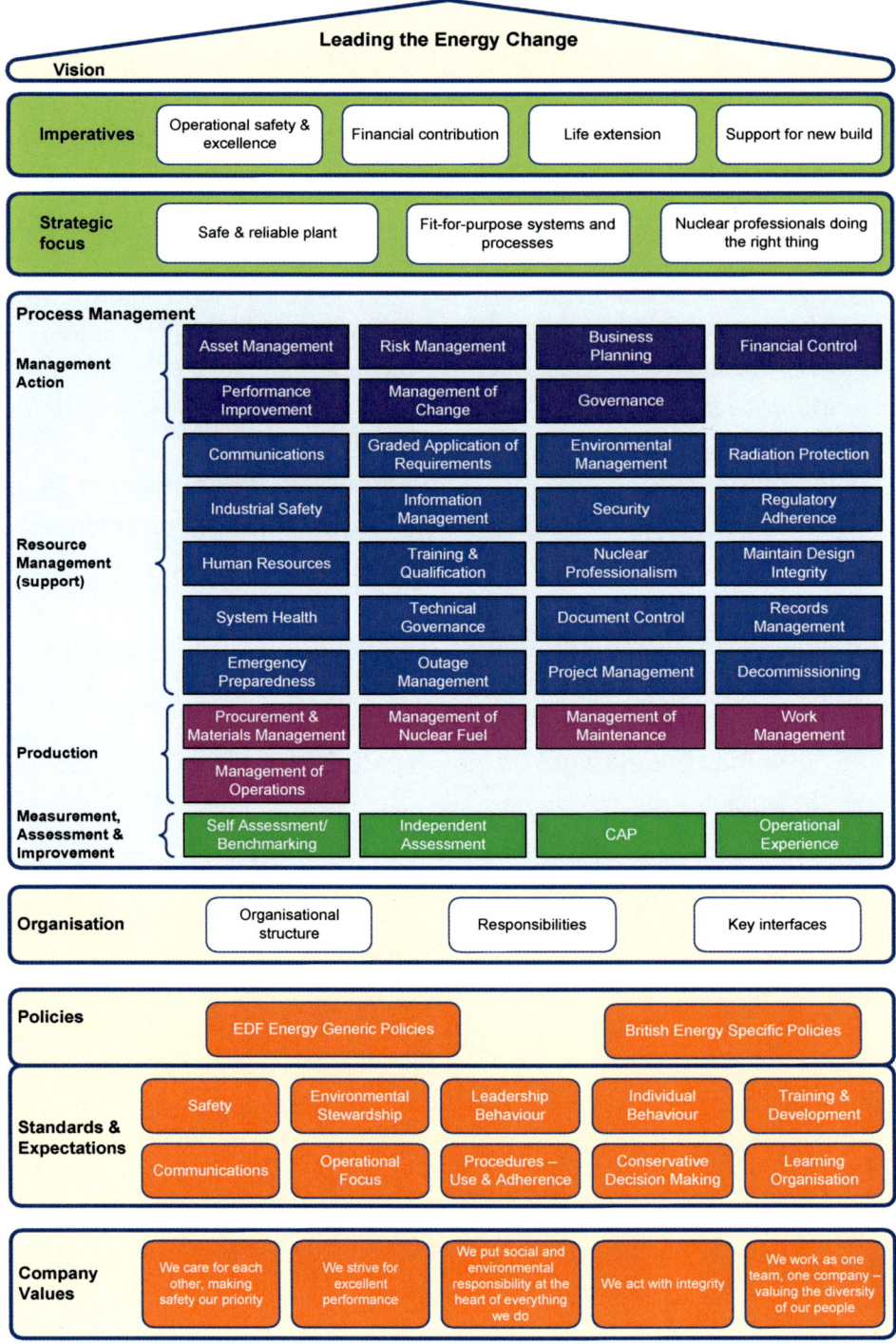

Nuclear Process Model – Point Lepreau Generating Station, Canada
[Ref. PLGS 2014]

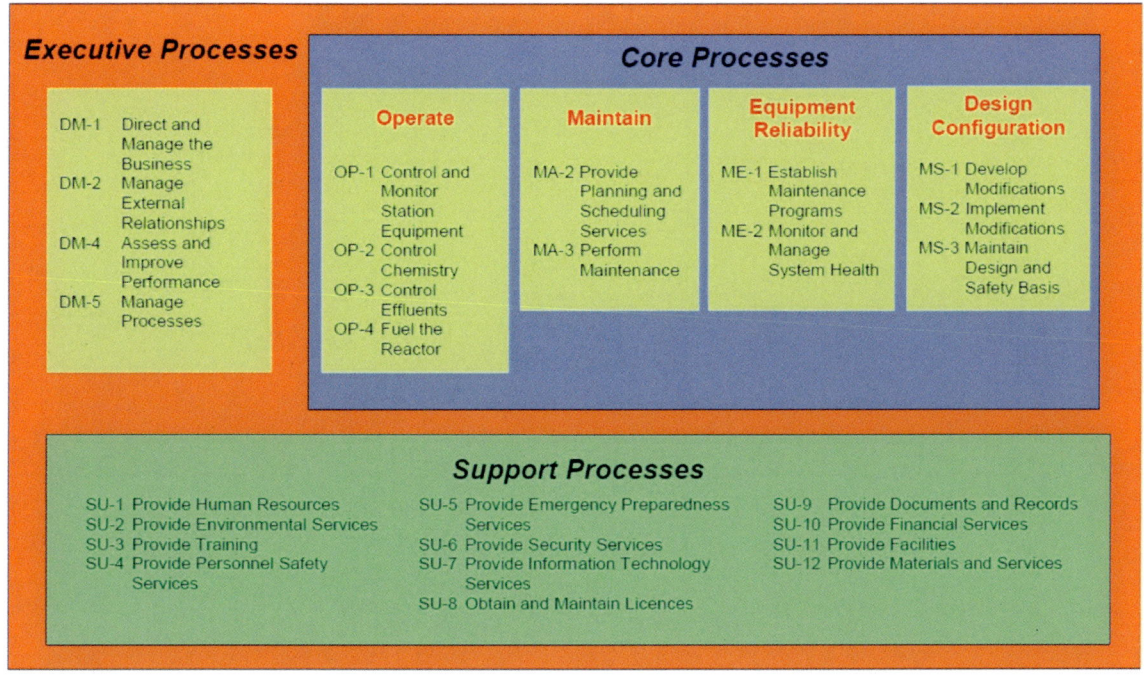

Nuclear Regulator Process Model – Canadian Nuclear Safety Commission
[Ref. CNSC 2013]

MANAGEMENT PROCESSES	CORE PROCESSES		
	Manage the Regulatory Framework	Manage Licensing and Certification	Assure Compliance
• Direct and Manage the Organization • Manage Communications and Stakeholder Engagement • Evaluate and Improve Performance • Manage Processes	• Administer the *Nuclear Safety and Control Act* • Establish and Maintain Regulations and Guidance Documents • Establish and Maintain Domestic and International Arrangements • Disseminate Scientific, Technical and Regulatory Information • Conduct Regulatory Research	• Assess Applications • Make Licensing and Certification Decisions	• Verify Compliance • Enforce Compliance • Report on Compliance

ENABLING PROCESSES

- Human Resources Management
- Occupational Health and Safety Services
- Learning and Development
- Information Management
- Information Technology
- Finance
- Internal Security
- Legal Services
- Physical Resources
- Procurement and Contracting

Nuclear Standard Process Model – INPO/NEI

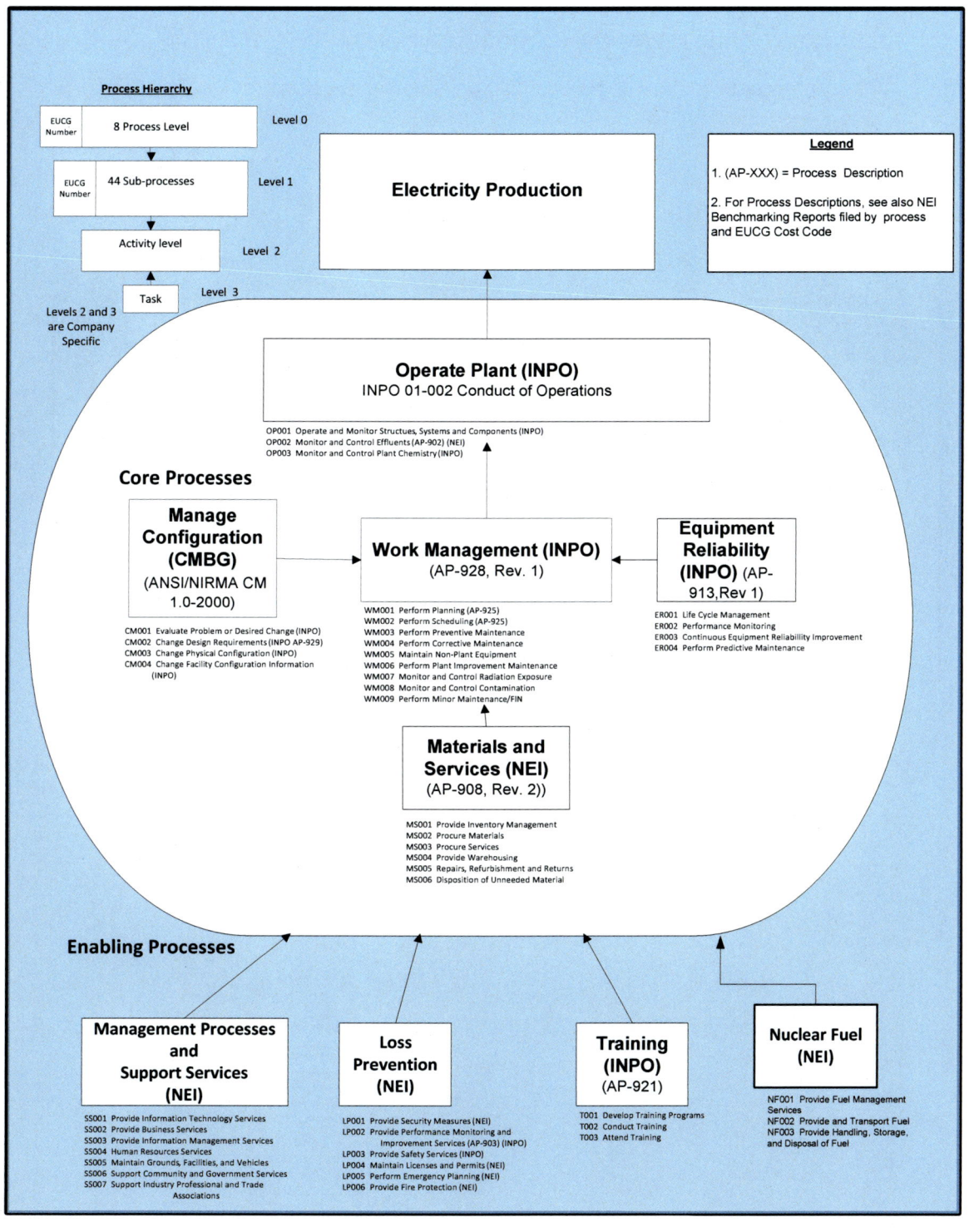

A-35

Nuclear Standard Process Model – INPO/NEI

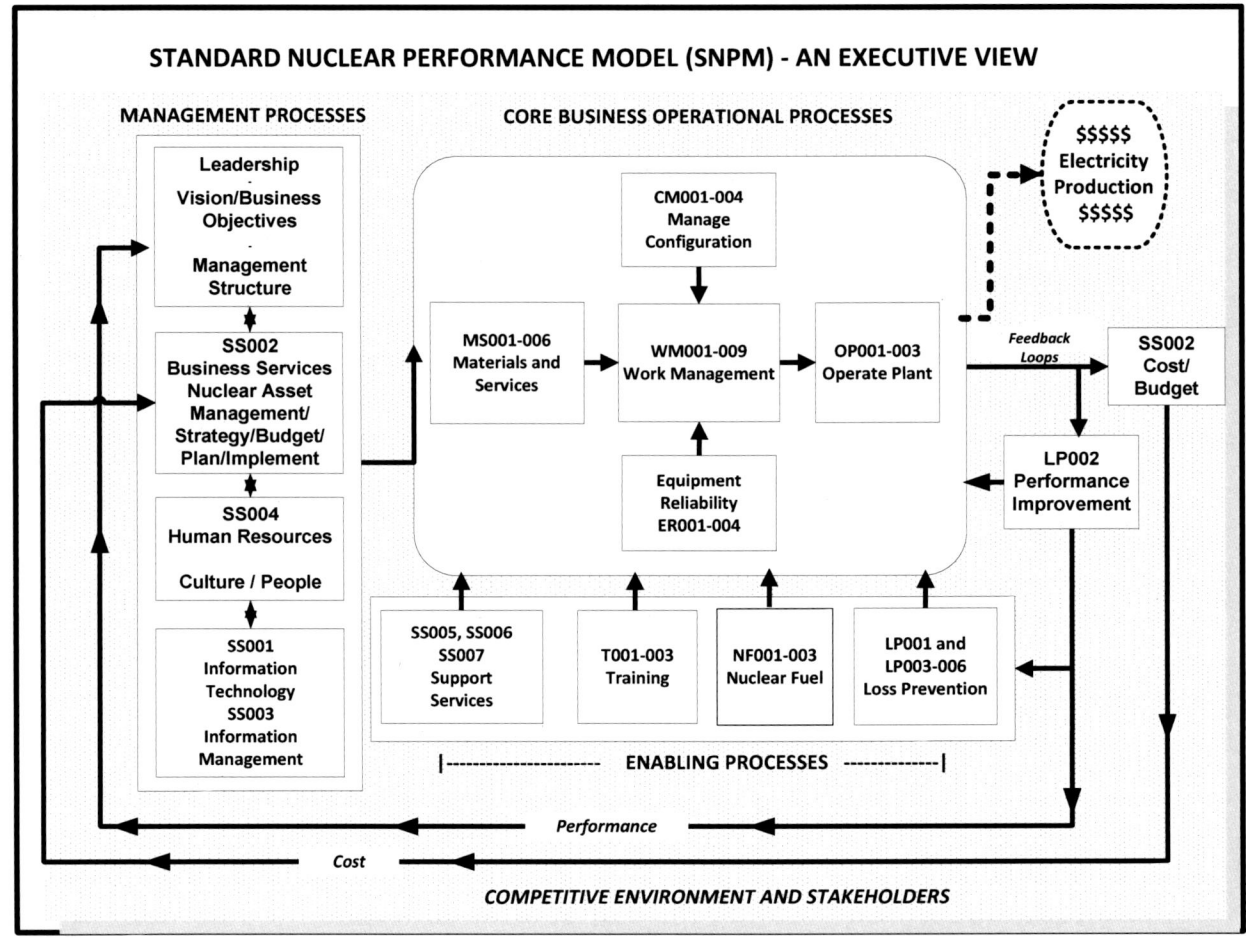

Nuclear Regulator Model – Federal Authority for Nuclear Regulation, United Arab Emirates [Ref. Grant, I.M. et al. 2013]

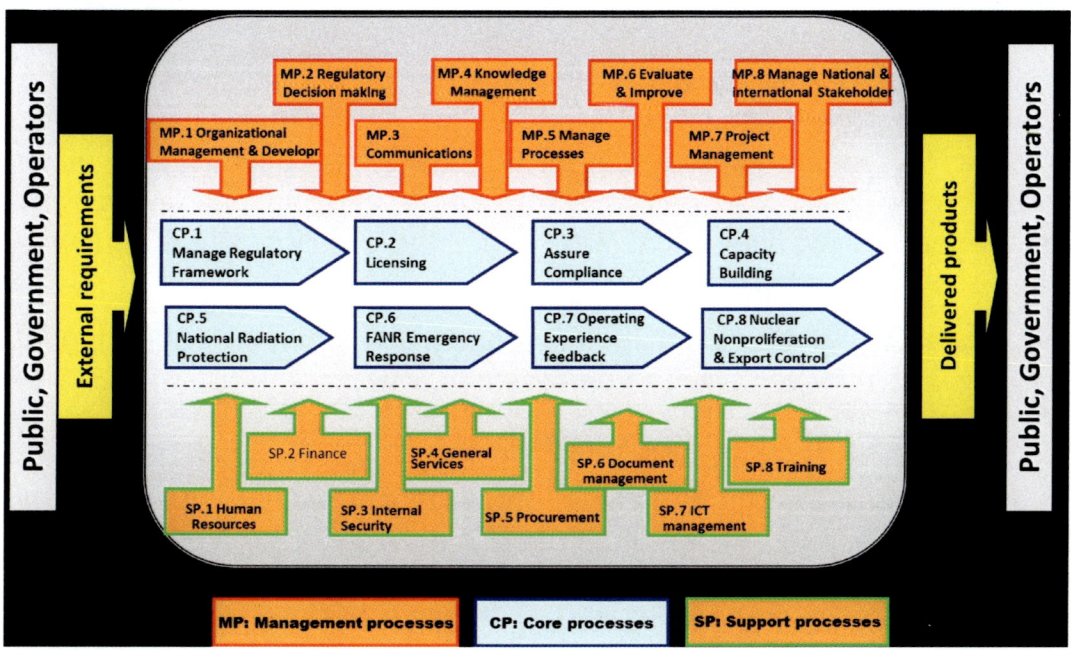

Appendix F

Organizational Assessment Questionnaire

This Appendix provides a method for assessing the current state of management systems using the models discussed in Part A. The questionnaire should be completed by people familiar with all aspects of the organization, either as a group or individually. It is desirable to have input at various levels across the organization to avoid biases that may occur if the questionnaire is completed only by senior staff or one department.

The purpose of the questionnaire is to identify areas that may offer opportunities for systematic improvement. The process has 5 steps.

Step 1 – Answer all these questions

On a scale of 1 through 5, indicate the extent to which your organization is compatible with each statement in the following table. Your choice should represent your current view of what <u>actually happens</u> in your organization rather than your view of what should happen.

Rating:

    1 – don't agree at all

    2 – don't quite agree

    3 – neutral (we're neither bad nor good)

    4 – agree somewhat

    5 – agree strongly.

No.	Rating 1 to 5	Question
1.		Procedural adherence is emphasized in the workplace.
2.		Most emergent issues are technical, engineering, or mechanical.
3.		Managers motivate personnel to improve performance.
4.		Supervisors are responsible for assigning experienced people to work activities.
5.		Managers routinely observe and evaluate personnel performance.

No.	Rating 1 to 5	Question
6.		Managers reinforce expectations and adjust priorities.
7.		Technical competence and skills are highly valued throughout the organization.
8.		Training focuses mainly on skills of the trade and technical competence.
9.		Work performance is routinely verified to confirm consistency with standards.
10.		We are conservative in our decision-making to ensure safe and reliable operations.
11.		In our organization, practical experience in the field is considered more valuable than education.
12.		Managers use performance indicators to monitor a variety of parameters.
13.		Managers set clear goals, priorities, and performance expectations.
14.		In our organization specialist expertise is more valued than being a generalist.
15.		Our primary focus is on reliable operation.
16.		Department roles and boundaries are well defined to ensure responsibilities and authorities are clear.
17.		Considerable emphasis is put on planning, scheduling and controlling work.
18.		Sound technical knowledge and experience are essential for promotion to senior positions.
19.		Quality assurance inspections and audits against standards are an important control mechanism.
20.		Our key focus is on our primary means of production and its efficient operation.
21.		Mobilizing metrics are mainly centered on production and equipment parameters.
22.		Craftsmanship, skill of the trade, and equipment knowledge are highly valued and respected for problem solving.
23.		Maintenance, operations, and technical work is identified, scheduled, documented, and trended.
24.		We purchase top quality maintenance, test, and inspection equipment to support production.

No.	Rating 1 to 5	Question
25.		Our organization is very pragmatic and focuses on solving immediate problems.
26.		We have strict controls on authorizations for equipment maintenance and operation.
27.		We take prompt corrective action in response to indications of abnormal equipment operation.
28.		Managers demonstrate a high level of commitment to safety.
29.		Information flow and logistics between departments is coordinated mainly at the manager level.
30.		Cost control is a significant factor in work allocation and performance.
31.		There is single point control for changes to the management system architecture and processes.
32.		Opportunities exist for individuals to partner with others possessing complementary leadership and behavioural preferences.
33.		Team leaders pay attention to staff growth and development.
34.		Our planning processes are effective.
35.		Team leaders engage teams in self-reflection on team dynamics, performance, and behaviours.
36.		Decision-making authority is delegated to the lowest practical level.
37.		My manager keeps our team apprised of emergent organizational and team issues.
38.		Desired outcomes are clearly defined and communicated.
39.		Senior leaders have a clearly articulated vision for the organization.
40.		Our management system is based on a top-level model that is easily cascaded to lower level processes and procedures.
41.		The organization pays visible attention to its responsibilities to society at large.
42.		Leaders are selected to match the required functionality and behavioural propensities of the team.
43.		Work assignments make use of team diversity.
44.		Our project management processes are effective.
45.		Senior leaders actively promote benchmarking beyond the organization.

No.	Rating 1 to 5	Question
46.		Our practices as a learning organization extend beyond 'find-and-fix problems' and 'learn from our and other's mistakes' to 'find innovative solutions'.
47.		I am in a right-fit job that fully utilizes my innate propensities and abilities.
48.		Our budgeting system is effective.
49.		My manager is an effective spokesperson for our team.
50.		Processes and procedures are user-focused, up-to-date, and easy to follow.
51.		Cross-discipline and cross-departmental cooperation and engagement are strengths in our organization.
52.		Information is easily accessible.
53.		The management system is considered to include organizational structure and culture.
54.		Leaders take a collaborative approach to resolving organizational issues.
55.		Users and stakeholders are engaged from inception to improvement to ensure effectiveness and efficiency.
56.		Process maps are easy to follow from a human factors perspective.
57.		We maintain our equipment and infrastructure to high standards.
58.		My manager delegates work without micro-managing.
59.		We have a designated management system owner-architect.
60.		Leaders create and communicate a unified message.
61.		Processes and procedures are developed using high levels of engagement, including cross-functional input.
62.		Our processes and our technology are aligned and compatible.
63.		The organization's human resources are a fluid asset shared according to organizational needs and individual suitability.
64.		Process interfaces are well defined.
65.		The organization has a means for identifying innate behavioural strengths.
66.		It is easy to retrieve the current process or procedural document needed for a particular activity.
67.		My manager is a role model for the organization's values.

No.	Rating 1 to 5	Question
68.		Teams define their own mobilizing metrics based on 'customer' needs.
69.		Outcomes go beyond profitability.
70.		Prior to purchasing new technology we evaluate its impact on the way we work.
71.		Team leaders manage power dynamics to create open communication.
72.		Supervisory, management, and senior management roles are recognized as distinct disciplines rather than a natural career progression.
73.		Our technology effectively supports information retrieval and retention.
74.		Leaders are engaged in improving the management system.
75.		There is little duplication of processes and procedures across the organization.
76.		There is single point ownership and accountability for every process and its associated procedures.
77.		My manager has a good understanding of the work processes of key groups that interact with our team.
78.		Our accounting and cost-control systems are effective.
79.		Process maps form the backbone of process documents.
80.		Process owners are credible, hands-on, knowledgeable individuals.
81.		There is organizational focus on engaging people in deciding how work is to be accomplished.
82.		We actively improve our technology.
83.		Managers and supervisors willingly share information with others.
84.		Organizational development staff are active partners in management system development, change, and assessment.
85.		Senior leaders demonstrate a strong capacity for strategic, systemic, and systematic thinking.
86.		Process owners engage others to continually improve their processes.
87.		The organization has a disciplined succession planning process in place.
88.		Organizational and process improvements identified by teams are acted on in a timely manner.
89.		We have adequate tools and equipment to do our work.

No.	Rating 1 to 5	Question
90.		Document types are defined and supported by standard templates used throughout the organization.
91.		Long-term sustainability is a key focus area for senior leaders.
92.		My manager routinely conducts team meetings, both planned and as needed.
93.		Consistent standards for process development are used across the organization.
94.		Team resourcing considers the requisite propensities for healthy team dynamics and functionality.
95.		The organization demonstrably values a broad range of individual talent and contribution.
96.		The organization goes beyond minimum compliance with standards.
97.		A well-defined document hierarchy is in place.
98.		Distributed or co-leadership is used to enhance team performance.
99.		Senior management pays attention to its responsibilities to external shareholders and stakeholders.
100.		Leaders encourage innovation.
101.		The management system is regarded as a key enabler for knowledge management, change management and oversight.
102.		Information is freely shared throughout the organization.
103.		My manager views human error as a learning opportunity.
104.		The organizational structure is aligned with our desired functionalities.
105.		Team leaders care about whether people are trained and competent to do their work.
106.		Leaders pay attention to developing internal talent at all levels.
107.		There is a concise top-level document that describes the organization and relationships between its work, principles, context, standards, structure, processes and responsibilities.
108.		Teams from different departments work well together.
109.		Our income exceeds our expenses.
110.		My manager welcomes feedback even when someone questions his or her actions or decisions.

No.	Rating 1 to 5	Question
111.		The organization provides learning and growth opportunities related to potential growth rather than just the current job.
112.		Oversight is pro-active, forward thinking, and goes beyond reacting to problems or resolving findings from audits.
113.		Leaders at all levels understand and apply the management system.
114.		The management system is regarded as a key repository for information.
115.		Consistent writer's guides are used across the organization.
116.		The organization actively makes use of diversity of reasoning and relating styles.
117.		Leaders routinely use participative engagement tools (e.g., facilitators, team meetings, open space forums, appreciative inquiry, focus groups, etc.) to help resolve organizational issues and improve organizational alignment.
118.		Our monitoring and measurement systems track the right performance indicators.
119.		My manager consults the team on optimal strategies for performing work.
120.		We have adequate facilities to support our work.
121.		Changes to the management system are considered from an organizational and cultural perspective.
122.		Job design considers interdependencies, interfaces, and relationships.
123.		Senior leaders pay attention to their meaning-making role.
124.		The senior management team has strengths in a variety of behavioural competencies in addition to technical expertise.
125.		My manager has a good understanding of our team's work processes.
126.		We have adequate financial resources to support our improvement agenda.
127.		The organization understands the benefit of connecting people who have complementary strengths.
128.		Silo mentalities are discouraged in our organization.
129.		Leaders pay attention to organizational culture.
130.		Core, support, executive, and governance processes are differentiated.
131.		Information is regarded as an asset.

No.	Rating 1 to 5	Question
132.		Leaders pay attention to the relationship and integration among departments and systems.
133.		Preparation and revision of processes and procedures are supported by competent technical writers.
134.		Positions are filled on the basis of potential gaps in the overall team attributes rather than solely from individual position descriptions.
135.		My manager acknowledges exceptional effort by the team or its members.
136.		Senior leaders set and communicate organizational direction based on a clear understanding of issues relevant to organizational health and sustainability.
137.		My manager spends sufficient time interacting with team members and is accessible when needed.
138.		Our organization manages large changes effectively.
139.		The management system is viewed as a primary vehicle for continual improvement.
140.		My manager resolves relationship issues promptly, fairly, and effectively.
141.		There are clear links between process activities, position description responsibilities, job analyses, training/development, and selection criteria.
142.		Document revisions and temporary changes are controlled effectively.
143.		We meet or exceed customer expectations.
144.		My manager pays attention to the emotional well-being of team members.
145.		Talent assessment and recruitment goes beyond qualifications and experience to include behavourial attributes.
146.		The organization does a good job of considering leadership competencies in relation to what the organization is trying to accomplish and how it is trying to evolve.
147.		Executive/management processes are well developed.
148.		An oversight mechanism is in place to ensure the overall effectiveness of the organization.
149.		The organization pays visible attention to its responsibilities to the local community.
150.		Interpersonal competencies are a factor in promotions to senior positions.

No.	Rating 1 to 5	Question
151.		An organizational design basis is used for development planning and assessing organizational changes.
152.		The organization recognizes different types of teams and resources them accordingly.
153.		In difficult or stressful situations managers in our organization guard against placing excessive pressure on any team or individual.
154.		We have established protocols for communicating with external stakeholders.
155.		My manager is an effective negotiator in terms of ensuring our team obtains needed resources.
156.		External factors have little impact on our organization.
157.		We have mutually respectful relationships with our regulators.
158.		The public generally understands and accepts the role of our organization.
159.		Our role in society is unlikely to change within the next decade.
160.		The regulatory structure and constraints are appropriate for our industry.

Step 2 – Complete the scoring table for the Maturity Model

In the left hand side of the table below, insert the rating number from the first 30 questions in Step 1 in the appropriate blank space. On the right hand side of the table, insert the rating from other selected questions, paying careful attention to the question number.

Question	Rating 1-5	
1.		
2.		
3.		
4.		
5.		
6.		
7.		
8.		
9.		
10.		
11.		
12.		
13.		
14.		
15.		
16.		
17.		
18.		
19.		
20.		
21.		
22.		
23.		
24.		
25.		
26.		
27.		
28.		
29.		
30.		
Total		
Divide by	15	15
Result		
Key	1	2

Question	Rating 1-5	
35.		
36.		
44.		
45.		
46.		
50.		
51.		
54.		
64.		
65.		
72.		
74.		
75.		
76.		
81.		
85.		
93.		
101.		
108.		
111.		
112.		
116.		
118.		
121.		
123.		
128.		
132.		
136.		
138.		
150.		
Total		
Divide by	15	15
Result		
Key	3	4

Perform the calculations at the bottom of the above table.

Step 3 – Place the scores on the Organizational Evolution Model

Before applying the results of step 2 to Figure F-1, on a scale of 1-5 record your gut sense of the extent to which each stage applies to your organization, where 1 is not at all, and 5 is a lot. Next, use the key in the last row of the table in step 2 to transfer the scores to the Organizational Evolution Model below.

The results provide an indication of your organization's predominant stage of evolution and its relative cultural preferences and orientation as described in Chapter 3. Typically the highest scores will be for Stage 1 and Stage 2. If the score for Stage 4 is higher than for Stage 3, this may indicate a positive bias or halo effect.

Explore any differences between your gut level estimate and the results transferred from the table in Step 2.

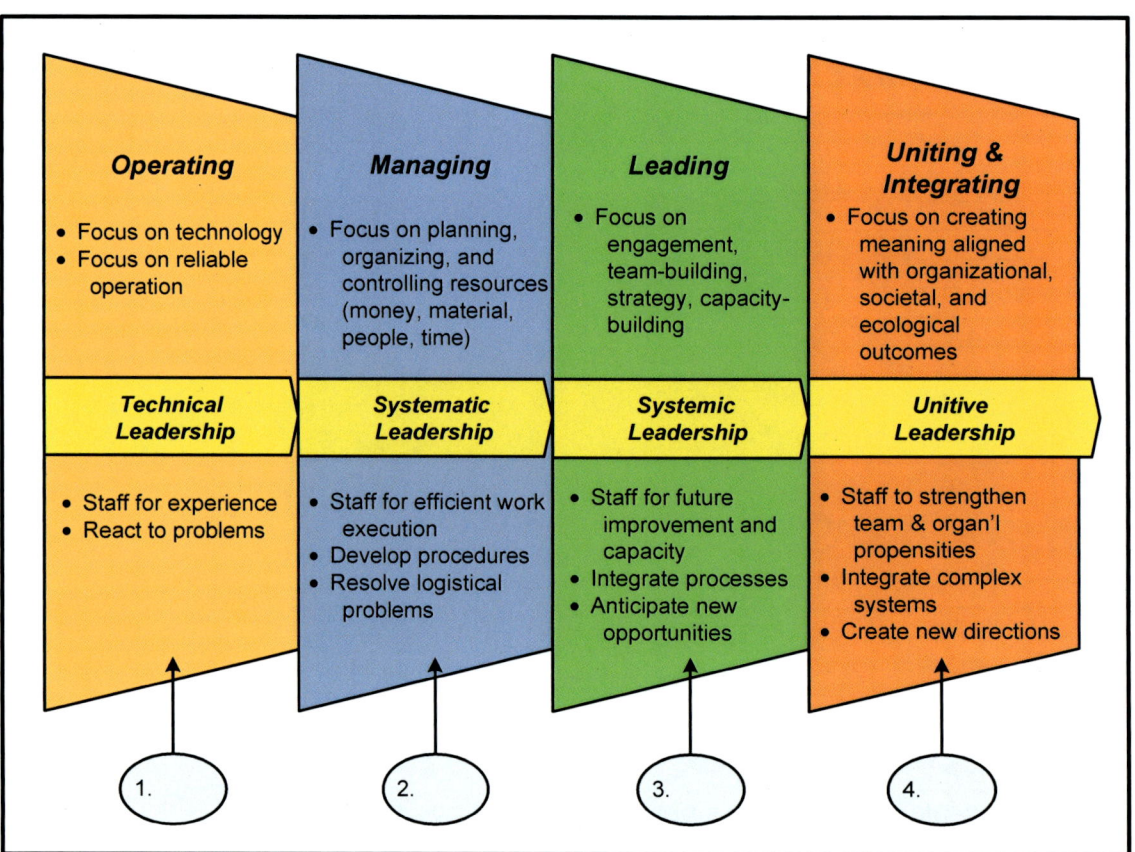

Figure F-1: Assessment scores against stages of evolution

Step 4 – Complete the scoring table for the Organizational Model

Transfer the rating from each of the questions in Step 1 to the appropriate blank in the following table. Transfer the subtotals of the scores from each page into the appropriate line near the end of the table.

Question	Rating 1 - 5											
31.												
32.												
33.												
34.												
35.												
36.												
37.												
38.												
39.												
40.												
41.												
42.												
43.												
44.												
45.												
46.												
47.												
48.												
49.												
50.												
51.												
52.												
53.												
54.												
55.												
56.												
57.												
58.												
59.												
60.												
61.												
62.												
63.												
64.												
65.												
66.												
67.												
68.												
69.												
70.												
71.												
72.												
73.												
74.												
Subtotal 1												

Question	Rating 1 - 5										
75.											
76.											
77.											
78.											
79.											
80.											
81.											
82.											
83.											
84.											
85.											
86.											
87.											
88.											
89.											
90.											
91.											
92.											
93.											
94.											
95.											
96.											
97.											
98.											
99.											
100.											
101.											
102.											
103.											
104.											
105.											
106.											
107.											
108.											
109.											
110.											
111.											
112.											
113.											
114.											
115.											
116.											
117.											
118.											
119.											
120.											
121.											
122.											
123.											
124.											
125.											
126.											
127.											
128.											
Subtotal 2											
Question	Rating 1 - 5										

	1	2	3	4	5	6	7	8	9	10	11	12
129.												
130.												
131.												
132.												
133.												
134.												
135.												
136.												
137.												
138.												
139.												
140.												
141.												
142.												
143.												
144.												
145.												
146.												
147.												
148.												
149.												
150.												
151.												
152.												
153.												
154.												
155.												
156.												
157.												
158.												
159.												
160.												
Subtotal 3												
Subtotal 2												
Subtotal 1												
Grand Total												
Divide by	16	3	28	3	10	5	4	16	11	16	5	13
Result												
Key	1	2	3	4	5	6	7	8	9	10	11	12

Complete the calculations in the above table by dividing the grand total by the number shown in the third to last row. This will normalize scores based on the number of questions in each category.

Step 5 – Place the scores on the Organizational Model

Before applying the scores from the previous table, examine Figure F-2 and record your gut level estimate of 1-5 beside each oval, where 1 is poor performance and 5 is excellent. Next, use the key in the last row of the previous table to enter the score into the appropriate oval. The results indicate how well your organization is doing related to each attribute. A score of less than 3.0 in any oval suggests there are opportunities to strengthen organizational approaches in the related area. If any of the scores differ from your gut estimate, consider why this might be.

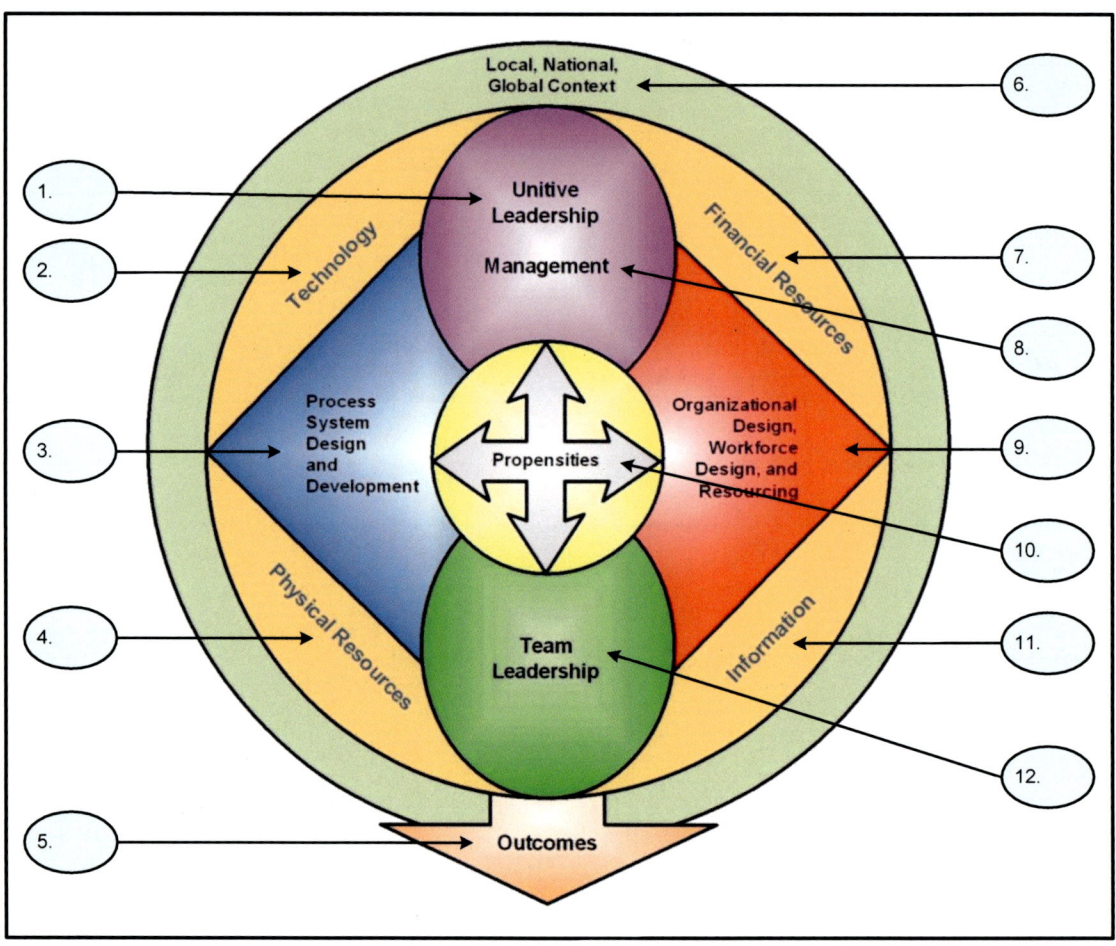

Figure F-2: Assessment scores against the generic organizational system model

Appendix G

Process Description Worksheet

This Appendix provides a template for describing the essential attributes of a process. It is a useful starting point for developing a specific process, particularly a top-level process.

The list of key activities in the template usually provides an indication of the main sub-processes required to implement the key process.

One can develop more detailed forms for such descriptions, however, our preference is to use a one-page approach whenever possible. The worksheet is intended as preparation for discussion with the process development team, and the content invariably changes with input from the group during its initial meeting. The worksheet is not a formal document to be updated and maintained, hence it can be discarded following process development. Any information derived from it is captured in the formal process documentation.

Process Description Worksheet Template

Process identifier and name	
Indicate the process name, beginning with an active verb. A process identifier or code may be used.	

Purpose
Describe the 'business' reason for the existence of the process

Application
Describe the scope of the process: who it applies to, and under what conditions such as when and where.

Key requirements
• *Bullet list of key requirements (e.g., applicable codes and standards, management requirements).*

Key activities
• *Bullet list of key activities*

Key inputs	**Supplied by**
• *Bullet list of key inputs*	• *Bullet list of suppliers or providers of the inputs*
Key outputs	**Provided to**
• *Bullet list of key outputs*	• *Bullet list of customers or receivers of the outputs*

Performers
List the main performers of the process by department or job classification

Key stakeholders
List the stakeholders who should be notified or consulted when planning significant changes to the process.

Key interfacing processes
List the interfacing processes that may be affected by a change to this process, or for which changes to an interfacing process may affect this process.

Process Owner (title)	**Responsible Manager (title)**

Appendix H

Table of Contents – Organizational Design Basis Document

This Appendix provides a sample Table of Contents for an Organizational Design Basis Document. Like the Management Manual described in Appendix I, the document is informational rather than procedural, and specifies guiding principles and requirements related to the organization and organizational changes. However, the level of detail will be greater because the basis document contains details on more positions.

1. Introduction
    1.1. Purpose
    1.2. Application (Scope)
2. Organizational Principles
3. Integration Strategy / Approach
    3.1. Human System
    3.2. Management System Processes
    3.3. Technology
4. Shared Meaning System
5. Rationale for Key Organizational Attributes
    5.1. Organizational Functionalities
    5.2. Organizational Groupings
    5.3. Organizational Levels
6. Rationale for Key Process-based Groupings
    6.1. Process-based Groupings (Mobilizing Constellations)
    6.2. Meeting Venues
    6.3. Relationships and Interfaces
7. Critical Propensities
    7.1. Leadership Level
    7.2. Team Level
8. Organizational Map
    8.1. Structure / Organigrams
    8.2. Key Position Responsibilities, Accountabilities, and Authorities
    8.3. Process Owner Responsibilities, Accountabilities, and Authorities
9. Organizational Support Systems and Programs
10. Organizational Development Strategy
11. Organizational Change Management

Glossary of Organizational Terms
Appendices
    A (*Example*) Terms of Reference – Template

Appendix I

Table of Contents – Management System Manual

This Appendix provides a sample Table of Contents for a Management System Manual. Not all sections apply to every organization, and it is important to design a manual that fits the needs of the organization. A well-designed manual can eliminate the need for additional policy statements, allowing the organization to focus documentation resources on processes and procedures that actually control work. The manual should be concise, typically in the range of 25-35 pages.

Statement of Executive Commitment
1. Introduction
    1.1. General
    1.2. Purpose of this Manual
    1.3. Application (Scope)
    1.4. Organization
2. Our Meaning System
    2.1. Operating Context
    2.2. Mandate
    2.3. Mission
    2.4. Vision
    2.5. Values
    2.6. Strategic Outcomes
    2.7. Our Culture
    2.8. Our Operating Philosophy
    2.9. Stakeholder Engagement
3. Our Technology
4. Our Management System
    4.1. Management System Basis
        4.1.1. Policy Statements
        4.1.2. Management System Requirements
        4.1.3. Grading
    4.2. Our Processes
    4.3. Process Ownership
    4.4. Governance Processes
    4.5. Executive/Management Processes
    4.6. Core Processes
    4.7. Support Processes

5. Our Human System
    5.1. Our Organization
    5.2. Responsibilities, Accountabilities, and Authorities
        5.2.1. Organizational Units
        5.2.2. Outcome-focused Process Groupings
        5.2.3. Senior Management Positions
    5.3. Health, Safety, and Environment
    5.4. Human Resources and Training
    5.5. Organizational Development
6. Resource Management
    6.1. Planning
        6.1.1. Strategic
        6.1.2. Annual
        6.1.3. Operational
    6.2. Finance
    6.3. Information Management
    6.4. Internal Security
    6.5. Legal Services
    6.6. Physical Resources
    6.7. Procurement and Contracting
7. Management System Documentation
    7.1. Documentation Framework
    7.2. Records
8. Monitoring, Assessment, and Oversight
    8.1. Performance Assessment
    8.2. Management Oversight
9. Proactive Adaptation and Continual Improvement

Appendix J

Example of a Graded Approach

This Appendix provides a sample framework for grading adapted from a system developed at the Point Lepreau Nuclear Station in Canada. Although there are many possible frameworks [IAEA 2014], the example in Figure J-1 is sufficient to illustrate a simple and practical approach to grading. Generally, organizations should resist developing complex grading systems that are difficult to apply in practice. For this reason, during development of the framework it is beneficial to include subject matter experts from the processes that have a key need for grading.

A framework such as Figure J-1 is used during the initial development of a process to ensure a graded approach is incorporated into each process or procedure as appropriate. For Grade 1 application, the full set of controls is applied as defined in the applicable procedure. For example, work on a safety related system would require in-hand procedures, higher level authorizations to perform the procedure, specific qualifications for the performer, control of replacement parts and configuration, and detailed recording of task progress and results. These controls would be explicitly identified in the applicable procedure or detailed work plan.

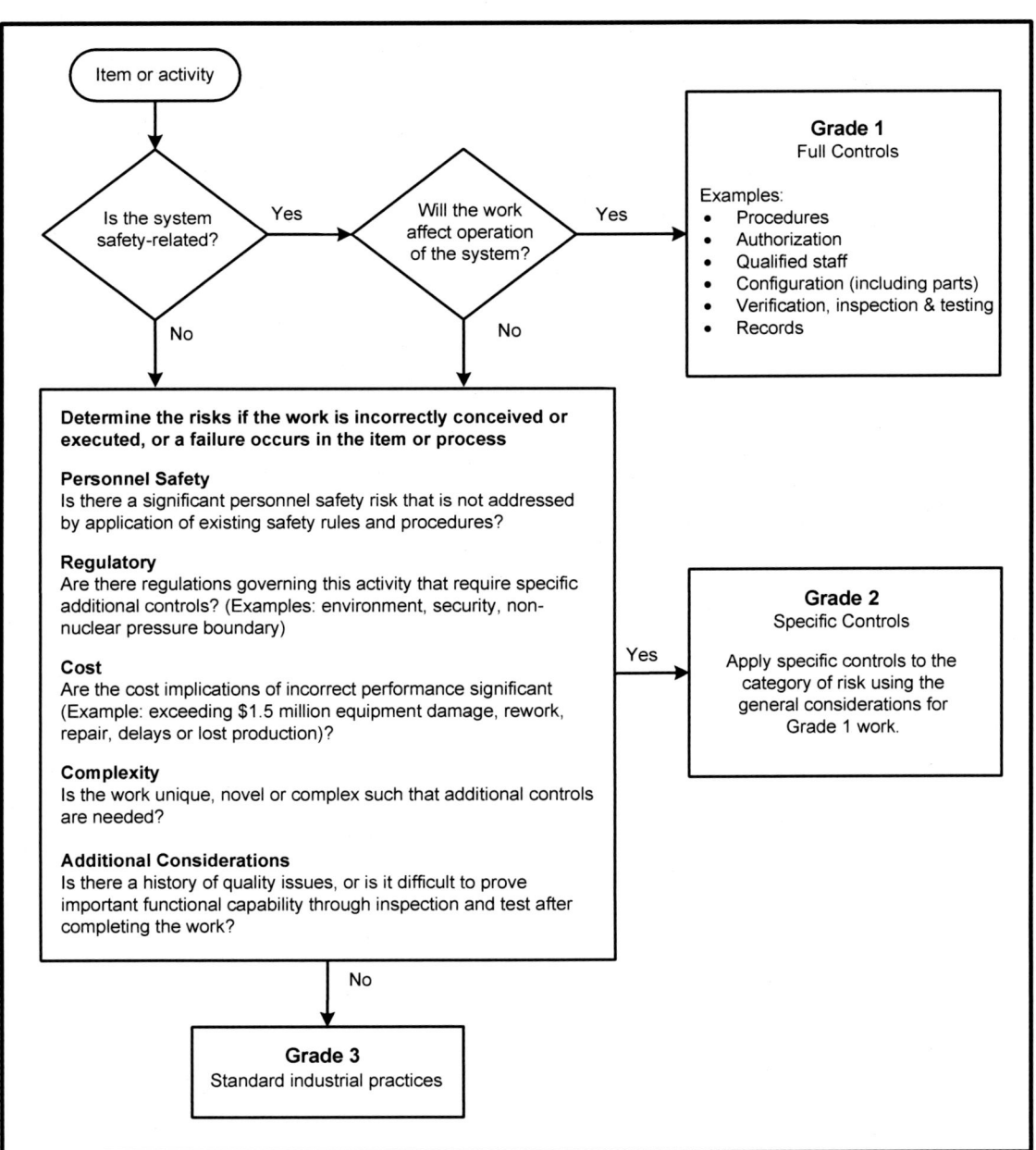

Figure J-1: Example Grading Framework

Appendix K

Tips for Writing Effective Process and Procedural Documents

1. Develop management system documents using a single, trained group of technical writers skilled in producing documents to best practices. This aids consistency, avoids overlap and duplication, and controls interfaces. It also ensures the most effective use of time for technical subject matter experts, since they are rarely efficient at writing documents.
2. Develop lean, activity-based documents free of information that is not of direct use for the specific application.
3. Use a one-page rule for process maps or flowcharts. This usually limits the map to about 10 activity boxes (somewhat more if there are parallel activities).
4. Design for the end user, rather than including everything anyone might ever want to know.
5. Design for online use, including tablets or other handheld devices.
6. For process documents, the map or flowchart forms the backbone of the content. Relate supporting text for detailed activities directly to the map. There should be a clear one-to-one relationship between the tasks and elements on the flowchart. Do not place flowcharts in an appendix as an afterthought.
7. Put background information, training information, or history in other documents such as training documents, information reports or technical basis documents. If the information has practical value for the user but is not directly part of the activities performed, put it in an Appendix.
8. Use active rather than passive or descriptive language.
9. Design processes and procedures for the repeat user, not the first-time user. Experienced users tend to skim documents that contain information they already know, increasing the likelihood of error through missed steps. Move sections that are referred to infrequently to an appendix. Train first-time users appropriately.
10. Don't write implementation documents and distribute them for review without first engaging cross-functional stakeholders to discuss the document's purpose and the activities it should contain.

11. Policies don't do real work. Keep them brief and eliminate them wherever possible. Most generic policy statements can be included in the Management Manual at Tier 1. Ensure policies are supported by lower level implementing documents.
12. All work processes should be defined within the management system, but not all work needs to be documented. A good guide is to cover 80% of anticipated situations to avoid unnecessary detail and complexity in documents. Supervision can provide guidance on the remaining 20% of unusual cases.
13. Processes are different from procedures. Procedures require 100% compliance if work is safety related. Processes allow for some flexibility provided governing requirements are met.
14. Processes should be simple. The extent of documentation depends on safety importance, complexity, and number of cross-functional interfaces.
15. Base the process on valid, traceable requirements (e.g., Acts, Regulations, codes, standards, policies) rather than on history or opinions.
16. Minimize non-value added steps such as unnecessary reviews and approvals.
17. Use process-based systems thinking rather than departmental thinking when examining work activities, interfaces and flow to prevent processes from evolving into another form of management by department.
18. Even when a flowchart is not needed in the document (e.g., equipment procedure), it is often useful to sketch one during document preparation to help ensure a logical sequence of steps.
19. Identify responsibilities after mapping the process to ensure the responsibilities reflect actual activities and vice-versa. When recording responsibilities, summarize rather than repeat activities in the process. Describe authority or oversight responsibilities.
20. If a document exceeds 30 pages, consider splitting it into two.
21. Processes don't have to be the perfect on first issue, otherwise continual improvement would be unnecessary. Implementing a process that is 80-90% correct may result in faster improvement since implementation always reveals unanticipated issues. (This does not apply to procedures or processes with safety implications which have to be verified or validated as 100% correct.)

22. Assign an owner by title or name to every document used to perform work. If no one owns a document it is unlikely to be kept current.
23. Keep forms separate from documents that use or refer to them. This allows independent revision.

Appendix L

Human Performance Enhancers and Error Reduction Tools

This Appendix provides a list of human performance enhancers and error reduction tools used in the nuclear industry. Many variations of these approaches exist. They are grouped in terms of the Management System Elements, Actions and Practices, and Knowledge Base. Items within each group are in alphabetical order.

Management System Elements

Item	Description
Audits and inspections	Routine audits and inspections of safety relevant equipment and materials, including contingency supplies.
Change management	Formal, consistent approach to assessing, controlling, and monitoring changes in human, technology, and process systems.
Configuration management	Rigorous control of design information, installation, and maintenance and operational states, including rigorous control of temporary changes.
Equipment identification	Unique, unambiguous labeling of equipment in the field and on design drawings, operational flow sheets, and procedures.
Fitness for duty	Criteria for optimal shift cycle design, limitations on hours of work, alertness to symptoms of impaired performance, including stress, and promotion of non-punishing self-identification.
Job safety planning and analysis	Comprehensive work planning, safety assessments, critical task analysis, contingency planning.
Operating experience usage	Easy access to relevant internal and external operating experience for job planning and briefings.
Performance indicators	Indicators related to safety and reliability, including precursors such as human performance error rate. Indicators are proactive and motivate desired behaviours (mobilizing indicators)
Procedure design	Modern human factors elements embedded in procedure design and checklists. Usage classification (in-hand, reference, information) applied to procedures.
Simulator use	Use of full scope and field simulators for training and testing.
Work management and controls	Effective work management systems, work permit controls, equipment tagging and lockouts.

Actions and Practices

Item	Description
Barrier analysis	A determination of the barriers in place to reduce the likelihood of an unintended event. Barriers may be physical, temporal, administrative, etc.
Blameless culture	Reporting of errors or omissions, including self-reporting, is valued by the organization and does not result in recrimination.
Challenge meetings	A meeting with the sole purpose of discovering potential weaknesses in a plan of action.
Checklist Usage	Itemized lists of actions that must be performed to accomplish a task in a safe and effective manner.
Conservative decision-making	Ensuring safety and reliability are included in decision-making as a matter of routine practice.
Contingency plans	Back-out criteria, redundancy, compensatory actions are included in the planning of work activities.
Distraction management	Minimization of parallel work activities or conversations, particularly during critical operations.
Field observations	Peers, supervisors, and management routinely conduct field observations to ensure work is conducted in a safe and effective manner. Some organizations have formalized observation programs.
Independent verification	Having an individual independent of the work perform an independent check, based on specific acceptance criteria.
Inquiring attitude	Willingness to ask questions, follow up issues, and expect answers. Also known as a 'questioning attitude'.
Inspections and Hold Points	These quality elements are built directly into procedures to indicate points at which work must be inspected prior to the next step being performed.
Just-in-Time training	Training on important aspects of a job within a reasonably short time period before performing the activity.
Mock-ups	A staged setup of a work area or activity to enable practice in the absence of hazards associated with the actual work. See also table-tops, walk-throughs.

Peer-checking	Having an individual familiar with the task confirming the accuracy of a peer's work at specific points. The individual may be involved in some aspects of the work other than the activity being checked. He or she may be from a different work group.
Phonetic alphabet	A standardized form (e.g., NATO) of expressing letters and numbers to help avoid communication errors. Letters that have similar sounds, such as i (India) and y (yellow) are less likely to be confused.
Place-keeping	Signing-off or check-marking specific steps in a procedure for which the sequence of operation is critical.
Procedural adherence	Following process and procedural documents, reporting procedural problems to enable correction, and obtaining approval for deviations.
Reporting culture	Implementation of a no-blame reporting culture in which errors, omissions, and concerns are raised with the aim of enhancing organizational learning.
Rigor of operations	Discipline in manipulating equipment. Rigor of operations includes maintenance and design activities.
Self-checking	Checking one's actions prior to execution. This includes variations such as STAR – Stop-Think-Act-Review; Touch-STAR in which the device to be manipulated is touched as the procedure is followed; touch-talk-STAR in which the added dimension of speaking the action and device identification are added, and STAR-C(ommunicate) in which the action is communicated to another during or after performance.
Table tops	A review of a new or changed process or procedure by a group representing typical performers. See also walk-throughs and mock-ups.
Three-way communications	The originator speaks, the listener repeats, and the originator confirms via an additional repeat, hence the message occurs three times.
Transparency	Willingness to share information laterally and vertically across departments and hierarchical levels.
Validation	Validation confirms that an activity achieves the intended outcomes under real or simulated conditions.

Walk-throughs	A simulated run through a new or changed process or procedure in which a group representing typical performers. Walk-throughs typically occur in the field rather than around a table. See also mock-ups and table-tops.
Workload management	Supervision should ensure workload balance to prevent high workloads or requirements to perform simultaneous tasks. In particular, individuals should not be subject to unnecessary time pressure that may impede concentration, thoughtful decision-making, or compromise safety.

Knowledge Base

Item	Description
Coaching and Mentoring	Constructive feedback aimed at improving performance
Defense in depth	A safety approach involving multiple barriers to prevent undesirable events. Barriers may be design, physical, human, temporal, etc.
Human performance	How humans behave under various work conditions. Motivators, detractors, and error-likely situations. Methods for enhancing and sustaining human performance in high reliability organizations.
Human propensities	Knowledge of underlying drivers to human behaviour that can compromise safety in terms of attention, clarity-lucidity, risk acceptance, stress-tolerance, confidence level, mental biases, spatial awareness, stamina, and foresight.
Management for safety	Essential elements that must be in place for an organization to maintain high levels of safety and reliability.
Professionalism	Values and behaviours that promote effective, accountable performance.
Risk management	How to identify, assess, and mitigate risk.
Safety culture	How to promote a natural inclination to make wise safety decisions at all levels within an organization under normal and off-normal conditions.
Safety leadership	Roles and responsibilities of leaders in promoting and sustaining safe operation.
Safety roles	Roles and responsibilities of individuals and specialists in promoting and sustaining safe operation.

Appendix M

Selecting Mobilizing Metrics

This Appendix discusses mobilizing metrics, measurement challenges, and ways of identifying mobilizing metrics aligned with human motivation. Although the focus of the handbook is on processes, process indicators are only one aspect of measurement. In the age of Google analytics and big data, nearly everything can be measured, and the temptation to do so pervades many organizations. Peter Drucker's saying that "what gets measured gets done/managed" is often accepted as gospel, despite ample evidence of human ingenuity when it comes to manipulating data to make them appear favorable. In a world of limitless options, how does one determine what is worth measuring?

Measurement systems are traditionally designed to identify the need to get others to act, i.e., motivate them to perform. Despite concrete evidence that intrinsic motivation is at the heart of sustainable performance, measurement systems often rely on extrinsic motivation in the form of team leaders and managers tasked to encourage or pressure employees to meet performance expectations. From the perspective of employees, this inherently creates a power dynamic that links self-esteem, social standing and confidence directly to a measurement. It is not surprising that upward flow of information is undermined by this dynamic.

In this chapter we begin with traditional approaches and transition to systems that foster self-motivation and mutual accountability.

TRADITIONAL APPROACHES TO PERFORMANCE METRICS

The following is an abbreviated account of common features of performance metrics (what we call mobilizing metrics).

Measure quantitatively when possible. Typical measurement parameters include:

- Time – an indication of responsiveness
- Quality – an indication of whether requirements are met or exceeded
- Safety – incident free performance
- Financial – income versus costs of implementation, operation, and maintenance
- Productivity – efficiency, effectiveness, reliability, quantity
- Employee satisfaction – perception of working environment, empowerment and opportunities

- Customer satisfaction – value to internal and external customers.

Essentially all measures attempt to evaluate effectiveness and efficiency. Effective means the activities meet legal and customer requirements. Efficient means the activities are accomplished with minimum resource cost and effort.

Each category of indicators can be examined from multiple perspectives. For example, indicators may be:

- Leading – suggest future performance (proactive) and are often obtained by trending low-level precursors such as near misses or low-consequence human performance errors
- Current – provide real-time status such as motor rpm and bearing temperature
- Lagging – indicate past performance (reactive) such as lost time accidents
- Time-averaged – recognize that short-term fluctuations occur, hence rolling averages are more useful (e.g., average absentee days per employee by month)
- Cumulative – indicates total impact over time such as cost versus budget.

Measurement may take place at various points:

- Input measures identify the effectiveness of transfers between processes or organizations
- In-process measures track process effectiveness and efficiency
- Output measures measure value-added organizational or business outcomes from the perspective of the internal or external customer.

Process indicators focus on attributes of the process related to effectiveness, efficiency and satisfaction.

Project indicators focus on deliverables, milestones, schedule, and work achievement curves.

Good principles and practices for selecting measures include:

1. Measure concrete, value-added outcomes.
2. Measure success, not failure.
3. Good measures drive the right work and the right behaviors.
4. Link measures to the business purpose or objectives of the process.
5. Develop a systematic measurement system, not a collection of unrelated measures.

6. Select the 'critical few' measures that will lead to informed decisions and actions. These should be linked to activities (how we do work).
7. Select measures that can be cascaded:
    – to the required organizational levels
    – from process to sub-process
    – from Business to Operational Plans.
8. Notwithstanding the above, avoid roll-ups, indices, and dashboards that obscure what is happening.
9. Select measures that someone 'owns' and are worth the effort to collect, analyze and report. Who is the customer of the measure?
10. Consider how the intended measure will it be used to adjust performance.
11. Select challenging yet achievable targets for key measures.
12. Use indicators for benchmarking performance against other organizations and the industry or profession at large.
13. Refine measures based on experience. They have a finite life and should be changed when no longer useful.

Consider the SMARTER attributes shown in the sidebar.

SMARTER attributes of good indicators and measures

Effective indicators and measures have a number of common features. They are:

- Specific – directly related to a process activity, area of interest, or output
- Measurable – quantitative rather than qualitative, even for behavioral measures
- Accountable – responsibility for results can be assigned to an owner who can take appropriate action
- Reasonable – the measure makes business sense, and collecting data is not burdensome
- Timely – provides early detection
- Effective – measures true intent related to the desired outcome
- Reviewed – someone cares about the measure.

BEYOND TRADITIONAL METRICS

We begin with four suggestions to keep in mind when thinking about measurements.

1. Design the measurement system so that it helps mobilize the organization to achieve the desired outcomes. This means it has to support collaboration and build on intrinsic motivation, rather than being reactive, punitive and based on short-term incentives.
2. Consider success and satisfaction related to the six simultaneously interacting complex systems in Figure 1-1. Use the systemic model developed by the organization as an overall guide.
3. Design indicators for the person or group who are most able to do something about the result. Each group will have different needs and roles e.g., chemistry control, equipment health, organization effectiveness. These may include:
    a. Subject matter experts who own the core issue
    b. Departmental units and teams
    c. Mobilizing constellations
    d. Management.
4. Consider the human system, not just technical, process and financial measures. Include required propensities, diversity, team capability, culture, relationships, etc., using the individual, team and organizational performance V's and Figure 5-2.

DESIGNING FOR OWNERSHIP AND INTENDED USE

An indicator is only useful if someone is interested enough to pay attention to it and willing to take action based on its result. To design motivating indicators, it is important to engage internal users to find out what would be meaningful indicators in terms of expectations they set for their own performance as well as expectations driven by their functionality within the organizational structure. For example, what indicators should a senior management team establish to monitor their own effectiveness and efficiency as a team accountable for defining the mission, establishing direction, securing resources, integrating structures and aligning staff?

Methods such as the balanced scorecard that link strategy, finance, internal processes, and learning and growth [Kaplan and Norton 1996], are a step in the right direction but need to become more comprehensive. Some metrics at the senior executive level are easy to quantify e.g., budgets, milestones and output rates. Unfortunately, these only measure explicit organizational performance and give no insight into the implicit human system effectiveness that is the accountability of senior management. How does one measure the effectiveness of inter-departmental relationships?

If one understands that measures are actually questions, one can broaden the assessment of management effectiveness by having the team ask itself 'provocative' questions. For example:

- Are the relationships on our team as strong as they should be?
- Are we accepting longstanding problems and issues?
- What indications do we have that our organization is healthy at all levels and in all dimensions e.g., physical, emotional, mental and spiritual
- How resilient is our organization?

In this way, the focus shifts from what others in the organization must do to what the senior leaders themselves can do to improve performance.

When applied to different levels and groups, this approach has the potential to create a system of self-accountable metrics that broadens understanding of how things are working and who needs to contribute what to enhance organizational performance.

Consider working with each of the groups below to develop metrics that will enable them to gauge their own performance:

- Board of directors
- Senior management
- Middle management and supervision
- Process owners
- Mobilizing constellations
- Organizational units or teams.

Obtain input from regulators in terms of their perceptions of the value and relevance of the indicators.

BUILDING AN INTEGRATED SYSTEM OF MEASUREMENTS

An important thing to recognize about indicators is that they indirectly become a form of governance, and hence should be treated as a system rather than a list of all things that the organization decides to monitor. A systematic approach to developing a coherent structure for indicators can help. There are many ways this can be accomplished. Some include systems or hierarchies based on:

- Business plans (long term, mid-term, short-term)
- Organization level (Board of Directors, Management, Process Owner)
- Organizational unit (Department, group, or team, mobilizing constellation)
- Management models (business model, process model, etc.)
- Socio-technical system model (e.g., Figure 1.1)
- Stage of organizational evolution.

For example, if one used the four stage organizational evolution model in (Figure 3.1), the indicator structure might look something like this:

Stage 1 – Operating – Technical leadership.

These metrics focus on core technology and physical infrastructure. They are pragmatic and generally easily understood and accepted because of their impersonal nature.

- focus on health of core technology and reliable operation
    - e.g., physical system health parameters, configuration, etc.

Stage 2 – Managing – Systematic leadership.

These include basic business and operating metrics. By their nature, these can have impact on the human system since they focus on controls and can be perceived as punishing. This makes them more prone to manipulation.

- focus on planning, organizing, budgeting and scheduling
- control of resources (money, material, time)
- identification of logistical problems to achieve efficient work execution per employee
- cost and skill of labour
- efficiency (absenteeism, attrition, schedule, planning, budget vs costs, time, backlog, work-down rates)
    - e.g., % training attendance, process indicators related to planning and scheduling.

Stage 3 – Leading – Systemic leadership

These metrics relate to organizational design, workforce design, capacity of resourcing, process system design and development. This shifts focus from task performance to individual and team performance, and inter-group relationships. Typical human reactions relate to the relevance/value and resource loading for an increase in indicators, and concerns regarding the potential for micro-management by measure.

- focus on engagement, team-building, strategy, capacity building – future improvement and capacity building, looking for opportunities to enhance effectiveness
- friction levels, conflicts, grievances, satisfaction/climate surveys, engagement practices (no. of safety meetings, daily meetings), process measures, reporting culture and mechanisms for participation
- management system and people-process interactions
    - e.g. qualifications completed, performance management, supervisor observations, succession planning, audits,
    - e.g., indicators for all processes, rollups, traffic lights, dashboards

Stage 4 – Uniting and Integrating – Unitive leadership

These relate to labour and market trends, organizational health, external relationships, self-assessment, and peer relationships.

- focus on creating meaning aligned with organizational, societal, and ecological outcomes – strengthening organizational propensities and integrating complex systems
- shift to organizational performance and outcomes, organizational communication systems, understanding interactions within the entire system, culture indicators
- trend external factors (local, national, and global context)
    - e.g., safety culture surveys, benchmarking mission implementation
    - e.g., propensities, competencies, and behaviours of leadership, management, and teams

Choosing Targets

Organizations commonly assign targets or goals to specific measures, often with a deliberate intent to select "stretch" targets to "motivate" performance improvement. If done without sufficient thought, such targets may be perceived as unrealistic or punishing, and promote human ingenuity to achieve the target at the cost of safety or quality. Setting arbitrary targets with unrealistic expectations of achievement (e.g., a 15% increase in output) is simply bad management.

It is beneficial to engage the workforce to establish targets, often because the discussion itself promotes ideas on how to improve performance through reducing duplication and inefficiencies. Systemic issues by definition are beyond the control of a single group for which the target is established. Appreciative Inquiry is an effective way to involve people in thinking about what works well and what can be enhanced. When applied in a cross-group setting, this approach can also clarify misunderstandings that disrupt shared space.

Performance trends can sometimes be more useful than targets since they are less likely to distort behaviours and may be used proactively to analyze the causes of the trends. Analyzing why a target isn't met is less useful. This is especially true when organizations establish many targets that routinely aren't met, and employees acclimatize themselves to treating targets as something managers set to appear effective as managers.

Management level targets are most useful when focused on key organization effectiveness parameters in relation to each of the seven lenses of the organization performance model. Targets that look at workforce propensity diversity, alignment of propensities to purpose, and the suitability of leadership styles to the structure and nature of work being performed are especially helpful for middle and senior managers to assess the effectiveness of their own functionality in the organization.

Made in the USA
Coppell, TX
11 December 2024